THE M & E HANDBOOK SERIES

Applied Economics

Edmund Seddon
MA
*Senior Lecturer in Economics,
Faculty of Business and Management Studies,
Liverpool Polytechnic*

J. D. S. Appleton
B.Sc(Econ), M.Sc.Dip.Ed
*Principal Lecturer,
Faculty of Business and Management Studies,
Liverpool Polytechnic*

SECOND EDITION

MACDONALD AND EVANS

Macdonald and Evans Ltd.
Estover, Plymouth PL6 7PZ

First published 1972
Reprinted (with amendments) 1973
Reprinted 1975
Reprinted 1976
Second edition 1978

Printed in Great Britain by
Hazell Watson & Viney Ltd,
Aylesbury, Bucks

Preface to the First Edition

This Handbook sets out to analyse the main problems which confront the U.K. economy today and to test the validity of theoretical solutions to these problems against the results which have been achieved. It is intended for a very wide range of students, from those taking G.C.E. "A" Level to those preparing for papers in Applied Economics in the examinations of both academic and professional bodies.

Part One establishes the theoretical framework of macro-economic analysis and appraises the techniques and effectiveness of fiscal policies designed to manage the level of demand.

Part Two continues this approach in the realm of monetary policy by way of examining the structure and operation of the whole monetary system.

Part Three considers the implications for domestic economic policy of external trade and payments transactions.

Part Four is concerned with *direct* Government intervention in specific segments of the economy in an attempt to improve the efficiency of their operation.

The authors are conscious that this is a field of study in which there is continuous change. Old problems assume new forms and require fresh solutions. Moreover, the institutional apparatus of the economy is evolving at a rate which quickly dates written material. Nevertheless it is hoped that this book will provide the reader with a systematic and critical approach to the solutions put forward to current economic problems. Judicious reading of newspapers, periodicals, journals, and Government and banking publications will enable the student to keep abreast of events.

Grateful acknowledgment is due to the following bodies for permission to reprint the examination questions which appear in Appendix III.

The Joint Matriculation Board of the Universities of Manchester, Liverpool, Leeds, Sheffield, and Birmingham (J.M.B.).

University of London.

Liverpool Polytechnic.

Institute of Bankers (I.O.B.).

Savings Bank Institute (S.B.I.).

Institute of Municipal Treasurers and Accountants (I.M.T.A.)

Institute of Cost and Management Accountants—formerly Institute of Cost and Works Accountants (I.C.W.A.).

Institute of Transport (I.O.T.).

Chartered Institute of Secretaries (C.I.S.).

January 1972

E.S.
J.D.S.A.

Preface to the Second Edition

In this second edition a new introductory chapter has been added. It outlines the development of economic thinking to the present time and seeks to establish the controversial nature of a subject which has continued to evolve in response to a changing environment. Attention is drawn particularly to a major area of disagreement in contemporary macroeconomic theory, the dispute between Keynesian and monetary economists. A further new chapter enlarges upon the differences in the theoretical foundations of the two approaches and the implications for Government policy.

In microeconomics it is generally agreed that the traditional "theory of the firm" does not give an entirely satisfactory account of the behaviour of today's large corporation. The problem is outlined in the introduction and taken up again in Part Four.

Elsewhere there have been substantial additions and modifications to the original text to bring it into line with the present state of economic theory and practice.

June 1978
E.S.
J.D.S.A.

Contents

PART ONE: THE MACROECONOMIC
APPROACH

From collectivism to individualism; Classical
market economics; The economics of John
Kenneth Galbraith; The response to Galbraith;
The Keynesian revolution; The counter-revolution in monetary theory; Politics and applied
economics

The business cycle; Analysis of the causes of the
business cycle; An elaboration of the macroeconomic model

A perspective of public finance; Stabilisation of
demand at full employment; Policies for economic growth; The stabilisation of prices; Incomes policy; Conclusions on demand management

A Keynesian view of money and national income
determination; A Keynesian view of money and
price determination; A monetarist view of money,
prices and national income determination; The
Phillips curve and the inflation/unemployment
trade-off

CONTENTS   xi

List of Tables

List of Illustrations

THE MACROECONOMIC APPROACH

CHAPTER I

An Outline of
Developments in Economic Analysis

FROM COLLECTIVISM TO INDIVIDUALISM

1. Introduction. The objects of this introductory chapter are two-fold. Firstly it sets out to define the subject area by showing how it originated and developed in response to a changing economic environment. Secondly it seeks to demonstrate that unlike the physical sciences the subject does not comprise a body of theory universally agreed by all economists. There has always been dis-agreement both in terms of the methodology appropriate to the analysis of particular problems and in the interpretation of observed economic phenomena. Controversy continues at the present time on a number of issues, particularly with respect to the importance of money in the economy. (The neo-Keynesian/monetarist controversy, *see* 37, 38.)

2. Origins of economics as an independent area of study. As an independent discipline, economics emerged from the great politi-cal, social and cultural upheaval which culminated in the Industrial Revolution. Its birth is to be associated with the transi-tion from a feudal society organised in small self-sufficient units to a much more loosely knit society producing for national and international markets.

3. Security, stability and collectivism. The principal character-istic of feudal society was the stability which it achieved through a highly structured collectivism. The problem of matching scarce resources to man's needs was tackled *locally* and by *collective* decisions, implemented in agriculture through the manorial courts and in industry and trade through the craft and merchant

guilds. In the event of unwise decisions responsibility and resulting hardships were shared collectively. Justice in dealings with
other groups was exacted collectively and penalties accepted
collectively. The *just wage* and the *just price*, strangely reminiscent
of today's prices and incomes policies, were imposed collectively.

The prevailing desire was for the security in life which stems
from the certainty that tomorrow will be the same as today. In a
spiritual age in which the authority of the church was absolute
hardship in this world would be recompensed in the next.

Hardship there was in abundance and in material terms the age
is marked by stagnation.

4. Progress, individualism and laissez-faire. The European
Renaissance is synonymous with the reawakening of the spirit of
enquiry, a questioning of accepted values, a resurgence of individualism. The implications for social organisation were far
reaching since feudal institutions were too inflexible to adjust to
change. In the towns, where the customs and practices of the
guilds appeared to conflict with the individual interests of mer-
chants and craftsmen, they were ignored and individuals pros-
pered. The age of geographical discovery brought in its train an
expansion of commerce and still greater prosperity for an emerging middle class of entrepreneurs, who began to organise production to meet increasing demand. Already there could be per-
ceived the separation of the functions of providing capital and
labour, the hallmark of capitalism.

A temporary check to the disintegration of collectivist society
was made by the state. As the regulatory powers of local institutions declined they were replaced by central government legislation. This process reached its zenith in the reign of Elizabeth I
with the establishment of a highly centralised nation state, subject to an absolute monarchy. However, the full flowering of
individual freedom, political, spiritual and economic was not
long to be delayed. The conflict of interest erupted in the Civil
War of 1688–9, a revolution in a unique sense. Where subsequent
revolutions simply substituted one authoritarian caucus for another, on this occasion a whole collectivist ethic was replaced by
an unfaltering belief in the right of the individual to free expression, politically, spiritually and economically. The age of
laissez-faire had dawned.

5. The implications of a market economy. The eighteenth century
contained all the ingredients for dramatic change. There existed

already a class of wage earners and a class of capital-providing entrepreneurs. The ethic of individual free enterprise was unchallenged and state interference minimal. The need was for technological advance and necessity became the mother of a spate of inventions, which could only be fully utilised in a factory system geared to large scale production for an expanding market. In the space of a few decades a subsistence economy was transformed to a highly specialised market economy composed of increasingly complex interdependencies. Much had been accomplished in overcoming the fundamental problems of scarcity and how to produce more, but the complexities of the new methods of social organisation themselves raised new problems. *These problems were to become the substance of the new subject of political economy.*

6. A tentative definition. We are now able to see that, while the subject of economics is rooted in the problem of scarcity, the economist only acquires an interest once that problem is set in the context of a particular system. It is, therefore, to be seen as a social or behavioural science concerning itself with all of the implications for the alleviation of scarcity of different methods of organising society.

CLASSICAL MARKET ECONOMICS

7. Adam Smith and the English classical economists. Smith provided the first rationale for a free enterprise economy, in which an optimal matching of available resources to individual wants would be secured through the operation of an "invisible hand", the market mechanism. Collective action through the state would be restricted to the maintenance of internal and external security.

This idea was subsequently explored and developed by the great English classical economists of the nineteenth century. The substance of this line of thinking can be summarised as follows.

(*a*) *The economic problem.* Economics is concerned with the optimal allocation of scarce resources between competing alternatives.

(*b*) *Individual choice.* The order of priority of these alternatives can only be determined with any accuracy by the individual.

(*c*) *The market mechanism.* The market will assure the direction of resources in accordance with this scale of priorities. A high priority will be signalled by a willingness to pay a higher price. In response to the higher price more resources will be drawn into that use. Conversely, a falling price will indicate an over-supply or a lower priority. Resources will now be directed to some other use.

(*d*) *The market clearing-price.* Assuming there to be no impediment to the market mechanism there would always be a price at which the market would be cleared. Hence there existed no possibility of long-term involuntary unemployment of resources. This proposition was supported by J. B. Say's "law of markets".

8. Say's "law of markets". This law reasoned that the decision of individuals to work and produce is motivated only by the wish to acquire the produce of others. An increase in the output of the individual will generate for him sufficient income to take from the market goods equivalent to those produced by his own efforts.

The fundamental assumption is that all income will be spent upon either consumer goods or capital goods at a rate sufficient to guarantee the full employment of all resources. Resources could remain unemployed in the short run but only because the supply price was too high. In the long run, a fresh equilibrium price established at a lower level would ensure that they were once more fully utilised.

9. Microeconomics and macroeconomics. The traditional aspect of the subject, which has been outlined so far, belongs to the area which the modern economist describes as microeconomics. It attempts to explain the principles which govern the direction of resource use and will, therefore, isolate parts of the economy, one consumer, one firm, one industry for close analysis.

Distinct from this approach is the attempt to explain the principles which govern the level of resource use in the economy as a whole. This aspect of the subject is referred to as macroeconomics and contributes the most significant element in the *twofold* revolution in economic thinking which occurred in the 1930s. It is to be particularly associated with the writings of John Maynard Keynes, "*the Keynesian revolution*".

Overshadowed by this drastic reappraisal of the classical model of the economy, but still of great importance, were the modifications to traditional thinking being made by a number of economists, in particular Edward H. Chamberlin in the U.S.A. (*The Theory of Monopolistic Competition*, 1933) and Joan Robinson in England (*The Economics of Imperfect Competition*, 1933).

10. Allowing for monopoly influence. Implicit in nineteenth century explanations of the market as the optimal allocator of resources, was the concept of "perfect competition". If price were permitted clearly to reflect our changing priorities and productive resources were not impeded in their consequent movement from one use to another, then the economy would remain flexible and capable of satisfying our needs with maximum efficiency. However, no attempt was made to prescribe exactly what conditions "perfect competition" had to fulfil. Once this analysis was made it became clear that in the real world of the twentieth century there was growing monopoly power, exercised not only by the suppliers of end products but also by the suppliers of the factors of production, land, labour and capital. If supply could be artificially restricted in order to secure a higher price and increased monopoly profits then the market was distorted. Price no longer established a natural harmony between the interests of buyers and sellers. Resources were no longer allocated in a way which fully represented the wants of individual consumers and the capacity of individual suppliers.

Recognition that economic activity in the real world took place in a variety of conditions, ranging between the hypothetical extremes of perfect competition and absolute monopoly, led to reformulation of the traditional model of the economy in terms of monopolistic competition by Chamberlin and imperfect competition by Robinson.

An even more radical challenge to the traditional view of markets and the behaviour of firms was postulated in the 1960s by John Kenneth Galbraith.

THE ECONOMICS OF JOHN KENNETH GALBRAITH

11. The firm's objectives. In *The New Industrial State*, 1967, Galbraith questions whether the modern industrial firm responds to a market or controls it; whether it is motivated by the desire to maximise profits or whether it has a range of quite different objectives. In the traditional market model the consumer was sovereign, while the pressure of competition obliged the firm to operate with that degree of efficiency consistent with the maximisation of profits. Galbraith argues that in industries where many small firms are producing in highly competitive conditions they are subject to the full authority of the market and will seek only to increase their revenues.

12. Monopoly objectives. Equally, says Galbraith, it has long been assumed that monopolies will behave in a similar way. Why should a monopoly seek to rid itself of the pressures of a competitive market only to settle for less than the maximum possible return.

The answer lies in the pressures which have obliged the large corporation to substitute planning for the market. Rapidly changing and highly specialised technology with the associated commitment of large sums of capital and extended periods of production time, compel the firm to free itself from the uncertainties of the market. It now seeks to control the prices that it pays for its inputs and which it receives for its outputs as well as taking steps to ensure that buyers take the planned quantities at those prices. In short, instead of being subject to the market, the large corporation has subordinated it to the goals of its planning objectives. Profit maximisation *may* still be a corporate goal but will no longer be enforced by the market while other objectives are likely to be of greater importance.

13. The motivation of senior management. Accepting the separation of ownership and control of the corporation, the profit motive in the conventional view produces a paradox. It is supposed that managers will not seek ruthlessly to reward themselves but to maximise the profits which will accrue to remote and powerless shareholders. Some concession may be made to the view that at the very top the pecuniary interests of managers and owners coincide since higher salaries can be justified by higher corporate earnings. Even this argument dissolves with the rise of "the technostructure".

14. The technostructure. As power passes down the organisation to the scientist, the engineer, the contract negotiator, the sales executive so profit maximisation disappears as the sole obligatory company objective. The members of the technostructure are rewarded to scale while an effective code of behaviour inhibits them from utilising confidential information for their own financial advantage. In short, while they must eschew personal profit the conventional view assumes that they will seek it for others.

15. The same goals for the technostructure, the corporation and society. The goals of the technostructure will be reflected in the goals of the mature corporation, which in turn will be conceded by a society which now makes those goals its own. For example, if a primary objective of the technostructure is autonomy and the level of earnings which sustains it, this will become a corporate goal and one which society will accept and applaud. The relationship will also work in reverse. If society holds rapid technical progress in high regard this goal will be mirrored in the goals of the corporation and of the technostructure.

What is important is an identity of individual, corporate and social purpose. The individual will identify with the goals of the corporation provided that they coincide with some socially laudable objective. There exists no such identity of purpose when the only corporate objective is making more money for shareholders, an activity which attracts no great social approval.

Significantly, while some social attitudes originate outside of the technostructure, many simply reflect its personal interests since individuals have a great capacity for endowing their own activities with social value. Company objectives will now be tailored to fit those personal social goals.

16. Survival and growth of sales. These personal goals will manifest themselves in a number of ways. Survival will be the primary objective and therefore the firm will require to maintain a minimum level of profits. This achieved the modern corporation will now seek to expand its sales at the expense of profit.

17. Growth and advertising. The firm wishes to grow and therefore society must be conditioned by advertising to believe that the acquisition of more things is a desirable social objective. The firm, in fact, creates demand for its own products and growth is deified.

Galbraith then comments that western society already has more things than it knows what to do with.

18. "The scientific and educational estate". Scientific and managerial intelligence are the key resources of the new industrial state. The Government supports the system through public provision for education and technological research. In this way material objectives are established and personnel trained to achieve them. This scientific and educational elite thus acquire a certain moral authority and being sufficiently intelligent to see through the cult of growth offer the promise of gradual change to a less philistine style of life.

19. Conclusion. The Galbraithian analysis represents a radical departure from the mainstream of economic thinking. The market exercises authority in only a very limited and diminishing area of the economy. It should therefore be abjured. Real power lies with giant corporations which in fact dictate the path of social and economic development. Observation suggests that this produces a rather unattractive way of life. The implication is clear. Government, advised by a cultured scientific and educational estate, should play a greater part in planning the way ahead to a better society.

THE RESPONSE TO GALBRAITH

20. General assessment. It is true that conventional theory is insufficiently sophisticated to give a very satisfactory account of the behaviour of today's large corporation. Attempts have been made to provide explanations which could be accommodated within the body of existing theory but none go so far as Galbraith. It is also true that Galbraith's work has attracted a great deal of interest but support for his views has been drawn from the wider public rather than from his professional colleagues.

Professional criticism has come from two main directions.

(*a*) *No systematic economic model.* While there may be important truths in much of what Galbraith says, his various points have not been incorporated in any systematic theory which explains the functioning of the whole economy. Until this happens his insights are unlikely to have any real influence upon the way in which economic problems are handled. At present this seems improbable since in contrast to Smith, Keynes, Friedman and others he has not attracted other economists to form "a school of thought".

(*b*) *Too many dogmatic generalisations.* Many of his hypotheses rest upon sweeping assertions which may be "felt" to be true but remain untested by scientific methods. Attempts have been made to provide such tests with results which have not been favourable to Galbraith's case.

21. The goals of stability and sales maximisation: Demsetz. Professor Harold Demsetz (U.C.L.A.) has tested two of Galbraith's central hypotheses on the structure of industry.

(*a*) *"Technostructure orientated firms sacrifice profits to accelerate sales."* Galbraith identifies such firms as those which are capital intensive, heavily advertised, oligopolistic, large and with an orientation towards military production. Demsetz measured the performance of 375 such firms to see if there was evidence of a trade-off of profits against sales. He found no evidence that this was the case.

(b) "*Management places stability above profits.*"A principal management objective will be to ensure that the firm's plans are not disrupted. Demsetz analysed a sample of thirteen stocks of leading defence contractors. He found that they offered to investors 21 per cent more risk in terms of annual fluctuations in the rate of return to investors than did randomly selected portfolios of thirteen stocks.

22. Planning for a minimum level of profit: McFadzean. Galbraith asserts that the technostructure will simply plan for the minimum level of profit necessary to keep the shareholders pacified.

Professor F. S. McFadzean levels the criticism that "the corporate planners in Galbraith's unreal world start off with a predetermined level of profit to meet the objectives he postulates and presumably juggle with proceeds, volumes, costs and investments to achieve this figure . . . it implies a control of events and markets which exists only in a monopoly situation and the imagination of Professor Galbraith".

McFadzean goes on to point out that profits are a residual which no firm can plan with any certainty since all the evidence shows that no firm can ultimately bend the consumer to its will.

23. The technostructure will place its own security above profit maximisation: Solow. Galbraith claims that the shareholder has no power to influence the objectives of the technostructure and that the latter will place its own security above profits.

Professor R. M. Solow argues that this is paradoxical. If managers earn less than is feasible with the resources at their disposal this will have a detrimental effect upon the company's share prices. Lower prices provide an incentive for takeover bids which will displace the existing management. It follows that indirectly shareholders do influence the company's objectives.

24. The mature corporation moulds the consumer to its will: Solow. Fundamental to the Galbraithian thesis is the view that the company through powerful advertising is able to dictate to the consumer.

Professor Solow responds that while much advertising may be thought distasteful or excessive, this is no evidence that the art of salesmanship has freed the large corporation from the need to meet the market test, giving it "decisive influence over the revenue it receives". Galbraith offers no evidence, only assertion.

Accepting that this is a difficult question to resolve it may be equally argued that much competitive advertising is self-cancelling and that much is legitimately informative contributing to competition in the market place.

25. Large corporations do not monopolise the whole economy: Solow. Solow concedes that large corporations may be typical of manufacturing industry but argues that Galbraith underestimates the amount of activity still undertaken by small firms. This is particularly true of trade and services, the sectors which show the greatest growth relative to the whole economy.

Moreover, Professor John Jewkes in *The Sources of Invention* rejects Galbraith's assertion that technological advance depends upon large monopolistic corporations. The evidence shows that much innovation has been by small competitive firms.

26. Conclusions. The Galbraithian controversy has been discussed at some length since it clearly has fundamental implications for economic theory. It must, however, be concluded that without much more research and the production of substantive evidence Galbraith's propositions remain hypothetical. In particular it has to be proved that markets no longer function in the way that mainstream economic thinking has postulated.

THE KEYNESIAN REVOLUTION

27. The depression of the 1930s. In the period 1921–39 only once did the proportion of insured persons unemployed fall below 10 per cent. In two years it was above 20 per cent and the overall average was in excess of 14 per cent. There was immense hardship, apart from which it was estimated that there was an annual loss of potential output of between £400 and £500 million measured at the prices current at that time.

The classical economic model could only explain equilibrium at full employment (*see* 7(*d*), 8 above). It could give no account of the long-term failure to utilise resources.

28. New economic thinking. The attention of economic theorists now shifted from the direction of the demand for resources (microeconomics) to the level of that demand (macroeconomics).

It seemed clear to some economists that despite falls in wages, and even if there were no interference in the process of wage bargaining, there would be no inevitable tendency to full employment.

The new macroeconomics was therefore concerned with analysing the relationship between certain variables expressed as aggregates, i.e. the volume of consumer and investment expenditures, the level of national income and employment and the volume of production.

29. John Maynard Keynes. Pre-eminent among the new economic thinkers was Keynes whose analysis is expressed most fully in *The General Theory of Employment, Interest and Money*, 1936.

Focusing upon aggregate demand for goods and services, he suggested that if this were to fall in the short term there would be over-production. As stocks accumulated some people would be thrown out of work. At least initially they would look for work at comparable wages. In the meantime their purchasing power would be reduced and demand would fall still further. They might, in due course, accept work at a lower wage but by this time the continuing fall in demand would have produced a situation in which even this low wage was too high to ensure employment for all. With some unemployment persisting and at a reduced level of activity demand might decline still further producing yet more unemployment.

Before long-run equilibrium was established at a level of wages sufficiently low to guarantee the employment of everybody the economy would have sunk into depression.

30. Key features. Certain features of the Keynesian system are immediately apparent.

(a) *Initial impact on output*. The initial effect of a fall in demand would be upon output rather than upon prices. Prices and wages would only begin to fall once it was clear that the decline in demand was more than temporary. The original loss of output and employment would now be magnified as demand continued to decline with an ensuing major recession.

(b) *Stickiness of wage rates*. This approach contrasted with the earlier view that the first impact would be upon wages and prices, which at a lower level would remove excess supply from the market.

In the labour market unemployment might in the long-run produce competition leading to lower wages and more employment.
In the short run determination to find a job at the same wage
would in fact lead to a period of zero wages and further falls in
demand. It followed that if the decline into depression were to be
halted, it was the demand for labour which was crucial.

31. Policy implications. Since the automatic equilibrating function
of the market was shown to be inadequate there was a clear case
for Government intervention. The shortfall in private sector demand would be compensated by increased public sector spending.

In the pre-war world, public opinion was not yet prepared to
accept such a dramatic change. *Laissez-faire* economic thinking
was rooted in the view that the state had no part to play in
economic affairs. Central economic planning was essentially collectivist and socialist.

32. A social and economic watershed. The 1939–45 war provided
the climate for a change of view. For the purpose of winning a war
total planning of the economy was accepted. Would it not, therefore, be reasonable to accept some degree of central planning if
this led to a fairer, more secure and stable society?

In 1942, the Beveridge Report provided the blueprint for the
Welfare State. Beveridge stressed that any prospect for a comprehensive system of social security founded upon the insurance
principle would have to be underwritten by the certainty of a
continuing high level of employment. Government gave a firm
commitment to this objective in the White Paper, *Employment
Policy*, 1944 and it subsequently became the first priority of all
succeeding Governments. The state was now responsible for the
level of economic activity. The age of *laissez-faire* had passed.

33. Economic intervention with social democracy. The Keynesian
analysis appeared to provide a mechanism through which the
main features of the market could be retained while its inadequacies were compensated by state intervention. In this way it
would be possible to avoid the illiberality of wholly planned
economies and the political totalitarianism which inevitably
accompanied them. Democracy would be preserved.

34. Keynesian policies in practice. Policies designed to sustain
aggregate demand at a level, consistent with a high level of employment, appeared at first to be remarkably successful. With

this encouragement, the "high level of employment" objective of the 1944 White Paper was now referred to more emphatically as "full employment". Never defined statistically, in practice it came to mean 1.2 per cent–2 per cent unemployment. Anything in excess of 2 per cent brought political pressures which required Government to take remedial action.

35. "Stop-go". A new problem emerged. In its anxiety to ensure that aggregate demand was sustained at an adequate level and encouraged in this by political pressures to spend more on social measures the tendency was to over-compensate. In the "go" phase, full employment output was soon achieved. The continued expansion of demand induced inflationary pressure which, in due course, brought imbalance in international payments. To restore the balance it was then necessary to damp down aggregate demand and the economy came to a "stop".

The periodicity of this cycle of events gradually increased along with the level of unemployment experienced in the "stop" phase and the rate of inflation occurring during the "go" phase.

It seemed that the new economic steering mechanism did not function with the precision which had been intended. Indeed for some economists Government intervention had itself become a de-stabilising agent.

36. A new phenomenon. Towards the end of the 1960s appeared the problem of escalating inflation accompanied by rising unemployment. It was now the new orthodoxy which could no longer explain events, since the theory developed by Keynes's successors postulated a trade-off between inflation and unemployment. When one rose, the other fell.

THE COUNTER-REVOLUTION IN MONETARY THEORY

37. Demand and supply, the short term and the long term. In the short term it is demand which is flexible and subject to instability. It is equally amenable to manipulation. On the other hand supply is inflexible, being dependent upon the availability of productive resources which can only be developed in the long term.

Inasmuch as the Keynesian analysis placed emphasis upon the treatment of unemployment, which resulted from a deficiency of demand, it concerned itself with the short term and tended to neglect the long term. A boost to demand would manifest itself in increased employment and output and hardly at all in prices.

Criticism of this preoccupation with the short term reflects the pre-Keynesian view that, in the long term, variations in demand work chiefly on prices and only indirectly on output. Variations in prices will, however, determine the proportion of productive resources which are employed. On this view the phenomenon of inflation with unemployment is explained. The continued and excessive expansion of demand in the long term results in price inflation rather than increased output. As inflation gathers momentum so the factors of production are priced out of the market and the economy stagnates.

38. The monetarists. It should be remembered that from the outset there were those who contested the validity of Keynes's analysis, in particular his contemporary, Friedrich Hayek. It was not however, until the 1950s that a powerful reaction began to develop in the thinking of the monetarist school of economists which is usually associated with Professor Milton Friedman and the University of Chicago. Their influence has steadily grown.

Their basic contention is that there exists a consistent relationship between the rate of growth of the money supply and the general price level. This in turn will affect the level of employment of resources. Government attempts at short term "fine tuning" of the economy are self-defeating, since they themselves prove to be the principal source of instability.

Long term equilibrium will depend from the side of supply upon the physical constraints which affect the availability of land, labour and capital. On the side of demand Government should confine its policies to holding monetary growth to a stable rate which would reasonably accommodate any *real* growth in output.

POLITICS AND APPLIED ECONOMICS

39. The relationship. Politics concerns itself with the organisation of society by methods which permit the expression of the popular will. Economics as we have established concerns itself with the organisation of society by methods which best alleviate the problem of scarcity. There is clearly a close relationship between the two and, not infrequently, a conflict between the two objectives. What economists may objectively consider to be the best solution to a particular problem may not be consistent with the politician's interpretation of the wishes of the electorate. In other words, economic solutions may only be applied within the limits of their political acceptability.

It will therefore be the function of the economist to provide a range of solutions from which the politician can choose. Arguably, he may go on to indicate that the selection of one solution rather than another may ultimately necessitate changes in the political framework itself. It is then conceivable that if this additional factor were taken into account such a solution might not be chosen.

40. Political and economic policies in the U.K. A characteristic of post-imperial Britain has been its increased introspection, an almost exclusive concern with its own internal problems which in the main have been economic. A large part of all political debate has therefore revolved around the solution to these problems and to this extent political policy has become identified with economic policy.

The Keynesian analysis provided a rationale for short-term remedial action but no foundation for a long-term development strategy. Since for electoral reasons the politician tends to think short term it was on that aspect of economic policy that he concentrated. Even when in the 1960s and into the 1970s the short-term manipulation of demand proved ever less effective in sustaining economic activity he was reluctant to look to the long term and alternative economic solutions which offered no immediate political reward. In other words, long-term economic problems continued to be treated with short-term political solutions.

The progressive failure of macroeconomic policy was met by an increasing number of *ad hoc* interventions to regulate prices and incomes, subsidise employment, create jobs and take into public ownership firms and industries in danger of liquidation.

41. The political market and the economic market. We have established that there exists a heavy overlap between economics and politics. However, when we examine the way in which the *"political market"* and the *"economic market"* serve as mechanisms for the allocation of scarce resources we discover that they function according to quite different and often incompatible criteria.

In the political market place, parties seek a return to power by trying to outbid each other. They will try to offer more of what they suppose the voter wants. However, there exists neither a mechanism which enables the voter to balance more of one good against more of another, nor any mechanism for ensuring that a majority of votes implies a commitment by the electorate of a quantum of resources to the fulfilment of an election programme. Every few years the voter is required to make a major decision which subsequently relieves him of the responsibility of making many smaller and much more frequent ones. The power to decide has been delegated. It follows, therefore, that the political market is highly imperfect and that the detailed economic decisions made by the party elected will only roughly approximate to the wishes of even their own supporters. The greater the share of productive resources pre-empted in this way, the less the likelihood that the electorate at large will be satisfied. In short, the political return to the collectivist ethic moves in advance of and conflicts with the innate individualism of liberal societies. As we have seen, this individualism works through the operation of the *economic* market.

Here, suppliers compete not for votes but for money, the resources or claim to resources which permits them to survive and expand. Individual consumers no longer commit by one major decision their income for a number of years to a single package of goods and services. Now, a vast number of spending decisions, each of which is marginal, commits £1 at a time to one good at the expense of £1 less of another. This method of resource allocation points to the crucial distinction between the two markets. "The political entrepreneur asks what most people want. The economic entrepreneur must ask himself what people want most": (Peter Jay). The consequent devolution of the decision making process provides the foundations of liberal economics.

42. A rationale for Chapters II, III and IV. The following two chapters will develop more fully the macroeconomic theory which in its application has been the principal instrument of Government economic policy for the past thirty years. An account of the criticisms of that theory will then be given in Chapter IV.

PROGRESS TEST 1

1. List the principal collectivist features of feudal society.   (3)

2. What are the characteristics of a free enterprise market economy?   (5)

3. What are the principal characteristics of classical economic thinking?   (7)

4. Distinguish between microeconomics and macroeconomics. (9)

5. What did Joan Robinson and Edward Chamberlin contribute to economic theory?   (10)

6. List the principal aspects of Galbraith's *New Industrial State*.   (11–19)

7. In what general respects may Galbraith be criticised?   (20)

8. What is the nature of McFadzean's criticism of Galbraith? (22)

9. How does Solow criticise Galbraith?   (23–5)

10. What do you understand by "the Keynesian revolution"? (27–30)

11. What was the importance for practical policies of Keynesian thinking?   (31–4)

12. What do you understand by "stop-go"?   (35)

13. Explain the nature of the "counter-revolution in monetary theory".   (37–8)

14. Compare the functioning of the "political and economic markets".   (41)

CHAPTER II

The Keynesian System

THE BUSINESS CYCLE

1. A general theory. The weakness of classical economics was as we have seen that it was only able to explain the working of the economy in a particular situation, full employment. Keynes provided a "general theory" in the sense that it explained how the economy might function at *any* level of employment. Writing in a time of massive unemployment it was natural that his primary concern should be with this problem. However, it is often forgotten that he provided an explanation of the whole business cycle and had a good deal to say about the problem of over-full employment and inflation.

2. Industrial fluctuations. Variations in the level of economic activity can be observed to occur in different time series and from different causes.

(*a*) *The secular trend.* This is the long-term trend which in Western economies in the nineteenth and twentieth centuries has been one of growth with rising production and consumption.

(*b*) *Seasonal variations.* As the name suggests, for climatic reasons variations occur within the space of one year, e.g. in the building trade.

(*c*) *Erratic fluctuations.* In a wholly unpredictable way variations result from forces external to the economy, e.g. natural catastrophes or political upheavals.

(*d*) *Long waves.* Since 1822 it is possible to define six periods, each averaging twenty-five years' duration, in which the prevailing trends of prosperity and depression alternated.

(*e*) *The business or trade cycle.* Within each long wave there can be discerned between two and a half and three and a half business cycles comprising a regular alternation of prosperity and depression.

Government economic policy since 1945 has aimed to reduce and, hopefully, eliminate cyclical fluctuations, the ultimate objective being a smoothly rising growth curve. The degree of success is to be observed in the less pronounced booms and the less severe depressions, referred to nowadays as "recessions". On the other hand the periodicity of the cycle has increased and "stop-go" economic policies have become subject to much criticism.

3. Phases of the business cycle. Four phases may be discerned:

(a) *The upswing.* A period of rising economic activity and prosperity. The general price level tends to rise.

(b) *The downturn.* The point of crisis at which expansion slows down or ceases.

(c) *The downswing.* A period of contraction. The general price level tends to fall.

(d) *The upturn.* The point of revival prior to the next upswing.

4. Manifestations of the business cycle. There are three principal criteria by which one may distinguish the phases of the cycle. They are the level of employment, the volume of production and the volume of consumption. At the outset it should be stressed that these indicators need not point in the same direction. If they diverge then the considerations set out below must be set against each other in order to arrive at a conclusion.

5. Level of employment. Because of their far-reaching social and political implications there has been a tendency to accept unemployment figures as the principal if not the only indicator of the phases of the business cycle. The reliability of this indicator must therefore be assessed. It must first be made clear that unemployment springs from a variety of causes:

(a) *Seasonal unemployment.* This corresponds to seasonal variations in certain types of business activity.

(b) *Frictional unemployment.* This is "short-term" structural unemployment. Within any industry there are always those firms which are contracting while others are expanding. It follows that in the short run there will be unemployment as some men move from one firm to another.

(c) *Secular unemployment.* This is "long-term" structural unemployment. In a dynamic society technological change brings new industries while old industries become obsolescent. Unemployment results for those men whose skills are no longer in demand.

(d) *Cyclical unemployment.* The figures rise or fall according to the phase of the business cycle.

In the period between the wars the hard core of chronic unemployment was secular in character and associated with the regions in which there had been excessive specialisation in industries such as cotton, coal, iron, steel and heavy engineering. Superimposed was the huge mass of unemployment of cyclical origin. In such a period the economy may move into an upswing while there remains a considerable volume of unemployment for secular, seasonal and frictional reasons.

Moreover, if there is downward pressure on wage rates during the downswing, unemployment figures need not necessarily rise. The same number of men continue to be employed at lower wage levels. This was commonly the case in the nineteenth century and in recent years has manifested itself in trade-union pressure for work sharing as an alternative to redundancies.

On the other hand during an upswing it is possible for the level of unemployment to rise if increased output is due to the improved productivity of labour.

Finally, in utilising this criterion there remains the difficulty of defining full employment as a norm upon which to base policy measures. The choice of figure must ultimately be arbitrary. Judged by Government policies in the years 1945–66 it would seem to have been accepted as lying within the range 1.2–1.4 per cent unemployed. There then appeared to be a realisation that such figures were excessively ambitious when the Prime Minister declared in the House of Commons that he did not think the House would find intolerable an unemployment figure of 2.4 per cent.

When in 1972 unemployment exceeded 1 million and in 1977 topped 1.6 million it seemed that the limits of political tolerance had previously been underestimated. There was also some acceptance that Government could not regulate unemployment to the degree that had previously been thought possible. Thus the Prime Minister asserted in 1976 that, "we used to think we could spend our way out of recession. That option is no longer open to us". With this failure of confidence disappeared any clear view of how full employment might be defined.

6. Criticisms of the use of unemployment statistics. During the 1970s criticism has been directed to the lack of analysis of the unemployment statistics in the returns of the Department of Employment. It is argued that the macroeconomic total of unemployment is a misleading indicator of the phase of the business cycle and therefore an unreliable guide to Government in formulating economic policy. Only a microeconomic division of the total by age, duration, sex and other variables can produce a reliable policy guide.

In his research monograph *How Much Unemployment?*, 1972 and his Hobart paper *How Little Unemployment?* (I.E.A., 1975) John B. Woods argues for a much closer analysis.

7. Distinct indicators for social and economic policy. New data published since 1972 clearly reveals certain features of the labour markets.

(*a*) *Diversity.* There are many markets in labour, not just one. Each displays its own characteristics, e.g. young and old, male and female.

(*b*) *Dynamism.* Even in times of relatively slack demand there is a brisk turnover of labour. This reveals a vital distinction between job changes and the long-term unemployed.

It is therefore argued that a clear distinction should be made between unemployment figures which may provide a guide for social policy and those which indicate how many unemployed are genuinely available for work. The present global figure is of little use as an economic indicator since it takes no account of the different types of unemployment noted in 5 above. Implicit in the official macroeconomic approach is the view that *all* unemployment is of cyclical origin.

8. A new strategic indicator of unemployment. Woods then suggests a new indicator which he defines as "the number in the male labour force aged 25 to 55 without work for more than six months".

His reasons for such a restricted definition are as follows.

(*a*) *Exclusion of those unemployed for under six months.* The issue of P45 forms by the Inland Revenue reveals some 10 million job changes annually. Only about one third of these jobs are found through the labour exchanges but even here the turnover is very brisk with each month between 300,000 and 350,000 entering the register and about the same numbers leaving it. The difference between the two flows shows the overall rise or fall.

Those who register fall into two groups, a majority who find work in under two months and the rest who take longer or remain permanently unemployed.

Changes in demand management policy can have no short-run effect. Therefore the short-term unemployed should be excluded from the indicator.

(*b*) *Exclusion of those over 55.* A substantial number of those in the 60–65 group comprise occupational pensioners who register either to receive social security or to have their national insurance contributions credited. With the extension of occupational pension schemes and the trend to earlier retirement the suggestion is to exclude those over 55 since there is even less likelihood of them being genuinely available for long-term employment.

(*c*) *Exclusion of those under 25.* There are two distinct groups.

(*i*) *Adult students.* During the 1970s increasing numbers of students have registered during vacation in order to qualify for certain social security benefits. This has clearly produced temporary distortions in the unemployment figures.

(*ii*) *School leavers.* There are approximately 750,000 school leavers each year of whom about 500,000 seek work. They present a special problem. They may take a long time to find their first job and even longer to find one that suits them. Initially, they swell the number of job changers disproportionately. However, in the period 1962–72 the median duration of unemployment for boys aged 15–17 was very low at 2–4 weeks.

(*d*) *Exclusion of women.* The trend is for women in all age groups to represent a larger proportion of the total work force. This proportion grew from 25 per cent in 1939 to 37 per cent in 1975. In contrast, male employment has declined not only relatively but since 1965, absolutely. In the following ten years there was a decline of 800,000 men in employment offset by an increase of 865,000 women.

Moreover, the evidence shows that on average female unemployment for more than six months stands at only 30,000 while female vacancies (when they were still advertised as such) repeatedly exceeded that figure.

The conclusion is that *long-term* unemployment is specifically a male problem.

(*e*) *Other exclusions.* It should also be recognised that a reliable strategic indicator should allow for:

(*i*) *Long-term unemployables.* Investigations suggest that there may be in the region of 250,000 people who for physical or psychological reasons are incapable of holding a job.

(*ii*) *Fraudulent registrations.* From successful prosecutions a "guesstimate" of 2 per cent of the total unemployed may be made.

9. Volume of production and consumption. We must next assess the validity of the other two principal indicators of the phase of the business cycle.

(*a*) *Volume of consumption.* It has been observed that during a downswing it is possible for a high level of employment to be maintained at the expense of lower wage rates. However, with lower earnings it is likely that expenditure on consumption will decline and this will be a more reliable index of the state of trade. Even so, it cannot be used in isolation.

(*b*) *Volume of production.* During the downswing the volume of consumption may for a time remain unaffected but expenditure on investment declines. In short, the nation is subsidising its standard of living by consuming capital. Conversely, in an upswing there may be a big increase in capital expenditure while consumption is little affected. The nation is adding to its capital.

10. Policy implications. The aim of macroeconomic policy will be to achieve continuous growth (i.e. eliminate the business cycle) at stable prices and with full employment. If the various manifestations of the business cycle point in the same direction there will be little doubt as to the phase of the cycle and *if* the Keynesian analysis is accepted, a clear indication of the policies to be adopted. Where they diverge the position is less obvious and it will be necessary to balance the evidence and to establish the order of priorities of the three policy objectives.

For example, during 1969 and 1970 the demand for labour was weak and unemployment rose although the volume of production continued marginally to rise. The balance of the evidence indicated that the economy was still in recession but since the policy priority was to counter inflation employment was sacrificed and no stimulus given to demand.

During 1971–2 the unemployment figures continued to rise suggesting that the recession was deepening. Employment now became the first priority and major reflationary measures were undertaken.

NOTE: In line with the criticism that the global unemployment figure has received insufficient analysis and has been incorrectly interpreted, it may be noted that while the *stock* of unemployment rose in 1971–2, from the spring of 1971 more men began to leave the register. From the end of 1971 the notification of vacancies increased. This reflected a new trend which passed unnoticed. Attention was focused upon the stock to the neglect of the underlying flows. This misinterpretation led to policies which were directly responsible for the inflation of 1973–4.

ANALYSIS OF THE CAUSES OF THE BUSINESS CYCLE

11. Business-cycle theories. The causes of the business cycle are complex and it would be idle to claim that any single explanation is adequate or that the same explanation is equally valid for all countries or for every cycle. This is generally recognised by most writers on the subject and differences are usually of emphasis rather than of principle.

There are five groups of theories which may conveniently be placed under the following headings:

(*a*) Psychological theories.
(*b*) Monetary theories.
(*c*) Over-investment theories.
(*d*) Under-consumption theories.
(*e*) Keynesian theory.

It is a merit of the work of Keynes that he gives due consideration to these other theories and having allowed for their validity in certain circumstances goes on to offer his own explanation. We shall confine our attention to Keynesian theory since this has provided the foundation for practical economic policy-making since 1945.

12. Effective demand, national income and the level of employment. The "General Theory" centres upon the concept of effective demand which comprises total national expenditure upon consumer goods and services and upon capital goods. The crucial thing to remember is that spending generates income and employment while saving does not. What one man spends represents demand for another man's employment and constitutes his income. Expenditure and income are two aspects of the same thing. A third aspect will be the money value of the total volume of production since this equates with both total money expenditure and total money income. Whatever is spent upon production will be distributed in wages, rent, interest and profits.

From these propositions three important conclusions follow:

(*a*) *The key indicator is the national income figure*. Employment according to Keynes is a function of national income. If income is declining so is employment and vice versa.

NOTE: This was a valid enough assumption in a period of depression. An increase in business activity would be reflected in the use of more labour. The proposition becomes more questionable once a high level of employment has been attained and emphasis is placed upon increasing national income through improved productivity. A post-war phenomenon has been the periodic rise in unemployment at the same time as national income has continued to rise.

(b) *The production of goods and services of a given value generates sufficient income to purchase them in their entirety if we so wish.* However, if we fail to spend the whole of that income then some goods and services will cease to be produced. Income and employment will decline.

(c) *Total effective demand determines the levels of income and employment.* It follows that where the figure of national income shows decline the remedy is to be sought in supporting effective demand.

13. The impact of saving. All income is divided between individuals and institutions in the form of wages, interest, rent and profits.

A part of this income will be devoted to current expenditure upon consumption. The rest will be saved. If a given level of income and employment is to be maintained the *whole* of these savings *must* be devoted to investment, i.e. in the Keynesian sense, expenditure upon capital equipment.

In short, the level of effective demand will be determined by the interaction of the rate of saving and the rate of investment. However, saving and investment are distinct functions governed by different motives and normally carried out by two different groups of people. It would be wholly coincidental if "intentions" to save and invest were to agree. It is essentially because of a discrepancy in these intentions that instability in the level of effective demand arises.

14. The propensity to save. While some savings are corporate and their volume is directly related to a decision to invest, the greater part are the product of decisions by individuals to refrain from current consumption. These decisions are governed by three factors.

(*a*) *Psychological motivation.* A wide variety of personal considerations motivate individual savings, e.g. prudence or the desire to satisfy some ambition. It should be stressed that none of these motives will be in any way related to the investment requirements of the entrepreneur. However, they will be broadly influenced by the prevailing economic climate. Keynes remarked upon "the paradox of thrift". In the downswing of the cycle, a sense of insecurity increases the propensity to save which in itself contributes to the descent into depression. Conversely, during the upswing, while the mood is optimistic, the propensity to save declines, thereby contributing to inflationary pressures.

(*b*) *The rate of interest.* It was assumed by the classical economists that investment and saving would be equated by a fluctuating rate of interest. An increased demand for investment funds by the entrepreneur would be reflected in a higher interest rate. More savings would now be called forth. The evidence of this century suggests that while there is some correlation between the rate of interest and the propensity to save it is not nearly so strong as was once thought.

(*c*) *The level of income.* The principal determinant of the propensity to save will be the level of income. As income rises the marginal propensity to save rises to the point where saving ultimately becomes automatic.

It follows therefore that the marginal propensity to save of the upper-income groups is high and of the lower-income groups low. Conversely, the marginal propensity to consume of the upper-income groups is low and of the lower-income groups high.

If the intention is to regulate total demand by an adjustment of consumer expenditure a redistribution of income may be accomplished in a way which affects the propensities to save and consume.

15. The rate of investment. Investment manifests itself in a demand for new capital goods in either the private or public sector. In the Keynesian sense it does not include the purchase of securities on the Stock Exchange since this normally implies only the transfer of ownership of existing capital.

The rate of investment depends upon the anticipation of business-planners of a profitable return to their outlay. This anticipation is governed by the "marginal efficiency of capital", the phrase Keynes employs to denote the relationship between the prospective yield of one more unit of investment and the rate of interest which must be paid for its use.

In making his assessment of capital's marginal efficiency the planner will take account of certain objective factors, e.g. the size of the existing stock of capital of a particular kind. Nevertheless, however sophisticated his techniques may be his prediction of the future ultimately involves a guess. The problem stems from the unreliability of this guesswork. In advanced economies, Keynes asserted, forecasting recurrently erred on the side of pessimism with the result that investment fell short of what would have been justified had the future been more clearly foreseen.

In order to compensate for this repeated shortfall in effective demand there was scope for periodic injections of Government expenditure, "pump-priming". While conceding that this expenditure might on occasion be designed to stimulate consumption Keynes argued that in the interest of long-term development it was preferable that it should be expressed in investment.

16. The multiplier. The significance of one unit of investment more or less is amplified when attention is given to the operation of the multiplier.

The investment of a further £100 will certainly increase income and employment in the capital-goods industries, but it will also stimulate the propensity to consume of the income recipients. If it is assumed that one-fifth is saved then £80 will be spent upon increased consumption. Income is now increased in the consumer-goods industries and further stimulus given to consumption. Still assuming a savings factor of one-fifth this will be of the order of £64. The multiplier gradually loses momentum due to the impact of saving until the total addition to effective demand has been £500 and to savings £100.

Seen in terms of the effect upon employment, at an average wage level of £10, the initial investment would give work to ten men. When the multiplier had run its course, employment would be increased by fifty men.

In the same way that the beneficial effect of an extra unit of investment is enhanced by the multiplier, the depressant effect of the withdrawal of investment is equally magnified. In any attempt to stabilise demand timing is therefore of vital importance. A lost unit of investment must be replaced before the multiplier can take effect.

17. Deflationary and inflationary gaps. We are led to conclude at this point that instability in the level of effective demand may be attributed to an apparent disequilibrium between saving and investment.

(*a*) *A deflationary gap* between saving and investment initiates the downswing of the cycle and is magnified by the operation of the multiplier. It may result from:

(*i*) *A decline in investment* unaccompanied by an increase in consumption.

(*ii*) *A decline in consumption* unaccompanied by an increase in investment.

Stabilising action calls for the support of effective demand.

(*b*) *An inflationary gap* emerges when the rate of investment exceeds the rate of saving. Total expenditure is now higher than necessary to maintain the economy at the previous level of activity and the cycle has turned into the upswing. It may result from:

(*i*) *Increased investment* unaccompanied by decreased consumption.

(*ii*) *Increased consumption* unaccompanied by decreased investment.

When resources are unemployed, stabilising action may not be required. The tendency for prices to rise consequent upon the increased pressure of demand may be largely offset by the increased flow of goods and services at the higher level of employment. Where resources are already fully employed, price inflation will be avoided only by improved productivity. If this is not forthcoming, stabilising action requires that effective demand should be curbed by restricting either consumption or investment or both.

18. Nature of the disequilibrium of saving and investment. Some economists have adhered to the view that cyclical fluctuations originate in a *real* disequilibrium between saving and investment. Keynes, however, insists that they must equate.

During the upswing the entrepreneur finances his increased investment on credit. At the higher level of income now generated and given a fixed propensity to save, a volume of savings sufficient to cover the increased investment is called forth.

Conversely, during the downswing a lower rate of investment reduces income. Savings must then be restricted to a level dictated by the rate of investment.

In short the position is not one in which investment waits upon saving. It is the rate of investment itself which determines the ability to save. The two must always equate but may do so at any level of economic activity.

19. Reconciliation of the two views of saving and investment. A reconciliation of the two views of saving and investment has been offered in the following terms. Any given period of production can be viewed from two positions:

(a) *The ex ante position.* At the beginning of any period of production society anticipates a certain level of income and plans consumption, investment and saving in a way which it hopes will fulfil this expectation. Since saving and investment plans are unco-ordinated it is unlikely that the two will equate.

(b) *The ex post position.* At the end of a period of production what *in fact* happened can be observed. Expenditure upon consumption and investment generated income sufficient to permit a volume of saving exactly equal to the volume of investment.

In the form of a simple equation:

Consumption expenditure+investment expenditure = National income = consumption expenditure+savings.

It follows that if *ex post* investment (which equals *ex post* saving) differs from *ex ante* saving there is a gap between anticipation and realisation which, if inflationary, moves the economy into the upswing and, if deflationary, moves it into the downswing. The momentum is then increased by the operation of the multiplier.

AN ELABORATION OF THE MACROECONOMIC MODEL

20. The circular flow of income. The real world is of course a good deal more complex than was suggested by the previous simple equation. Figure 1 develops in a rather more elaborate way the central macroeconomic concept of the circular flow of income.

The figure shows two fundamental aspects of the flow which are utilised in the presentation of the national accounts in the annual Blue Book, *National Income and Expenditure*. They are firstly the broad classification into income, production and expenditure accounts and secondly the more detailed division into sectoral accounts. The latter provide an insight into the economic

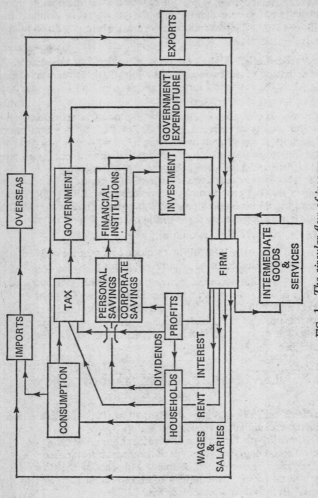

FIG. 1   *The circular flow of income.*

behaviour which may be expected in different sectors, e.g. the spending decisions of households will have a different motivation to those of firms or Government.

21. Sectoral relationships. The relationship between the sectors is shown in Fig. 1.

(a) *Distribution of the firm's revenue.* The firm's revenue will be distributed directly to households in wages and salaries, rent and interest. Interest will also be paid to other firms and this will be retained in the productive sector. Revenue may also be allocated to imported goods and services. The residual, profit, will be distributed to households as dividends, to Government in tax or to corporate savings.

(b) *Distribution of the household's income.* Household income will be devoted first to consumption. A part of this expenditure will be directed to imports and a part to the payment of expenditure taxes. The remainder will be returned to the productive sector to generate further distributions by the firm.

(c) *Government expenditure, investment and exports.* The productive sector receives further revenue from Government expenditure on goods and services, from the spending of firms and financial institutions upon fresh investment and from exports, both visible and invisible.

22. Double counting, leakages and injections. We are now able to see from this analysis that the production, income and expenditure accounts should show the same value after certain complexities have been resolved.

(a) *Double counting.* Firstly, in calculating the value of total production we must avoid the double counting of intermediate (or semi-finished) goods and services and include only the value of the end product. (Hence in Fig. 1 the small circular flow which is confined to the productive sector.) This will be achieved by calculating the value added at each stage.

(b) *Leakages.* Secondly, we must allow for leakages from the system caused by expenditure on imports (both finished and intermediate goods and services) and by the payment of indirect taxes.

(c) *Injections.* Thirdly, we must include injections into the system which result from private investment, total Government spending and exports.

Our equation now assumes a rather more detailed form,

$$Y = C + I + G + X - M - T_I$$

where Y is national income/output; C is private consumption; I is private investment; G is Government current and capital spending; X is exports; M is total imports; T_I is indirect taxes.

Some further refinement is still necessary. As we have seen, the propensity to save or consume is determined primarily by the level of income but more exactly by the level of *disposable* income after the payment of direct taxes, (*see* **14**(*c*) above). We should therefore add a simple consumption function to elaborate the meaning of C.

$$C = b(Y - T_D)$$

where b is the proportion of disposable income spent on consumption and T_D is direct taxes.

We will next note that *all* income is spent on consumption, paid in taxes or saved.

$$Y = T_D + C + S$$

where S is savings. Bearing this equation in mind and remembering our refinement of the consumption function (C) the national income equation may now be expressed as

$$T_D + C + S = C + I + G + X - M - T_I$$

This equation can be simplified and rearranged as follows:

$$S + T + M = I + G + X$$

where T is total taxation, $T_I + T_D$. The significance of this rearrangement is that we can see quite clearly the sources of leakage from the circular flow of income on the left-hand side of the equation and the sources of injection on the right. The injections will be largely autonomous since they are little affected by the existing level of income. Investment depends upon future predictions of profitability, Government expenditure upon current policy, exports upon overseas demand. In contrast, the leakages are primarily determined by current national income. The higher the income the greater the volume of savings and taxation and the greater the demand for imports.

23. The multiplier and the equation of injections and leakages. From our earlier discussion of the multiplier (*see* **16** above) it will be remembered that the effect of an autonomous injection of fresh expenditure will be magnified in further rounds of increased spending.

With each rise in income, however, there occur leakages in an increased volume of savings, taxes and imports. The situation is only stabilised when total leakages equal the new injection of expenditure. The same will be true when there is an autonomous withdrawal of expenditure.

It follows that if the Government is intent upon achieving equilibrium at a high level of income and employment it will seek to influence the autonomous factors in the equation.

This may mean an attempt to stimulate exports (X) through an exchange rate policy which keeps British goods internationally competitive, a feature of the Government's strategy for recovery in 1976–7. The emphasis has however, been upon the manipulation of the factor over which it has closest control, its own expenditure (G), followed by attempts to encourage private investment (I). Since the latter is conditioned by predictions of future consumer demand, consumption (C) has also been regulated.

24. The instruments of control. It was Keynes's view that the most precise control over the various components of aggregate demand could be exercised only through the public finances, i.e. the manipulation of taxation and public expenditure.

Monetary policy on the other hand, lacked precision and was uncertain in its results.

Lower interest rates might or might not induce more spending. Below a certain level, however, the evidence of the 1930s suggested that it was highly improbable. Moreover, interest rate policy was of little use in guiding spending injections into what might be considered the most appropriate directions and in any case it was likely to have a delayed impact.

In Chapter III we shall consider the part played by the public finances in the management of aggregate demand and return to the role of money in the Keynesian system in Chapter IV.

PROGRESS TEST 2

1. Point out the main features of five types of industrial fluctuation. (2)

2. Distinguish between four types of unemployment. (5)

3. What is the essence of John B. Wood's criticism of the use of unemployment statistics? (6)

4. Why should there be different indicators for social and economic policy? (7)

5. Outline the main features of a more accurate unemployment indicator. **(8)**

6. What determines the propensity to save? **(14)**

7. Explain the importance of the concept of effective demand. **(12)**

8. What governs the rate of investment? **(15)**

9. Explain the operation of the multiplier. **(16)**

10. Reconcile the two interpretations of the relationship between the rates of saving and investment. **(19)**

11. Account for the circular flow of income. **(20)**

12. For what reasons may there be leakages and injections? **(22)**

CHAPTER III

The Management of Demand

A PERSPECTIVE OF PUBLIC FINANCE

1. Objectives. The study of macroeconomics places emphasis upon the use of fiscal policy for the purpose of managing demand. Nevertheless, it should not be forgotten that there are other objectives.

Modern public finance may be said to have three aspects. It is:

(a) *The instrument for the satisfaction of collective wants.*
(b) *An instrument of social policy.*
(c) *An instrument of economic policy.*

2. Satisfaction of collective wants. We should not lose sight of the primary purpose of public finance, which is to raise revenue for expenditure upon collective wants. It has always been considered appropriate that certain services should be provided by collective action in the public sector rather than in response to market forces in the private sector.

In the *laissez-faire* society of the eighteenth century the view was that such services should be limited to external and internal security, i.e. defence and the preservation of law and order. A changing view of society has subsequently brought a gradual extension of the public sector, most dramatically since 1945.

3. Definition of the public sector. In this segment of the economy the production of goods and services depends upon the decision of central or local government. In arriving at a decision, while reference will be made to the cost of production, social objectives will be paramount. Resources will be deployed in a way which would not be achieved by the free operation of the price mechanism, e.g. it is reasonable to assume that a far higher proportion of resources is devoted to education than would be the case if all education were provided by private enterprise.

4. Two types of public expenditure. In the public sector the State commands resources in two ways:

(a) *Exhaustive expenditure.* The State directly employs a vast number of people, e.g. civil servants, teachers, soldiers, etc. Indirectly it employs as many in the private sector in the production of goods and services for the satisfaction of collective wants, e.g. defence equipment, schools. Such expenditure is exhaustive in the sense that resources have been diverted as a result of Government decision from the use which free market forces would have determined.

(b) *Transfer expenditure.* When income is redistributed from tax-payer to beneficiary in the form of pensions, family allowances, etc., the recipient is free to dispose of his benefit in response to the pull of market forces.

5. Public enterprise. Since the late nineteenth century local and central government have extended their economic interests, providing goods and services in response to market forces and sometimes in competition with private enterprise, e.g. water-supplies, local transport, the B.B.C. The scope of public enterprise was greatly expanded after 1945 with the nationalisation of major industries.

At this point the frontier between public and private enterprise becomes indistinct. To the extent that public corporations follow pricing and output policies dictated by the market, their behaviour parallels that of privately owned companies and they lie *outside* a strictly defined public sector. To the extent that social and political considerations determine that they should provide a service even at the expense of a loss to be shouldered by the tax-payer, they fall *within* the public sector, e.g. the subsidisation of uneconomic British Rail services.

6. Public revenue. Government has three sources of income from which it may pay society's collective expenses.

(a) *Taxation.* Taxes are levied upon the income and expenditure of individuals and corporate bodies in both the private and public sectors.

(b) *Profits of public enterprise.* While public corporations are not generally required by their acts of incorporation to do more than pay their way, occasionally there are trading profits.

(c) *Borrowing.* Until 1945, this source of income was considered appropriate only in times of national emergency. Sound public finance required that the Budget should always be balanced. Subsequently it was seen that a deflationary gap could be closed most effectively by loan-financed public expenditure. Government borrowing therefore developed as a means of financing both short-term indebtedness on current account and long-term capital investment by public corporations and local authorities.

7. An instrument of social policy. The social objectives of public finance are open to debate and will vary from time to time. A first objective will be the preservation of society and for the exponents of *laissez-faire* philosophy the security of the State was the only legitimate sphere for intervention.

In the nineteenth and twentieth centuries the view gradually developed that society had an obligation to guarantee minimum standards of welfare to all its members. Public finance was then faced with the problem of determining the proportions in which individual contributions should be exacted and benefits allocated. The commonly agreed aim was to secure some reduction in the inequality of income and wealth. The structure of public revenue and expenditure is therefore designed to make a positive contribution to this objective.

8. The principle of progression in taxation. The older view of equity in taxation rested upon the "principle of proportionality". It was argued that if all contributed in the same proportion then income and wealth relationships between individuals remained undisturbed by taxation. When it was appreciated that this approach imposed a greater real burden upon the poor another principle was sought and progression was introduced into the British tax system in the Budget of 1893. Applied first to estate duty it subsequently became a feature of income tax. Progressive taxation requires a more than proportionate contribution from those who are better able to pay.

It will be noted that apart from satisfying modern notions of equity this principle provides a positive instrument for effecting a more equal distribution of income and wealth.

9. Public expenditure. Public expenditure may be classified as:

(*a*) *Defence and environmental expenditure.* The benefits of public expenditure upon defence and the maintenance and improvement of the environment by both local and central government are enjoyed equally by all. No attempt is made to equate real net incomes.

(*b*) *Social service expenditure.* It is in the area of social service expenditure that there has been most growth since the war. Under this heading is included outlay upon education, national health, pensions, unemployment insurance, supplementary benefits, etc. While guaranteeing certain benefits to *all* citizens as of right, the intention is nevertheless to concentrate expenditure upon those most in need, i.e. to achieve a more equal distribution of real income.

10. An instrument of economic policy. Public finance may be instrumental in the pursuit of economic policy.

(*a*) *Protection of industry.* Historically, customs duties were viewed not only as the principal source of revenue but also as a means of limiting foreign competition. Only in the mid nineteenth century did Britain embark upon a period of free trade. In 1932, free trade was abandoned and a protective tariff established. Since 1945, there has been close international co-operation aimed at restoring free trading conditions (*see* X, 19–34). Nevertheless, in certain conditions a protective customs duty may still be considered legitimate (*see* X, 14–18).

(*b*) *Support for private enterprise.* Expenditure may be of two types:

(*i*) *Common services.* Certain services are provided which are of general benefit to all firms, e.g. the Departments of Employment, Trade and Industry.

(*ii*) *Specific assistance.* Specific firms or industries may be singled out for support with investment grants and loans on favourable terms.

(*c*) *Development of public enterprise.* In developing a country's economic infrastructure certain industries may be considered so vital that it is felt that their services should be guaranteed by the State and not left to the uncertainties of market forces, e.g. railways, postal services.

(*d*) *Demand management.* It has been explained in Chapter II that since 1945 fiscal policy has been considered the most powerful instrument for the management of demand. Ideally it will be deployed in a way which secures the optimum utilisation of resources, continuous growth and stable balance of payments.

11. The reconciliation of objectives. It will be seen from the foregoing discussion that public finance has a variety of objectives which the Chancellor of the Exchequer must reconcile. Of paramount importance will be the need for a structure which encourages the most effective economic performance. Within this framework the detailed pattern of revenue and expenditure will seek to deploy resources between public and private sectors in a way which secures the most rapid attainment of social objectives. It is worth emphasising that, however desirable the social objectives, if the means of achieving them are inappropriate or the pace too fast the subsequent strain upon the economy may make those same objectives unattainable. We shall therefore return to the use of public finance as an instrument of economic policy.

12. Economic policy aims. A system of public finance will seek to manage total effective demand in a way which is conducive to:

   (a) *Full employment.*
   (b) *Growth.*
   (c) *Stable prices and a balance of payments equilibrium.*

In the present imperfect state of economic knowledge it may prove impossible to achieve these objectives simultaneously and socio-political considerations will establish priorities. The record would seem to indicate that during the post-war years the main concern was to stabilise demand at a level consistent with full employment, if necessary at the expense of some inflation and associated balance of payments problems and also at the cost of an unsatisfactory growth rate. A "stop-go" cycle of events emerged. During the upswing unemployment fell towards 1 per cent but demand continued to outstrip full employment output. The subsequent rise in prices and incomes induced an unfavourable balance of payments sufficient to warrant the restriction of demand by fiscal and monetary means and a mild recession ensued.

When unemployment began to rise towards 2 per cent reflationary measures were adopted which moved the economy into the next upswing.

After 1962, emphasis shifted to the management of demand in a way which would produce more rapid growth. The net result was to escalate the rate of inflation and produce more serious balance of payments crises in the middle years of the decade.

The devaluation of 1967 brought a further shift of emphasis. Priority was now given to a restraint of domestic demand sufficient to stabilise prices at a level consistent with a favourable balance of payments at the new rate of exchange. The incoming Conservative Government of 1970, despite a favourable balance of payments, placed still more emphasis upon the need to check inflation as a precondition for the long-run attainment of the other policy objectives.

In 1972, with unemployment rising above one million for the first time since the 1930s the economy was given a massive reflationary stimulus in the hope of inducing a much more rapid growth rate. In recognition that the upsurge in domestic spending would draw in more imports and bring pressure upon the sterling exchange rate and hence the foreign exchange reserves the £ was floated, (*see* XI, 26(*b*)).

By 1974, with production stagnant and unemployment rising it was apparent that the increased level of spending was being absorbed almost wholly in a rapidly rising price level. Rather than check spending the Government now relied upon stricter controls over prices and a voluntary incomes policy, the social contract. These measures alone were insufficient to check inflation and the continuing depreciation of sterling. As a condition of a massive loan in the winter of 1976 the International Monetary Fund required assurances that the growth in aggregate demand should be restrained, specifically by reducing the rate of monetary growth and the Government's borrowing requirement which induced it.

During 1977 there was some evidence that Government had less confidence in its ability to "fine tune" the economy by the methods which will now be discussed. Nevertheless, it should be recognised immediately that even though compensatory budgetary policy may be in doubt such is the scale of modern taxation and public spending that they inevitably have major implications for the three principal policy aims.

STABILISATION OF DEMAND AT FULL EMPLOYMENT

13. The revenue and expenditure approaches. Total effective demand may be stabilised by varying the structure and volume of taxation or public expenditure. Both approaches will aim to influence consumption expenditure by altering the propensity to consume or investment expenditure by affecting the marginal efficiency of capital.

Adopting the revenue approach, taxes may be classified under two headings:

(*a*) *Automatic stabilisers* (*see* **14** below).
(*b*) *Policy-effected stabilisers* (*see* **15** below).

14. Automatic stabilisers. Certain fiscal devices automatically regulate the level of demand without the need for policy decisions. They include:

(*a*) *Unemployment insurance contributions.* In the upswing excess purchasing power is removed and contributions accumulate. Conversely, in the downswing the failure of demand is partially compensated by the payment of benefits.

(*b*) *Capital depreciation allowances.* Where allowances are based upon "initial" and not "replacement" cost, during the upswing more than true profit is taxed. The opposite is true during the downswing.

(*c*) *Capital gains taxation.* In an inflationary situation any given rate taxes more than the true gain. During the downswing, if there is a falling price level, then *if* tax is paid it will be on less than the true gain.

Automatic stabilisers have the advantage that they are continuously at work without the need for publicly announced changes in economic policy which in themselves may have an adverse effect upon business confidence. On the other hand they cannot be considered as powerful as decisions to change rates of taxation or to introduce new taxes or delete old ones.

15. Policy-effected stabilisers. It will be generally true that the manipulation of the tax structure is likely to be more effective in closing an inflationary gap than in countering deflation and unemployment. The argument is that higher taxes remove purchasing power which clearly cannot then be utilised. On the other hand while lower rates of tax will increase disposable net incomes there is no certainty of a corresponding rise in demand. The increase may be saved.

Disinflationary taxation may seek to check consumption or investment.

16. Restricting consumption expenditure. Taxes may be varied upon income or expenditure.

(*a*) *Income taxes.* It has been argued that higher rates of income tax are in fact inflationary, since they lead to more militant wage claims which if conceded are reflected in higher prices. For this proposition to be true there is an assumption that the consumer is able to pay the higher price and therefore that credit will always expand ahead of tax liability. It follows that higher income-tax rates should be supported by a sufficiently strict monetary policy if consumption expenditure is to be curbed.

A more widely held view of the effect of high income taxes relates to their possible disincentive influence, which may adversely affect the volume of production. It is argued that the tax structure should encourage earning and saving while penalising spending.

(b) *Expenditure taxes.* In practice, most reliance has been placed upon higher expenditure taxes designed to discourage consumption. Much use has been made of the "regulator", the power the Chancellor has to vary the rate of V.A.T. by a maximum of 25 per cent of the rate between Budgets.

The argument against such taxes is that they are regressive. Little account is taken of "ability to pay" and the burden will inevitably fall more heavily upon the lower-income groups.

17. Restricting investment expenditure. Expenditure of any kind represents demand for limited resources. While it is clearly desirable that in the long run adequate resources should be directed to investment it is possible that in the short term investment may exceed the rate which the economy can comfortably sustain. In this case investment allowances may be made less favourable or an investment tax introduced, e.g. in Sweden an arrangement has worked where a tax upon investment was levied during the upswing of the cycle and the proceeds disbursed during the downswing.

18. Reflation. When unemployment figures begin to rise there is invariably political pressure for lower levels of taxation which it is hoped will stimulate demand. It has already been observed that there can be no certainty that an increase in net disposable income will increase the level of demand. Nevertheless, if expenditure taxes on the products of certain key industries are reduced a general expansionary effect will be anticipated provided that demand is elastic, e.g. a reduced purchase tax on motor vehicles may be expected to stimulate demand throughout that industry and also the general level of consumption in the areas in which the industry is located.

Similarly, it may be hoped to induce an "investment-led boom" by lowering the taxation of capital. If net profit margins are widened then not only will investment be encouraged but the liquidity of companies is improved. Funds are available for self-financed expansion.

On the other hand lower levels of direct personal taxation are unlikely to prove very expansionary. While it is possible that greater incentives may now exist the principal benefits will be derived by the upper-income groups who have a high propensity to save. Because of the progression in the tax system relatively little advantage accrues to the lower-income groups who have a high propensity to consume.

19. Varying the level of public expenditure. Variations in taxation depend very largely for their effect upon the uncertain responses of the private sector. A much more positive result may be expected from decisions to increase or diminish public spending.

Two factors are of importance:

(*a*) *The multiplier.* It should be remembered that the consequence of an addition or a withdrawal of a unit of public investment will be magnified by the operation of the multiplier.

(*b*) *Timing.* Precision in the management of demand depends upon appropriate timing. This implies intervention which forestalls the multiplier. A criticism of the application of these techniques has been that all too frequently Government has acted too late, e.g. expansionary measures have been adopted when the economy has already moved into the upswing, thus inducing unwanted inflationary pressures. Certain practical difficulties obstruct the correct timing of intervention:

(*i*) *Delayed information.* There is, inevitably, delay in the preparation of statistics upon which policy decisions will be based.

(*ii*) *Planning time.* A decision having been made there will be an interval before plans to increase or scale down expenditure can be completed.

(*iii*) *Implementation of plans.* For wholly practical reasons fresh work cannot be started nor existing work stopped without warning.

(*iv*) *The operating time of the multiplier.* Even when the variation in public expenditure has begun to bite there will be a time-lag before the impact on demand has worked its way through the whole economy.

Decisions to change the level of public expenditure may be applied through four channels (*see* **20–23** below).

20. Direct central Government expenditure. The great expansion of the public sector since the Second World War has made it easier for Government to have a direct influence on the rate of investment. All the nationalised industries have investment programmes, the pace of which can be regulated in accordance with the needs of demand management.

21. Local authority expenditure. Since most local authority investment is heavily dependent upon Government financial support, it is possible to regulate the rate at which plans for schools, roads, urban renewal, etc., are implemented.

22. Private investment. It may be possible to influence investment decisions in the private sector with the inducement of a system of cash grants. Government agrees to pay in cash a proportion of the total cost of investment. Such a scheme offers the advantage of selectivity both in the industries and in the regions in which the incentives are to apply.

23. Private consumption. Transfer payments in the form of family allowances, pensions and other social security benefits are made to those who may be expected to spend rather than save.

For socio-political reasons it is unlikely that any attempt would be made to curtail demand (i.e. pursue disinflationary policies) by reducing benefits. On the other hand there may be scope for a more prudent administration of social security in a way which ensures that only those in real need receive benefit.

As a means of providing stimulus for expansion it is certain that the level of consumer demand will be increased by raising benefits and this course of action may be followed if it is not at the expense of the desired rate of investment.

POLICIES FOR ECONOMIC GROWTH

24. Objectives. It has been observed that during the 1960s although the goal of full employment had been achieved there was growing dissatisfaction with the growth rate which had tended to centre upon a figure of about 2 per cent per annum. This compared very unfavourably with most advanced industrial nations and it was felt that the economy should be able to sustain a real expansion of about 4 per cent per annum. Recognition of the greater priority now given to growth policies was implied by the establishment in 1962 of the National Economic Development Council (N.E.D.C.) (*see* XIV, 9(*a*)), the creation of a new Department of Economic Affairs (1964) which placed emphasis upon expansion and the publication in 1965 of a National Plan for growth.

25. Determinants of the growth rate. The rate at which the economy grows depends upon:

(*a*) *The availability of labour and capital.*
(*b*) *The efficiency with which labour and capital are utilised.*

Ideally, the structure of public finance will be disposed in a way which is most conducive to improvement under both headings. It should be stressed, however, that in an essentially private-enterprise economy Government can only attempt to create the right conditions for expansion. It cannot guarantee that growth occurs.

26. The availability of labour and capital. In the first place the growth rate is governed by the availability of labour and capital of the right quality at the right place at the right time.

(*a*) *Labour.* Under this heading falls labour of all kinds, skilled and unskilled, managerial and entrepreneurial. Its availability hinges upon:

(*i*) *Size and structure of population.* Absolute size and rate of increase of population together with its distribution between age groups and sexes are factors governing the flow of labour on to the market.

(*ii*) *Geographical and occupational mobility.* These are considerations which determine whether labour is of the right kind and in the right place. Implicit is the need for movement not only between occupations or industries or even firms but also movement between jobs within the same firm, i.e. adaptability to new working methods and procedures.

They are in turn influenced by a country's cultural attitudes and social and economic institutions, e.g. class and sex prejudices, the educational system, the trade-union structure.

(*b*) *Capital.* The creation of capital equipment of the right kind to assist in further production depends upon:

(*i*) *Rate of saving.* Factors governing the rate of saving have already been considered (*see* II, **14**). However, the saver now requires some inducement to surrender his liquidity by investing in some tangible asset.

(*ii*) *Rate of investment* (*see* II, **15**). Before the entrepreneur will invest he must anticipate sufficient net profit to recompense both himself and those whose savings he utilises.

(*iii*) *Research*. It should not be forgotten that the purpose of all production is consumption. The creation of capital is not in itself an objective and if it is to assist in satisfying future demand it must be of the right kind. To this end there should be adequate market research to produce a reasonable prediction of demand. Secondly, there should be adequate technological research to ensure that the most productive capital equipment is created.

27. Efficient use of labour and capital. To maximise the productivity of labour and capital it is necessary that they should be both fully employed and combined in the optimum proportion appropriate to any given stage of technology. This accomplished, expansion is then limited by technological and organisational change which permits the progressive substitution of capital for labour. Implicit is the need for flexibility in the deployment of the factors of production.

28. Flexible deployment of labour. Post-war experience suggests that there is a conflict between the objectives of full employment and mobility. When the economy is run at a high level of demand, the balance of industrial power shifts from management to labour. The employee resists change which dislocates his own economic life and which may offer no immediate recompense. He is supported by trade unions which are not disposed to accept redundancies. For the sake of industrial peace the employer continues to use his labour force uneconomically and there is a strong tendency towards overmanning. He is able to hand on higher costs in higher prices since demand continues to be sustained at a sufficiently high level.

29. Flexible deployment of capital. Ideally, it is desirable to have investment which is immediately responsive to the needs of new technologies and new markets. In practice it is very difficult to achieve this sensitivity. Much investment is of a highly specialised nature, large in scale and undertaken well in advance of the demand for the consumer goods at which it is directed. A decision to construct a steel-mill in a particular location cannot be easily reversed although technological or market changes may invalidate the premises upon which the decision was based.

The best that can be said is that sudden and large-scale changes in the direction and volume of investment should be avoided.

30. A tax structure to improve the availability of labour. It may be possible to vary the incidence and the weight of taxation in a way which improves the availability of labour.

(*a*) *Direct personal taxation.* The disincentive effects of a complicated and steeply progressive system of income tax and surtax have been the subject of recent discussion but the conclusions must remain imprecise. Nevertheless, the strategy of the changes in taxation proposed by the Chancellor in December 1977 is based upon the assumption that simpler and lower direct taxation will provide an incentive to work harder.

(*b*) *Indirect taxation.* In general it may be thought that direct taxation which penalises earnings is likely to be more disincentive than indirect taxation whose incidence is upon spending. Moreover, if the incidence of this taxation is upon those luxury goods which are complementary to improved leisure pursuits there may be some incentive to work harder in order to attain them.

31. A public expenditure structure to improve the availability of labour. Public expenditure may be directed in two ways to the improvement of labour's availability:

(*a*) *Personal direct transfers.* The level of various social security payments may or may not have a direct bearing upon retirements or returns to work. There is a general assumption that they do and governments have periodically attempted administrative adjustments to make payments more stringently, e.g. in 1970, the first three days of sickness were disqualified from benefit on the grounds that absenteeism was being encouraged.

A similar approach to the payment of supplementary benefits to firemen during their strike in the winter of 1977 met with less success.

(*b*) *Improvement of the economic infrastructure.* It is from expenditure in this field that the most positive long-term results will be expected although they will not be quantifiable. An effective education service coupled with adequate retraining facilities will improve the quality, the adaptability and the mobility of the labour force. An efficient health service will reduce the number of days lost through sickness and extend the working life of the population. Expenditure upon housing and communications may be expected to improve geographical mobility.

32. A tax structure to improve the availability of capital. The taxation of profits must have regard to the need to leave sufficient

incentive to the saver to surrender his liquidity and to the entrepreneur to invest (*see* **26** (*b*)).

(*a*) *Taxation of company profits.* When costs rise more rapidly
than the general price level, profits may be squeezed to a degree
which is incompatible with the desired rate of investment. Capital
cannot be renewed from the reduced volume of retained company
profits. There is no incentive to raise fresh equity capital for the
purpose of expansion. In such a situation there is a strong argument for the reduction of profits taxation.

Assuming that companies have ample profits they may be induced to reinvest by favourable allowances which can be offset
against tax liability, e.g. variable capital depreciation allowances.

(*b*) *Taxation of investment income.* British taxation normally
discriminates against distributed profits in the hope that companies will retain a larger proportion in order to finance their own
capital requirements. There is further discrimination against dividend income upon which the recipient pays a higher rate than he
does on earned income. It may be anticipated that beyond a certain point the incentive to the individual investor is removed and
fresh capital will not be forthcoming.

The principal point is that if the net return to risk capital falls
below a certain level the willingness to undertake risk upon which
change and growth ultimately depend will be inhibited.

33. Public expenditure and the supply of capital. Saving and investment may be encouraged by:

(*a*) *Cash grants* to firms on the condition of further investment,
e.g. the Investment Incentives scheme of 1966. The objection to
this method is that it distorts market forces and may encourage
investment which is not genuinely profitable. The scheme was
abandoned in 1970.

(*b*) *Support to local authorities* for the purpose of improving
the local economic environment may encourage private investment.

(*c*) *Investment programmes of public corporations.* The Government is in a powerful position to force saving and investment by
increasing taxation and devoting the proceeds to investment in
the nationalised industries.

**34. Financial policy and the optimum deployment of labour and
capital.** It has been observed (*see* **27** above) that the efficient use
of labour and capital involves their combination in optimum pro-

portions in the wake of changing technologies and markets. While the principal instrument will be "productivity bargaining" between management and labour, public finance may provide a context which is conducive to such improvements.

(*a*) *Structure of taxation*. The object will be to influence the labour/capital cost ratio in a way which promotes the substitution of capital for labour.

The criticism has been levelled that compared with our European competitors it has been *artificially* cheaper to employ more labour rather than more capital. For example, the proportion of the social insurance contribution borne by the State is considerably higher in the U.K. than elsewhere. Moreover, food subsidies and the pricing policies of the nationalised industries weighted in favour of the consumer have all tended to relieve the employer of the *full* cost of labour. On the other hand, the taxation of capital in the U.K. has been severe compared with European countries.

In the middle 1970s the cost ratio has further deteriorated. Inflation, incomes policies designed primarily to hold down unemployment together with employment premiums and employment protection legislation have all militated in favour of a labour intensive economy.

It will be seen that at least in theory the ratio might be reversed by discriminatory taxation.

(*b*) *Structure of public expenditure*. There are a number of directions in which public funds may be used to secure a better utilisation of labour and capital:

(*i*) *Housing*. Support for private and municipal building programmes may be expected to contribute to labour mobility.

(*ii*) *Adequate unemployment benefits* when coupled with redundancy payments may relieve the resistance to the redundancies which inevitably follow change.

(*iii*) *Education and training* when soundly based will improve skills and aptitudes which in turn will increase mobility.

(*iv*) *Government-sponsored research and development* which encourages selective investment of the most productive kind.

THE STABILISATION OF PRICES

35. The nature of the problem. The stabilisation of prices has been an economic policy objective for two main reasons:

(*a*) *Arbitrary redistribution of incomes.* In a period of rapid inflation there is a redistribution of "real" income from those whose money incomes are fixed to those whose money incomes respond to price change; from weak and badly organised labour to strong and militant trade unionists; from lenders to borrowers.

(*b*) *Imbalance in foreign payments.* As inflation progresses export prices lose their competitive edge while the high domestic price level invites an increase in imports. A balance of payments crisis ensues necessitating restrictive policies which retard growth and increase unemployment.

36. A majority view of the causes of inflation. During the 1960s the most widely held view of the cause of inflation rested upon the connection between a high pressure of demand in a tight labour market and rising costs and prices which in turn gave a further twist to the wage/price spiral.

(*a*) *Demand in the labour market.* It was argued by A. W. Phillips that there exists a positive relationship between the rate of change of wages and the demand for labour which in turn is inversely related to the percentage rate of unemployment. It then follows that the rate at which wage rates change will be determined by the unemployment percentage. (*See* IV, **14.**)

(*b*) *Inflated wage costs.* Since wages are a major cost in all forms of production and since all firms in an industry are likely to accede to a wage increase agreed by one there will be a squeeze on profit margins and a strong incentive to raise prices.

(*c*) *Wage/price spiral.* The general rise in prices which was initiated by an excessively low unemployment percentage now gives rise to further wage demands and inflation gathers momentum.

37. Disinflationary policies. If the foregoing explanation of inflation is accepted there are four possible courses of action.

(*a*) *A general restriction of demand* (*see* **38** below).
(*b*) *Regional development* (*see* **39** below).
(*c*) *Structural improvements* (*see* **40** below).
(*d*) *Incomes policy* (*see* **41–43** below).

38. A general restriction of demand. The fiscal measures appropriate to a reduction of the pressure of demand have been considered (*see* **13–23** above). The intention will be to stabilise the economy at a higher level of unemployment.

Three objections arise:

(a) *Social cost.* There are obvious social objections to policies deliberately designed to raise unemployment.

(b) *Loss of potential output.* At current prices a rise of 0.2 per cent in the rate of unemployment may be associated with a loss of production of about £600 million.

(c) *The phenomenon of inflation and rising unemployment.* In the post-war years the fiscal weapon has been regularly used to check the rate of inflation and this has generally been achieved at about 2 per cent unemployment. However, by 1970, despite severely restrictive taxation the rate of inflation had escalated to $8\frac{1}{2}$ per cent at the same time as unemployment rose to 3 per cent, its highest point since the 1930s. The immediate implication was that to contain inflation by a further restriction of demand would result in unemployment of a wholly unacceptable level.

A more radical view was that the accepted analysis of inflation was invalid. The inflation/unemployment trade-off postulated by Phillips did not occur. Inflation was purely a monetary phenomenon. This explanation will be examined fully in Chapter IV.

39. Regional development. The distribution of unemployment is by no means even and many areas of the country, e.g. Merseyside, Cumbria, have figures well above the national average. It is argued that inflation may be relieved by regional policies which increase unemployment in areas where there is excessive demand for labour at the same time as unemployment is decreased in the depressed areas. Thus unemployment is simply "transferred," the national figure remaining the same.

Financial incentives e.g. favourable tax treatment, discriminatory investment grants can be built into the fiscal system in an attempt to achieve this objective but the results will be unpredictable.

40. Structural improvements. Inflationary pressures arise from impediments in the functioning of labour markets. Government may assist occupational and geographical mobility with re-training schemes and housing programmes.

More fundamentally, the improvement of industrial relations may ease the problems of damaging and inflationary industrial disputes.

This has been a major theme for some years. In 1969 Government attempted, without success, to implement the proposals of its White Paper, *In Place of Strife*. These aimed to improve the collective bargaining process in a way which would reduce strike action.

The following Government's Industrial Relations Act of 1971 which had broadly similar objectives was equally unsuccessful.

It is a matter for debate whether trade unions exercise too much or too little power, whether the leadership is more or less militant than the membership, whether they are constrained too much or too little by the law. The conclusions reached will determine the extent to which Government may actively contribute to improved industrial relations and the usefulness of this approach in reducing inflationary pressure.

INCOMES POLICY

41. Incomes policy objectives. Incomes policies have been seen variously as short-term expedients for arresting inflation and associated balance of payments problems; as a longer-term method of avoiding inflation at full employment and of achieving a more equitable distribution of income and more recently as the principal Government instrument for checking inflationary wage rises which in a period of monetary restraint would price more men out of work.

42. Chronology of U.K. incomes policy. There have been six attempts to establish policies in restraint of prices and incomes.

(*a*) *1948.* Following the 1947 balance of payments crisis, the Government applied its remaining wartime powers to check price rises at the same time as it secured the co-operation of the trade unions in postponing wage claims. This policy met with some success until the 1949 devaluation brought inflationary pressures which forced the unions to abandon restraint.

(*b*) *1956.* The Government asked for a voluntary and temporary "wage pause" but was unsuccessful in gaining union co-operation. An independent and purely advisory body, the Council on Productivity, Prices and Incomes, was then set up but met with little success.

(*c*) *1961.* A pay pause was initiated, followed in 1962 by the setting up of a National Incomes Commission (N.I.C.) to review pay claims, and the publication of "guiding lights" for wages and salaries. Without union support, N.I.C. proved uninfluential.

(*d*) *1964.* A "declaration of intent" on productivity, prices and incomes was signed by employers, unions and Government as a pre-condition of economic policies which would permit more rapid growth. Finally, the machinery of a full-scale incomes policy was provided in 1965 with the establishment of a National Board for Prices and Incomes (N.B.P.I. or P.I.B.) which replaced N.I.C. and was to review price and pay increases. Its criteria were set out in a White Paper, *Prices and Incomes Policy*. A norm for wage increases was established at 3–3½ per cent. In 1966, statutory effect was given to a six-month wage and price freeze followed by six months of "severe restraint". A return was made to a voluntary policy in 1967. In 1970 the incoming Conservative Government declared its lack of confidence in a formal incomes policy and announced that the P.I.B. would be disbanded.

(e) *1972.* A statutory policy was imposed in November, 1972 with an enforced pay standstill. Subsequently a Pay Board and Prices Commission were established to apply the rules through the three stages of the Government's policy. Statutory incomes controls were abandoned with the outgoing Conservative Government in 1974.

(f) *1975.* A new "voluntary policy" took the form of the "*social contract*". The T.U.C. and the Labour Government agreed the broad social and economic policies which were to be pursued. In return the T.U.C. supported a policy limiting pay increases to £6 per week with no increases for those with annual income in excess of £8,500. Stage II of the policy was again based upon a flat rate increase, on this occasion £4 per week. During 1977, after much discussion by the T.U.C. of the need for "an orderly return to free collective bargaining", Stage III emerged as a general indication by Government that average pay increases should not exceed 10 per cent. In practice this has been interpreted as a 10 per cent norm with Government selectively applying a variety of sanctions to firms exceeding the norm.

In December, 1977 the Chancellor gave some indication that he was looking for a formula upon which to base a permanent incomes policy.

43. Income policy problems. From the preceding account it will be observed that all income policies have been short lived. The evidence points to a number of practical problems.

(a) *Do income policies cure inflation?* The prevailing assumption has been that inflation is rooted in rising wage costs induced by running the economy at an unrealistically low level of unemployment. This view is opposed by monetary economists who see rising wages like rising prices as a *symptom* and not a cause of inflation (*see* IV).

(*b*) *Voluntary or statutory?* The trade union movement has not been prepared to accept statutory policies other than for a strictly limited period of time. There is also some suggestion that co-operation in a voluntary policy may be more easily achieved with a Labour rather than Conservative Government.

(*c*) *Voluntary policies.* In the first instance there may be some doubt about a *voluntary* policy which is supported by non-statutory sanctions such as those applied by Government in 1977. Secondly, tripartite agreements between Government, T.U.C. and C.B.I. or still more significantly, bipartite agreements between the Government and T.U.C. would seem to give undue weight to some sectional interest at the expense of others and for this reason may not command the support of the whole country. Thirdly, such agreements disintegrate when the T.U.C. cease to receive the support of their membership.

(*d*) *Percentage increases.* The experience has been that the declared maximum or average percentage increase has in practice been treated as the minimum which negotiators would accept. This inflexibility has borne heavily upon the very low paid whose *absolute* increases have been correspondingly low.

(*e*) *Flat rate increases.* Conversely, flat rate increases erode differentials and reduce incentives. Evidence in 1976–7 suggests that this approach may be a major cause of industrial disputes.

(*f*) *Labour market distortions.* A severe criticism of flat rate increases is that imperfections in the labour markets are increased. It becomes more difficult for successful, expanding firms to attract the labour which they need since they are unable to bid up wages. Labour becomes that much less mobile.

(*g*) *Public sector pay.* As the most important employer it is of course inevitable that Government should have a pay policy in respect of its own employees. With the majority of pay agreements concluded nationally and with increased emphasis upon comparability, awards made in the public sector are clearly of great significance to pay levels in the private sector.

It will be equally true that any acceleration of private sector wage rates will induce pressures in the public sector. Government is therefore obliged to have an interest in the whole spectrum of incomes.

CONCLUSIONS ON DEMAND MANAGEMENT

44. A faulty steering mechanism. It has been observed that during the 1960s the steering mechanism of demand management operated with less and less precision (*see* I, 35–36). After 1966, the new phenomenon of rising prices and incomes accompanied by increasing unemployment put in doubt the possibility of steering a middle course between too much inflation and too much unemployment, trading one off against the other (*see* IV, 14–17).

45. Ad hoc interventions. This loss of confidence led in the 1970s to increased reliance upon direct interventions to deal with immediate problems as they arose.

Rising unemployment was checked by subventions for failing firms and industries under the Industry Acts of 1972 and 1975, by employment subsidies, the extension of public ownership, job creation schemes and employment protection legislation.

The strategy for checking inflation rested almost entirely upon phased incomes policy which was accepted with increasing reluctance.

46. Monetarism. The failure of demand management to achieve its goals was from a monetarist point of view entirely predictable, (*see* I, 38). Their criticism is directed to the role in the economy which Keynesians have assigned to money.

This controversy will be examined in Chapter IV.

PROGRESS TEST 3

1. In what senses may public finance be employed as an instrument of social policy? (7, 8, 9)

2. Point out four areas in which public finance may be employed in support of economic policy. (10)

3. At what policy objectives will "demand management" be aimed? (12)

4. What do you understand by an "automatic stabiliser"? (14)

5. Compare income taxes and expenditure taxes as means of restricting consumption. (16)

6. Is it ever justifiable to restrict investment? (17)

7. What practical difficulties are encountered in using public expenditure as an instrument of demand management? (19)

8. Through which agencies can central government expenditure be channelled? (20–23)

9. Analyse the determinants of the economic growth rate. (25–29)

10. Compare the effectiveness of direct and indirect taxes as means of improving the availability of labour. (30)

11. Suggest how taxes may be varied to improve the flow of capital. (32)

12. How might public expenditure improve the rates of saving and investment? (33)

13. How might financial policy improve the labour/capital cost ratio? (34)

14. Explain the generally held view of the causes of inflation. (36)

15. What do you understand by "incomes policy"? (41)

16. Do you consider that an incomes policy has any future in the U.K.? (43)

CHAPTER IV

The Role of Money in the Economy

A KEYNESIAN VIEW OF MONEY AND NATIONAL INCOME DETERMINATION

1. A synthesis of the real and monetary worlds. Our account of the Keynesian analysis of national income determination and its implications for public policy has so far neglected the role of money. In fact, a highly important aspect of Keynes's work was to show the impact of financial mechanisms and institutions upon output and employment.

In the classical model of the economy money played a minor role. It was simply a medium of exchange. Production created its own demand for the output and employment of others (*see* I, 8). *Real* factors determined the level of *real* national income. On the other hand in the world of money, monetary factors determined the general level of prices (*see* 5).

Keynes attempted a synthesis of the two, making money a central feature of his analysis. For him it was more than a medium of exchange. It was a unique financial asset, the only one with complete liquidity and instant purchasing power. This being the case, significantly it would be held for *precautionary motives*.

2. Transactions money and liquidity or precautionary money. Classical monetary policy centred upon the effect of a moving interest rate which served as a price mechanism. An expansion of the money supply would be consistent with lower interest rates, supply having outstripped existing demand. Cheaper money would in turn encourage businessmen to invest in more capital goods. The higher level of investment would increase national income and employment through the operation of the multiplier (*see* II, 16).

The implication of this reasoning is that an expansionary monetary policy would lead to growth in income, output and employment. A restrictive policy would have the opposite effect.

Keynesians argued that these predicted results would not

necessarily occur. They based their criticism upon a distinction between *transactions money* and *liquidity or precautionary money*.

(a) *Transactions money*. This is money in its capacity as a medium of exchange. It is required to conduct everyday business, the amount needed equating with the volume of that business. In other words, it is the national income measured in money terms. We have now to recognise that a monetary expansion which initiates lower interest rates and higher national income necessitates more *transactions* money to finance the increased volume of business. Whether such money is available from a given growth in the supply now depends on the demand for money for liquidity or precautionary purposes.

(b) *Liquidity or precautionary money*. A proportion of the total money stock is always required to satisfy the preference in the economy for liquidity. In some part this preference will be determined by the instinctive precaution to have some purchasing power instantly available. For the rest, we shall expect liquidity preference to be geared to the rate of interest. When rates are high liquidity preference will be low, any increase in cash balances being invested in income yielding financial assets. When rates are low the opportunity cost of holding assets in liquid or cash form has been reduced and the risk of holding financial assets of variable value totally eliminated. Liquidity preference consequently increases.

It will now be noted that when liquidity preference is low and excess cash is invested in financial assets, interest rates are driven down. For example, if the market bids up the price of a 5 per cent £100 bond to £200 then the yield falls to £2.50 per £100. If on the other hand liquidity preference is already high then monetary expansion which expresses itself simply in higher cash balances will not reduce interest rates further, since there is no increased demand for financial assets. With interest rates the same the incentive to invest is unaltered. National income does not increase.

This phenomenon was referred to by Keynesians as the *liquidity trap* and explains their belief that monetary policy was incapable of curing a depression. It followed that the thrust of Government policy would necessarily depend upon the more direct methods of influencing aggregate demand through the public finances. These were considered in Chapter III.

3. Lower interest rates and an adequate money supply. On this analysis monetary policy would still have a subsidiary role. In the first place, low interest rates were desirable both to encourage investment and to minimise the cost to Government of sustaining aggregate demand through deficit public finance, i.e. the servicing charge of an expanding national debt.

Secondly, with a low interest rate high national income economy there is a correspondingly high demand for transactions money, less being left for precautionary purposes. Interest rates may however, fall to a level at which liquidity preference is increased. Some people will wish to exchange financial assets such as bonds for cash. Since the stock of precautionary cash is limited heavy sales will depress capital values, i.e. force up interest rates. At higher rates, investment, national income, employment and the demand for transactions money all decline. Of a given money stock more is now available to satisfy the demand for precautionary purposes. A new equilibrium is established albeit at a lower level of activity. It follows from this argument that attempts to sustain full employment by fiscal methods should be supported by an expansionary monetary policy.

A KEYNESIAN VIEW OF MONEY AND PRICE DETERMINATION

4. Money national income and the price level. In Chapter II we examined the factors which determined *real* national income. To this equation we have added the Keynesian explanation of the influence of money and the interest rate. Still adopting the Keynesian analysis we must now explain the determinants of *money* national income. To do so, we should not only understand the factors which determine real income (Q) but also those which govern the *general or average price level* (P). Money national income will then be $P \times Q$.

5. The classical view. The classical explanation of price determination is usually referred to as the *quantity theory of money* expressed in the formula

$$M \times V = P \times Q$$

where M is the quantity of money, V is the velocity of circulation, (the number of times the money stock changes hands), P is the general price level and Q is the *real* national income of goods and services.

It was further postulated that Q would be determined by

physical considerations such as the availability of the factors of production and technological efficiency. Velocity was also determined by outside forces in the shape of institutional arrangements, e.g. whether wage payments were made weekly or monthly.

Since V and Q were already determined it followed that movements of P depended upon changes in M. It was the money supply which governed the general price level.

6. Keynesian rejection of quantity theory. Criticism is ultimately aimed at the presumed stability of the velocity of circulation and is based upon the fundamental distinction between transactions money and liquidity money.

Quantity theory is accepted in respect of transactions money. Under a given regime of institutional arrangements this element of the money supply will correspond to money national income, $P \times Q$.

As we have seen, however, the demand for liquidity money varies with the rate of interest. As rates fall so liquidity preference increases and higher cash balances are held. Put another way, the *velocity of circulation of liquidity money varies with the rate of interest*.

It follows that what is true for one aspect of the money stock is relevant to the whole. This view leads to the conclusion that velocity is not a stable factor governed by institutional arrangements alone but that *it is influenced by the rate of interest*.

At this juncture the causal connection between M and P is broken. If interest rates are already low an expansion of the money supply will not express itself in a further reduction. We fall into the liquidity trap and simply add to our cash balances. In short, an increase in M is offset by a decline in V which leaves $P \times Q$ unchanged.

7. An extreme Keynesian view of price determination. The extreme position is one in which the quantity of money is of very little consequence. It may be added that Keynes himself did not subscribe to this view and was fully aware of the effects upon price of monetary expansion once full employment had been achieved.

However, from this extreme position, *money* wages are established by collective bargaining. Simultaneously, the level of employment will have been determined by the size of *real* national income. Real wages, i.e. the share of output accruing to labour will be in line with labour's marginal productivity. Since money wages *and* real wages are known, we have a fairly good idea of the general level of prices.

Thus, with real national income determined by consumption, investment and Government expenditure and prices determined by money wages, money national income will be $P \times Q$.

Money measurements of wages, prices and incomes are thought in any case to be of only minor interest and this analysis gives no attention to any influences which money and prices may themselves exert.

8. The significance of money and prices further developed. Modern monetarists have argued that the Keynesian explanation of equilibrium with low national income and employment depends upon the presence of market imperfections, e.g. the monopoly power of labour unions. Too little attention is paid to the power of flexible prices. If prices and wages were free to move downwards then employment and output would rise.

This claim is disputed by the Keynesians, who argue that their analysis holds good even in a situation in which wages and prices are flexible. A fall in wages and prices will result in a fall in *money* national income. With a given money stock, less is now required for transactions and more is available for liquidity purposes. Some of the extra liquidity money *may* be converted to financial assets, thus increasing capital values and forcing down interest rates. In this case investment will be stimulated and income and employment will rise. *Such a sequence of events will, however, only occur in the absence of the liquidity trap.* In an economy which is already depressed extra liquidity money may be held as cash leaving interest rates unaltered. Flexible market prices are thus no more effective in restoring full employment equilibrium than is monetary policy.

9. A rejoinder. Professor Friedman has responded to this argument by pointing to the work of Professors Pigou and Haberler. The "Pigou effect" describes the way in which the value of money varies in direct proportion to systematic movements in prices and wages. Clearly, if the price level is halved the value of *cash balances* is doubled.

It is then argued that if prices continue to fall a point must ultimately be reached at which the appreciation in the value of cash balances induces holders to increase consumption expenditure.

When this happens, Friedman continues, the liquidity trap is by-passed. Changes in the real quantity of money (purchasing power) directly influence aggregate demand without any dependence upon changes in interest rates.

If it can then be shown that changes in the *nominal* quantity of money govern the price level and hence the purchasing power of money, i.e. the *real* quantity, then it follows that variations in the money stock have a significant bearing upon aggregate demand.

These perceptions provided a starting point for the *counter-revolution in monetary theory*.

A MONETARIST VIEW OF MONEY, PRICES AND NATIONAL INCOME DETERMINATION

10. The price level and money national income are determined by the quantity of money. The modern monetarist position is neatly summarised in the argument developed by Professor Friedman in *The Counter-Revolution in Monetary Theory* (Occasional Paper 33, Institute of Economic Affairs).

(*a*) *A consistent relationship between monetary growth and nominal incomes*. A mass of evidence points to the universal truth of this assertion. Currently, he claims, the time lag between the two is of the order of six to nine months.

(*b*) *Relationship between monetary growth, output and prices*. Initially, the impact of an expansion of the money supply will be absorbed almost wholly in higher output with hardly any effect upon prices. After a *further* six to nine months prices will begin to rise.

(*i*) The *immediate* effect is not upon nominal income but upon liquidity. Cash balances increase relative to other financial assets such as bonds, equities, property. In this assertion, Keynesians and monetarists are in agreement.

(*ii*) Holders of extra cash will now attempt to restore the previous ratio of cash to other assets. For the economy as a whole the attempt will be frustrated since one man's purchase is another man's sale. However, the brisker turnover of financial assets will push up capital values, i.e. drive down interest rates.

(*iii*) Lower interest rates are conducive to increased borrowing and spending both on new assets and on current goods and services. Thus over some six to nine months the effect of monetary expansion has been to increase aggregate demand, nominal incomes, employment and output.

(*iv*) During the same period there has been little change in prices. There are as yet no inflationary expectations and future wages and prices have been set in advance. Subsequently, when entrepreneurs perceive that business remains good they will attempt not only to overcome the physical difficulties of increasing output but also to widen profit margins. Characteristically, the prices of goods and services will therefore respond to an unanticipated rise in nominal demand more rapidly than the prices of the factors of production, e.g. nominal wages. What in fact has happened is that *real* wages paid by employers have fallen and it is this reduction, unperceived by labour, which has made possible the higher level of employment.

(*c*) *The short term and the long term.* Monetarists recognise that in the short term which may be as long as five to ten years the overall impact of monetary expansion will be upon money incomes, output and employment. Over a period of decades, however, it is prices which are primarily affected. Expectations are adjusted and labour demands higher money wages to compensate for higher anticipated prices. Increased wage costs now make that expectation a reality.

Since the quantity of money has determined the price of the national output it follows that it has also determined the size of *money* national income.

11. Real factors determine real national income and the level of employment. Professor Friedman's argument continues that in the long term "what happens to the level of output depends upon real factors: the enterprise, ingenuity and industry of the people; the extent of thrift; the structure of industry and Government; the relations among nations and so on."

It is these real factors which at any time will determine "the natural level of unemployment". Fundamentally, this level is governed by imperfections in the market, the inability rapidly to redeploy resources to meet changing conditions coupled with the downward inflexibility of wages.

It is impossible to reduce unemployment permanently below this level (which would have been determined in a free market) by either monetary or fiscal stimulus.

12. Implications for public policy. It can be seen from the discussion so far that the differences between Keynesians and monetarists are fundamental. While the former perceive a central stabilising role for fiscal and monetary policy the latter view such attempts at "fine tuning" as being themselves the principal destabilising agents.

(a) *Fiscal policy.* Monetarists consider the measures which were outlined in Chapter III as ineffective. If a stimulus to aggregate demand is given through tax financed public spending then there is a corresponding reduction in private sector spending, immediately in consumption or indirectly in savings which would have been lent to other spenders. There is a similar result when public spending is financed by borrowing private savings. Resources are simply transferred from private to public sector use.

"To discover any net effect on total spending, one must go to a more sophisticated level—to differences in the behaviour of the two groups of people or to effects of Government borrowing on interest rates. There is no first order effect." (Friedman.)

(b) *Monetary policy.* While recognising the potency of monetary policy, monetarists maintain that too little is known of the *precise* relationship between money and *real* magnitudes such as *real* national income and the level of unemployment for even monetary "fine tuning" to be feasible. The best that can be done is to ensure that variations in the money supply are not themselves the source of instability, e.g. the monetary contractions in the U.K., 1925–31 and the U.S.A., 1929–33 which may be seen as the true cause of the slump.

However, nominal magnitudes such as the price level, the money national income and the exchange rate are in principle more amenable to control by the authorities through the money supply. Of these, a stable price level is thought to be of greatest importance since by reducing the risk of forward planning business confidence is increased. Once again however, the precise relationship between money and prices is ill-understood. The most realistic monetary policy is, therefore, one which prescribes, publicises and adheres to a fixed rate of monetary growth sufficient to accommodate any real economic expansion, e.g. 5 per cent. Long-term price stability would now be assured.

13. Conclusion. In conclusion the fundamental difference between the Keynesian and monetarist approaches should again be stressed. While the former postulates a major role for Government in guiding the economy the latter denies the validity of any discretionary macroeconomic policy. A genuine equilibrium will be achieved only through a more perfect functioning of the market.

This conclusion, they say, is based not only upon the logic of their analysis but also upon observation of the inherent instability and structural distortion of economies where discretionary policies have been most widely practised.

This criticism will be developed more fully in the next section with particular reference to the U.K. economy.

THE PHILLIPS CURVE AND THE INFLATION/ UNEMPLOYMENT TRADE-OFF

14. Steering a middle course. In 1958, Professor A. W. Phillips published the results of extensive research in an essay, "The Relation between Unemployment and the Rate of Change of Money Wages in the United Kingdom, 1861–1957" (*Economica*, Vol. 25, 1958).

He sought to show a regular inverse relationship in which wages rose more rapidly in periods when unemployment was low. Since wages constitute a major element of all costs, when they rose rapidly so would prices.

It followed that a lower rate of inflation could be bought at the expense of a higher level of unemployment and vice-versa. Since the Keynesian analysis provided an instrument for determining employment levels it should be possible to steer an acceptable course between the two extremes.

In the early 1960s this thinking was quantified with the suggestion that "full employment" should be reconceived in terms of 2.4 per cent unemployment, approximately twice the previously acceptable figures. With this margin of unused resources we should be able to enjoy a high and stable level of activity without inflation. By 1966, the proposal had been accepted by Government.

After 1966, emerged the new phenomenon of rising unemployment accompanied by escalating inflation. There was now apparently no trade-off. Since it was considered politically impossible deliberately to advocate still higher unemployment as a check to inflation, Governments during the following ten years have relied even more heavily upon incomes policies in the view that the immediate cause of inflation is wage cost push (*see* III, **41–6**). In contrast, as we have seen, monetarists maintain that "inflation is always and everywhere a monetary phenomenon".

15. The Phillips curve.

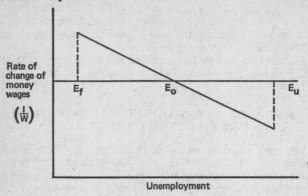

FIG. 2 *The Phillips curve.* The curve postulates an inverse relationship between the rate of unemployment and the rate of change of money wages and, hence, prices.

In Fig. 2, E_o is the "natural level of unemployment" consistent with neither upward nor downward pressure on wages and prices. At E_f there is overfull employment inducing upward pressure on wages and prices. At E_u with excessive unemployment wages are falling.

16. The fallacy in the Phillips curve. Monetarists argue that no economist has ever maintained that demand and supply were functions of *nominal* wages. It is the *real* wage (what the money will buy) which relates to both the demand for and the supply of labour. When the vertical axis is correctly labelled Real Wages (W/P) then the curve tells us nothing of the relationship between the level of unemployment and the rate of change of *money* wages and prices. In other words, it provides no explanation of inflation, the origin of which must be found elsewhere.

Thus, in Fig. 3, at E_o there is equilibrium with neither upward nor downward pressure on *real* wages. *But* that equilibrium will remain undisturbed with money wages and prices separately constant *or* rising at 10 per cent or falling at 10 per cent provided that they both change in the same proportion. It is of course the rise in money wages which is symptomatic of inflation.

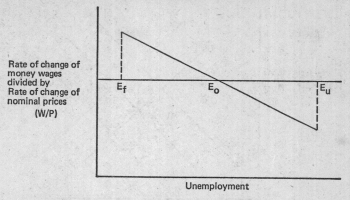

Rate of change of
money wages
divided by
Rate of change of
nominal prices
(W/P)

Unemployment

FIG. 3 *The fallacy in the Phillips curve.* The vertical axis now represents real wages (W/P). This curve tells us nothing about the relationship between unemployment and the rate of change of money wages.

The explanation of this simple error, say the monetarists, is to be found in the Keynesian view that increased demand would express itself in increased employment and output. *Prices would remain stable.* It followed therefore that a rise in *money* wages implied an equal rise in real wages.

Phillips himself was in fact being rather more subtle. He was suggesting that an *anticipated* change in money wages would equate with an *anticipated* change in real wages even though that expectation might not be fulfilled.

17. Unemployment cannot be permanently reduced by accepting a higher but stable rate of inflation. From a monetarist standpoint we have established that inflation cannot be checked simply by accepting a higher rate of unemployment. Equally, unemployment cannot be permanently reduced by accepting a higher but *stable* rate of inflation. This aspect of the case is summarised in Fig. 4.

We have shown that monetarists assume that in the long term the main impact of an increase in aggregate demand is upon prices rather than upon employment and output (*see* **10**(*c*)). For simplicity, in Fig. 4 it is assumed that there is *no* increase in output.

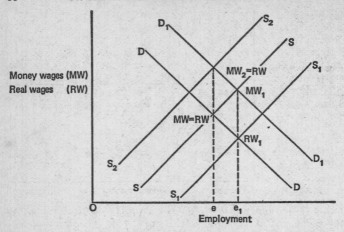

FIG. 4 *Long-term effect of stimulating demand to reduce unemployment.* Employment will be increased only for as long as labour accepts lower real wages.

At O_e employment and money wages (MW) equalling real wages (RW) there is equilibrium without inflation but with ee_1 unemployment, "the natural rate" in monetarist terms.

If it is desired to reduce this unemployment by an orthodox stimulus to aggregate demand, the demand curve (DD) is shifted to the right to D_1D_1. The very short term effect is the establishment of a new equilibrium at money wages of MW_1 and employment of O_{e1}. Concealed is the fall in real wages to RW_1. While labour was unwilling to accept a lower *money* wage in order to increase employment it has unwittingly accepted a lower *real* wage. The labour supply curve (SS) has in effect moved to the right to S_1S_1 and the true equilibrium lies at RW_1.

The higher level of employment will be sustained only for as long as labour is prepared to accept lower real wages. When expectations adjust to the higher prices associated with higher money wages and no increase in output there will be pressure for still higher money wages to restore living standards. The labour supply curve shifts to the left to S_2S_2 where a fresh equilibrium is established at money wages of MW_2 to equal the original real wage of RW. Unemployment reverts to its "natural" level of ee_1

albeit at a higher level of money wages and prices. A *given* rate of inflation has not sustained the higher level of employment.

The manoeuvre can only be successfully repeated provided that inflation is kept ahead of labour's expectations, i.e. the demand curve is moved to the right more rapidly than the response of the supply curve to the left. This implies a policy of deliberately accelerating inflation since in the long term labour's response to downward pressure on *real* wages becomes increasingly sensitive.

18. A perspective. In the U.K. in 1978, it is accepted that the fiscal instruments of "fine tuning" are not capable of operating with anything like the precision which was originally thought possible. It is also evident that the administrative machinery for exercising accurate control over these instruments is far from adequate. Attention will be given to this particular problem in V.

Beyond this and as we have observed, the whole theoretical foundation of demand management policy has in recent years been subjected to powerful criticism. Partly in consequence of this criticism and partly in consequence of British experience after 1966 it is generally recognised that it is no longer possible "to spend a way out of recession".

In the 1970s emphasis has been given spasmodically to monetary restraint. This was particularly true during 1977 when the International Monetary Fund made stringent control of the money supply a condition of a large loan granted in December 1976. It would, however, be far from true to say that monetarist doctrine had been accepted. Even were this view to prevail there are formidable practical problems, firstly in determining what exactly money is and secondly in devising effective methods to regulate its growth. These problems we shall consider in VII–IX.

PROGRESS TEST 4

1. What did Keynes consider to be the unique feature of money? **(1)**
2. Distinguish between transactions money and liquidity money. **(2)**
3. Explain why interest rates fall when capital values rise. **(2(b))**
4. Explain the quantity theory of money. **(5)**
5. Why did Keynesians reject quantity theory? **(5)**

6. What do you understand by "the liquidity trap"?   (2(*b*))

7. Why in the Keynesian view will lower wages not necessarily restore full employment equilibrium?   (8)

8. Explain "the Pigou effect".   (9)

9. Outline the steps between an increase in the money supply and a rise in the general price level as seen by the monetarists. (10)

10. How is real national income determined in the monetarist system?   (11)

11. What economic policy conclusions will be drawn from monetarist thinking?   (12)

12. What theoretical reasons would lead us to believe that unemployment cannot be permanently reduced by accepting a higher rate of inflation?   (17)

CHAPTER V

The Machinery of Demand Management

THE POLICY-MAKING ORGANISATION

1. The Treasury. The modern Treasury originated in 1714 when the medieval office of Treasurer to the Crown was "put into commission," i.e. a number of Lords Commissioners shared the office as a Board of Treasury. The Prime Minister is the First Lord of the Treasury and the Chancellor of the Exchequer is the Second Lord with the special responsibility of placing before Parliament the Government's financial policy.

2. Treasury responsibilities. Since the powers and responsibilities of the Treasury are not defined by statute it is difficult to delineate the scope of its work with precision.

Traditionally, its first and central task is to raise money to finance Government expenditure but in the twentieth century the Treasury's influence has extended into many other fields determined by the interests and personal stature of its Permanent Secretaries. In the inter-war period there was a total rejection of the idea that Government expenditure could relieve the problem of unemployment and the principal preoccupation lay with the Treasury's function in managing the Civil Service.

During the war, Government intervention in the economy resulted in the formation of the Central Statistical Office and the Economic Section of the Cabinet Office, both of which played a major part in the co-ordination of the work of departments with economic interests under the general direction of the Lord President of the Council. In 1947, the latter's economic responsibilities were taken over by a new Ministry of Economic Affairs under Sir Stafford Cripps. When six weeks later he moved to the Treasury he took with him his new economic functions. By 1950, any post-war notions of detailed central economic planning had been abandoned and Cripps himself stated that "the Budget itself can be described as the most important control and the most important instrument for influencing economic policy".

Keynesian doctrine had been accepted and the Treasury was to provide the machinery for its implementation. Apart from 1964–9, the lifespan of a revived Department of Economic Affairs, these macroeconomic functions have remained with the Treasury.

3. The other economic Departments. The Treasury has never been the only Department with economic interests although the division of functions between other Ministries has varied very frequently. Nevertheless, these functions have remained basically the same and include trade-union relations, regional policy, local government, housing, public works, power, transport, commercial, industrial and incomes policy.

After 1971, four large Ministries covered these responsibilities. They were the Department of Trade and Industry, the Department of the Environment, the Department of Employment and the Department of Health and Social Security. These have since been further re-organised.

Attached to the Cabinet office is an institution of great importance, the Central Statistical Office. It is responsible for collating and presenting figures for the national income, the balance of payments and factors influencing the money supply.

4. The problem of co-ordination. The Treasury lies at the centre of the economics Ministries and exercises control through its responsibility for Government spending and for demand management. However, the range of economic problems is so great that it would be impossible for the Chancellor alone to co-ordinate the work of the various Departments.

The attempt is made to overcome this problem through a series of inter-departmental committees. Since the war there has always been one main economic policy committee (currently known as the "Steering Committee on Economic Policy") attended by the Prime Minister, the Chancellor and the principal economic Ministers. This is paralleled by an official committee of Permanent Secretaries. Additionally, there are numerous special committees dealing with specific issues such as environmental planning and regional policy.

5. Treasury organisation. In view of the range of Treasury responsibilities the Chancellor is supported not only by a Permanent Secretary but also by three Ministers each responsible for an aspect of the Department's work.

(a) *Finance*. This group is responsible for Government borrowing and lending, the balance of payments and international financial negotiations.

(b) *National Economy.* This section is concerned with demand management (i.e. fiscal policy), economic assessment and industrial and incomes policy.

(c) *Public Sector.* This group is concerned with control of all central Government expenditure.

NOTE: The old responsibility for management of the Civil Service has been transferred to a new Department.

6. The position of the Bank of England. The Bank occupies the somewhat anomalous role of an independent institution which sees itself as the City's representative in Whitehall and yet which behaves very much like a Government Department, making known the views of Whitehall to the City.

The Treasury's Finance Group provides the main Government links with the Bank through highly confidential meetings of senior officials.

It should be noted that the Treasury has no direct links with either domestic or foreign financial markets. The Bank operates on its behalf.

7. International financial relations. In the post-war world it has not been possible to determine domestic economic policy without reference to its implications for other countries. There are seven important international financial organisations at which the U.K. viewpoint is represented by delegations normally composed of Treasury and Bank officials.

(a) *International Monetary Fund* (*see* XII, 31–41).

(b) *The Group of Ten* (*see* XII, 39).

(c) *Organisation for Economic Co-operation and Development* (*see* X, 41).

(d) *Working Party Three.* This is a sub-committee of O.E.C.D., made up of the Group of Ten less Belgium but with the addition of Switzerland, which meets in Basle. Its function is to exercise surveillance over members' domestic policies in respect of demand management and the balance of payments.

(e) *Bank for International Settlements.* Formed in 1930 for the purpose of facilitating German war reparations it became an instrument for co-operation between European central bankers.

(f) *International Bank for Reconstruction and Development* (*see* XII, 50).

(*g*) *International Development Association* (*see* XII, 51).

8. The Treasury Economic Service. Professional economists are spread throughout the three Treasury groups although the majority are concentrated in the National Economy Section. This vitally important group subdivides into four.

(*a*) *Economic assessment.* Short- and medium-term forecasting.

(*b*) *National economy* (*general*). Advice and briefing on any economic topic.

(*c*) *Fiscal policy.* The co-ordination of the Budget.

(*d*) *Industrial and incomes policy.* Prices and incomes movements, monopolies and mergers, investment, consultations with unions and employers through the medium of the National Economic Development Council.

9. Economic forecasts. The most important function of the Treasury economist is to provide forecasts upon which economic policy can be based.

(*a*) *Spot assessments.* Since 1967, the Treasury has published a monthly economic report containing current data on the most important variables such as employment, output, imports and exports.

(*b*) *Short-term forecasts.* In February, June and October, the Treasury in conjunction with the other economics Ministries prepares a National Income Forecast for the following year together with a Balance of Payments Forecast.

These are essentially predictions of business-cycle movements made on the assumption of no change in Government policy.

(*c*) *Medium-term forecasts.* These are made annually during the summer and normally for a five-year period. They are based on the assumption that Government policy will determine the level of activity and take account of underlying growth trends in population and productivity. From this prediction of the increase in future output an assessment can be made of the required allocation between consumption and investment in both private and public sectors. Guidelines are thus established for demand management.

THE FORMULATION OF THE BUDGET
JUDGMENT

10. The Budget and the financial year. For the purpose of the Budget Report and Financial Statement, the financial year begins on 1st April and ends on 31st March. (For the purpose of income-tax assessment, the year begins on 6th April and ends on 5th April.)

The Chancellor will normally make his Budget speech in April after the close of the old financial year. In it he gives a brief review of the previous twelve months' expenditure, but the vital part of his statement is concerned with his tax proposals for the coming year.

Since the object of a modern Budget is not only to raise revenue but also to regulate the nation's spending, it has become conventional to build the speech round a theme.

11. Financial Statement and Budget Report. When opening the Budget the Chancellor lays before the House the Financial Statement and Budget Report. This comprises four sections:

(*a*) *The economic background to the Budget*. A review of developments and trends during the previous year.

(*b*) *Public sector transactions*. The accounts of the public sector as a whole, they comprise the current and capital account transactions of the central Government (including the Consolidated and National Loans Funds and the National Insurance Fund) and of local authorities and nationalised industries. Provisional figures are given for the previous year's out-turn and estimates made for the following year.

NOTE: These accounts rather than those of central Government alone are considered of vital importance in assessing the impact of the public sector upon the economy (*see* VI, 12–17).

(*c*) *Central Government transactions*. All central Government receipts are paid into a central account, the Consolidated Fund, and all payments are made from this fund. This section is a record of these transactions for the previous year and an estimate of transactions for the forthcoming year.

(*d*) *Annex*. Details are given of the Chancellor's proposed tax changes which are intended to produce the estimated revenue and to achieve the economic objectives outlined in his speech.

12. Preliminary estimates. In February of each year, Government Departments first send into the Treasury their preliminary forecasts of their expenditure for the next financial year but one. At about the same time the Inland Revenue and Customs and Excise Departments send in their revenue forecasts. Revisions are made during the spring and in the early summer the Treasury Accountant is able to prepare his first Exchequer Prospects Table. This outlines revenue and expenditure for the coming year and is submitted to the Budget Committee in July.

13. The Treasury Budget Committee. The Committee meets continuously from July until March under the chairmanship of the Permanent Secretary. It comprises the Heads of the Public Sector and Finance Groups, senior Treasury economists, the chairmen of the Inland Revenue and Customs and Excise Departments and is attended by the Deputy Governor of the Bank of England.

In July it has at its disposal the summer National Income Forecast and the preliminary Exchequer Prospects Table, on the basis of which its primary concern at this stage is the possible need for the use of the regulator during the summer.

14. The Queen's Speech. Parliament reassembles in the autumn and is opened by the Queen's Speech in which the Government's legislative programme is outlined and some idea given of the revenue necessary to implement it.

Meanwhile, early in October, the Budget Committee has already agreed figures for public investment in schools, hospitals, roads, etc. It has also discussed the need for an autumn "mini-budget" in the light of what has so far transpired during the year.

15. Autumn National Income Forecast. In November the autumn Forecast predicts the way in which demand and output will grow in relation to productive capacity and the way in which the balance of payments will respond, both on the assumption that no change is made in the forthcoming Budget. A basis is thus given for an assessment of the sort of changes which will be desirable.

16. Firm estimates of revenue and expenditure. By early December Government Departments have sent into the Treasury firm expenditure estimates and the Revenue Departments have sent revised revenue estimates. The Treasury Accountant is then able to revise his Exchequer Prospects Table by the end of the month.

By the end of January the Treasury has approved the estimates of the spending Departments and in February they are introduced into Parliament for debate on the allocated "supply days".

Once the estimates have been approved by the Treasury, the Chancellor receives his first recommendations from the Budget Committee and from then on plays an active part in its deliberations. At this stage the "Budget judgment" begins to take shape and by mid February the Chancellor is receiving advice on the precise size of the deficit or surplus at which he should aim.

17. The Budget outline. During February and early March the main outline of the Budget has been agreed and much of the detail of the tax proposals has been firmly formulated. In the case of indirect taxation, it is necessary to agree changes well in advance since they are effective from Budget day. Since income-tax changes are not immediately applicable changes can be made up to about a week beforehand.

18. The Budget speech. By mid March, the main Budget judgment will have been made and the remaining weeks are occupied in the preparation of the Budget speech. A provisional outline is drawn up by the Chancellor's Principal Private Secretary and sections contributed by experts in the Treasury and other Departments. The Chancellor adds his own ideas on presentation and vets the various drafts until one is finalised. On the morning of the Budget, the Treasury Accountant checks the speaking copy of the speech to ensure that all figures are correct.

THE CONTROL OF PUBLIC EXPENDITURE

19. Consolidated Fund Standing Services and supply services. Each year Parliament reviews certain recurrent items of expenditure but is obliged to sanction them. They are known as the "Consolidated Fund Standing Services" and include interest payments on the National Debt, Royal Household expenses, judges' salaries and post-war credits. These standing commitments are agreed without much discussion by means of a "financial resolution".

All other annual current expenditure comes under the heading of "supply services" and falls into two groups. "Civil supply" comprises eleven classes of expenditure corresponding to the work of different Ministries or groups of Ministries. Secondly, there is the "defence budget".

20. Summary of procedure for supply services. Supply services are "voted" annually by the House of Commons. The procedure passes through five stages:

(a) The spending Departments submit estimates of their

proposed expenditure to the Treasury which approves, rejects or modifies them.

(*b*) The Crown submits the estimates for the consideration of Parliament.

(*c*) The House of Commons debates the estimates and "votes" sums for agreed purposes.

(*d*) The House authorises drawings upon the Consolidated Fund to meet agreed expenditure.

(*e*) In order to ensure that all drawings are utilised only for agreed purposes an Appropriation Act is passed.

At each stage there is opportunity for control and the whole procedure is underwritten by House of Commons Standing Order No. 78.

21. Standing Order No. 78. This famous Standing Order dates back to 1713. "This House will receive no petition for any sum relating to public service or proceed upon any motion for a grant or charge upon the public revenue, whether payable out of the Consolidated Fund or out of money to be provided by Parliament, unless recommended from the Crown."

The Government alone has the power to propose expenditure, a factor which militates in favour of coherent and effective financial planning. It follows that the Government alone is responsible for the success of the plan to Parliament and the electorate.

22. Treasury control. The spending Departments have always viewed the Treasury as a body whose primary concern is to restrain expenditure. The Treasury's authority to do so rests ultimately with the influence of the Chancellor in Cabinet, for it is here that his decisions may be overridden.

Subject to this proviso the Treasury's power is based upon two rules:

(*a*) Since 1861, it has been formally agreed that in the light of Standing Order No. 78, proposed departmental expenditure should first be sanctioned by the Treasury. When reviewing the estimates the Treasury attempts in a commonsense way to produce a balance between competing demands so that the country is given the best value for money.

(*b*) Since 1924 it has been agreed that no proposal for increased expenditure can be circulated in Cabinet without prior discussion with the Treasury.

It can thus be seen that the Treasury is in a very powerful

position to exert pressure at the stage where the estimates are first submitted.

23. Parliamentary debate of the estimates. Twenty-nine "supply days" are set aside for discussion of the estimates between February and the end of July. The Opposition are free to choose the estimates which will be debated but will be concerned to challenge the Government's overall strategy rather than to achieve detailed economies. In July or August an Appropriation Act is passed which authorises the Treasury to make advances to the Departments from the Consolidated Fund.

24. Committee on Expenditure. This Committee has now superseded the Select Committee on Estimates which had been appointed annually since 1921. The intention is for an inter-party committee to examine the estimates in more detail than is possible on the floor of the House.

Select Committees have performed a useful function in subjecting departmental administrations to external criticism, e.g. a Select Committee was responsible for a highly critical examination of Treasury control methods in 1957–8 which led to the Plowden Report on Public Expenditure (*see* **28** below).

25. Exchequer and Audit Department Act, 1921. This Act requires that each Department to which supply grants have been provided should prepare "accounts of appropriation" by a given date. The Departments and not the Treasury are therefore responsible for their own day-to-day spending but must show that public funds have been utilised only for purposes designated by Parliament.

26. Comptroller and Auditor-General. The appropriation accounts are submitted for auditing to the office of the Comptroller and Auditor-General. The office has a staff of over 500 divided into eight divisions, each responsible for auditing the accounts of a group of Departments.

Their function is not only to verify the technical accuracy of the accounts but also to look for waste and inefficiency.

27. Public Accounts Committee. The verified accounts are placed before the House of Commons in January and are referred to the Public Accounts Committee. This very powerful body comprises fifteen members with an Opposition M.P. as chairman. It scrutinises the accounts and publishes a report upon which the Treasury must take action.

LONG-RANGE PLANNING AND CONTROL

28. The Treasury and forward planning. We have so far considered the methods by which during the course of the financial year public expenditure is regulated. However, it had long been apparent that twelve months was far too short a period for the effective planning and control of expenditure, e.g. current expenditure on the building of a teacher-training college must be viewed in the light of continued expenditure over a number of years before there is any benefit in an increased supply of teachers.

The present approach to forward planning derives from the report of a 1961 committee under the chairmanship of Lord Plowden which fostered the concept of a five-year programme rolled forward at the end of every financial year.

29. The Plowden approach in practice. In 1961, the first comprehensive survey was made of the anticipated total of public expenditure in all sectors set against an estimate of the probable growth of national income. At this stage the surveys were forecasts rather than instruments of policy but, from 1965, the Cabinet began to make positive decisions on the portion of anticipated national income to be appropriated for use in the public sector.

The first survey to be published was in 1963 followed by a second in 1966. In 1969, a White Paper, *Public Expenditure 1968–9* to *1973–4*, began a regular annual series of such surveys.

In practice the Treasury maintains that in any five-year programme the third year is the earliest at which major changes may be made without serious dislocation. Plans for the fourth and fifth years are viewed as provisional.

30. Public Expenditure Survey Committee (P.E.S.C.). Each summer an inter-departmental committee makes a survey of public expenditure intentions costed on the basis of the previous year's projections. To this is added the best available estimates of total private-sector expenditure and the grand total is set against the anticipated growth of national income. If it exceeds the expected growth rate then the conclusion is that the total claim on real resources is too heavy and there will have to be a cut-back in public expenditure or a general increase in taxation.

31. Appraisal of public expenditure surveys. During the 1960s the inaccuracy of public expenditure surveys stemmed from the recurrent tendency to underestimate future costs. From 1963 to 1968 the percentage increase in public expenditure regularly exceeded that which had been planned. Only in 1968–9 was the annual increase brought under control. Subsequently, for a variety of technical and political reasons, the tendency to underestimate the growth of public expenditure remains.

(a) *The problem of forward projections at constant cost.* Certain public sector activities (e.g. education) do not lend themselves to measurable productivity increases which can offset the effects of inflation. It follows that not only will the expansion of such services need to be borne by an expansion of G.N.P. but also that the maintenance of existing services at inflated prices is also a charge upon growth. In short, the share of public expenditure in G.N.P. increases with inflation. Forward projections must therefore take account of this difficulty.

(b) *The problem of changed expenditure classifications.* An example of this difficulty is found in the change from investment allowances to investment grants in 1966 and back to accelerated capital depreciation allowances in 1970. While grants are classed as expenditure, allowances are treated as offsets against revenue. Although the net effect may be the same, for accounting purposes the abolition of grants reduces public expenditure. In calculating percentage rates of increase of public expenditure it is therefore necessary to make allowance for such changes.

(c) *The problem of a standardised system of costing.* Plans may be costed for different purposes employing different sets of definitions and therefore producing different results. None of these may be of value in checking the actual cost of the completed work. The Treasury is currently engaged in standardising definitions so that they may be used equally for forecasting, operational control and checking results.

(d) *The problem of public expenditure not wholly within the control of central Government.* The Supply Estimates represent only about half of total public expenditure. Local authorities control about a quarter and while central Government is in a position to influence their capital expenditure there remains a good deal of autonomy in respect of current expenditure.

32. The problem of demand management. One major problem not amenable to treatment by improved accounting methods remains

unresolved. This concerns the extent to which public expenditure
may be expected to play its part in the regulation of total demand
without wasteful disruption of existing programmes. The theoretical solution of a "bank" of projects which can be advanced or
slowed down as occasion demands has still to be achieved in
practice.

PROGRESS TEST 5

1. Explain the relationship of the Treasury to the other
economic Departments. (2–4)

2. What are the three main divisions of the Treasury? (5)

3. Explain the nature of Treasury economic forecasts. (9)

4. Outline the contents of the Financial Statement and Budget
Report. (11)

5. What are the "preliminary estimates"? (12)

6. What is the importance of the autumn National Income
Forecast? (15)

7. What do you understand by the "Budget judgment"? (16)

8. What are the Consolidated Fund Standing Services? (19)

9. What is the significance of Standing Order No. 78? (21)

10. Describe the function of the Comptroller and Auditor-
General's Department. (26)

11. What is the function of the Public Accounts Committee?
(27)

12. In what way is the Treasury concerned with long-range
economic planning? (28)

13. Explain the operation of P.E.S.C. (30)

14. What practical problems arise in respect of longe-range
planning? (31)

CHAPTER VI

The National Debt

PRINCIPAL FEATURES OF THE U.K. NATIONAL DEBT

1. Nature. On occasion Government may not find it convenient to finance its expenditure wholly from taxation and may supplement its revenue by borrowing, normally from its own citizens. It should therefore be noted that while the term "National" Debt is the one in common usage it is misleading since it suggests a debt owed by the nation to the rest of the world. Since the bulk of the Debt is held by U.K. residents it is more appropriate to think of it as the sum owed by citizens collectively (i.e. the Government) to citizens individually, in short the Government Debt.

2. Size and structure. In December of each year, the Bank of England as manager of the Debt, publishes its estimated figures up to the 31st March of that year. At 31st March, 1977 the *nominal* total of the National Debt (including foreign currency debt) was £68 billion, an increase of £10.5 billion on a year earlier. The bulk of this increase (£9.7 billion) was in market holdings; official holdings rose by only £0.8 billion (*see* Table I).

The December 1977 presentation shifted the emphasis from a contrast between marketable and non-marketable debt to the distinction between official and market holdings (*see* 3 below).

The foreign currency debt comprises direct Government borrowing in Europe, post-war reconstruction loans from North America and German assistance with the support costs of B.A.O.R. This amount is normally excluded from conventional Debt analysis.

Of the remaining *sterling* debt, official holdings have a different significance to those of the market which may be analysed as follows.

(*a*) *Funded debt.* Strictly speaking the phrase "funded debt" applies only to those stocks for which no redemption date has been set. The most important example of debt incurred on these

TABLE I. TOTAL OFFICIAL AND MARKET HOLDINGS OF NATIONAL DEBT, MARCH 1977

	£m.	% of market holdings
Official holdings	14,418	
Market holdings		
Sterling marketable debt:		
Government and Government guaranteed stocks	36,813	68.7
Treasury bills	3,637	6.8
Sterling non-marketable debt:		
National savings securities	5,285	9.9
Interest free notes due to the I.M.F. and I.D.A.	3,429	6·4
Other	22	
Total	49,186	91.8
Foreign currency debt:		
H.M.T. euro-currency loans	2,034	
North American Government loans	2,265	
Anglo-German offset agreement	73	
Total	4,362	8.2
Total market holdings	53,558	
Total	67,976	100.0
of which nationalised industries stock guaranteed by Government	808	

(*Source: B.E.Q.B. December 1977.*)

terms is $3\frac{1}{2}$ per cent War Loan (1952 or after). The Government is under no obligation to repay although it was at liberty to do so at any time after 1952.

Used in the broader sense, the phrase includes dated stock, i.e. all other Government and Government-guaranteed stocks. They are of varying maturities and are publicly quoted. A single repayment date may be set or there may be two dates, after the earlier of which Government can repay if it wishes and on the second of which it must repay.

Prior to the First World War, Government borrowed only

TABLE II.   STERLING MARKETABLE AND
NON-MARKETABLE DEBT, MARCH 1977

	£m.	% of sterling debt
Marketable debt:		
Funded debt	36,813	74
Floating debt	3,637	8
Non-marketable debt:		
National savings securities	5,285	11
Interest free notes due to the I.M.F. and I.D.A.	3,429	7
Other	22	
	49,186	100

(*Source: B.E.Q.B. December 1977.*)

against undated stock. Subsequently dated stock came to be the
principal component of the National Debt.

(*b*) *Floating debt.* Government requires to borrow regularly
on a short-term basis in order to accommodate the uneven influx
of tax revenue to the fairly even flow of departmental expenditure. This it does by borrowing against Treasury bills which are of
two types, "tap" and "tender". Tap bills represent lending by
Government Departments back to the Treasury. Bills payable
after ninety-one days are offered for tender every Friday on the
London Discount Market.

(*c*) *Non-marketable debt.* The biggest part of non-marketable
debt is in the form of securities which are not publicly quoted and
which have no redemption date set, although normally the holder
is able to claim repayment after giving a period of notice. Included are national savings certificates, defence bonds, premium
savings bonds, and the contractual savings schemes of the Department for National Savings and the Trustee Savings Banks.

Other non-marketable-debt instruments include certificates of
tax deposit and Ways and Means Advances. The latter item
represents the only method by which the Bank of England lends
directly to Government, lending which is on a very short-term
basis (*see* Table II).

3. Distribution of sterling debt ownership. An analysis of ownership gives further insights into the implications of the Debt, providing a basis for examining the extent of the burden placed upon the taxpayer (*see* Table III).

TABLE III.   OWNERSHIP OF THE NATIONAL DEBT,
MARCH 1977 (£m.)

Official holdings	Public bodies	Banking sector	Other financial institutions	Overseas holders	Other
14,418	66	4,757	18,898	7,125	18,340

(*Source: B.E.Q.B. December 1977.*)

(*a*) *U.K. Official holdings.* Of the approximate 25 per cent held by Government Departments or agencies about one half was attributed to the National Debt Commissioners, who administer the two funds, through which is invested money deposited in the ordinary department of the National Savings Bank and the Trustee Savings Banks as well as the proceeds of national insurance contributions.

More than one third was held by the Issue Department of the Bank of England as backing for the note issue. The balance was held by the Bank of England banking department. Government Departments with a temporary cash surplus and the Exchange Equalisation Account. The latter, when it supports the sterling exchange rate by using the hard currency reserves to buy up surplus sterling on the world's exchange markets, invests the proceeds in National Debt.

(*b*) *Public bodies.* A very small amount is held by local authorities and public corporations other than the Bank of England.

(*c*) *Banking sector.* This includes deposit and other banks, the discount market and the National Giro.

(*d*) *Other financial institutions.* The most important category of market investors, it includes insurance companies, building societies, the investment accounts of the National Savings and Trustee Savings Banks, local authority and other public sector superannuation funds, private sector superannuation funds, investment trusts and unit trusts.

(*e*) *Overseas holders.* There are three elements. The International Monetary Fund and the International Development

Association accounted for £3,601 million of the total of £7,125 million. This portion is made up primarily of non-interest bearing sterling notes held by the I.M.F. as a counterpart to U.K. drawings upon the Fund. Secondly, central monetary institutions held £1,719 million, the official sterling reserves of overseas countries. The remainder was held privately.

(f) *Other*. Of £18,340 million, individuals and private trusts held £12,480 million, the rest being divided between public trustees, various non-corporate bodies, industrial and commercial companies.

THE BURDEN OF THE DEBT

4. Real burden of the external Debt. It has been observed that £7,125 million of the total sterling Debt is held overseas. To the extent that interest payments are made abroad and principal repaid there are implications for the balance of payments. Goods and services must be diverted to foreign use without any compensatory imports. Alternatively, if foreign demand for the debtor nation's goods is inelastic, there will have to be a corresponding reduction in the volume of imports. Either way there will be a real loss to the debtor nation's standard of living.

5. Real burden of the internal Debt. It has been stressed that by far the greater part of the Debt is owned internally. It follows that no increase or decrease in the size of the Debt can make the country as a whole either poorer or richer. Payment of interest or repayment of principal involves simply a transfer from tax-payer to security-holder. To the extent that the debtor (i.e. tax-payer) is worse off, the creditor (i.e. security-holder) is better off.

If all securities were evenly distributed throughout the community and all tax-payers made an equal contribution to the cost of servicing the Debt, the real burden would be nil since for every interest receipt of £1, the recipient would make a tax contribution of £1.

In practice, the ownership of the Debt is not evenly distributed and a real burden arises to the extent that the cost of debt servicing involves a transfer from tax-payer to security-holder which increases the inequality of incomes. Despite the fact that a broad cross-section of the community may benefit from an interest in that part of the Debt represented by national savings and the holdings of the institutional investors, on balance it is likely that the greater part of the benefits will be directed towards the upper-income groups whose propensity to save will be correspondingly increased. Conversely, as a result of their tax contributions, the propensity to consume of the lower-income groups will be reduced, i.e. they must accept a real cut in living standards.

6. Indirect effects of Debt charges. Annually, substantial sums must be raised in taxation for the purpose of servicing the Debt. The level of this taxation will have implications for the management of the economy as a whole.

(*a*) *Incentives.* It may be argued that the extra volume of taxation can reduce the incentive to work of the tax-payer while that of the security-holder is reduced by his unearned income receipts.

(*b*) *Demand management.* More significantly, redistribution of income will influence both the level of total effective demand and its structure.

PRINCIPLES OF DEBT MANAGEMENT

7. Objectives. The aims of Debt management policy will be threefold:

(*a*) To minimise the real burden (*see* 8–11 below).

(*b*) In any fiscal year to budget for a surplus or a deficit (i.e. decrease or increase the Debt) in line with the broad aims of economic policy (*see* 12–17 below).

(*c*) To manage the size and composition of the Debt in a way which accords with the needs of monetary policy (*see* IX, 33–8).

8. Repudiation or repayment. It can be argued that if the cost of servicing a national debt becomes excessively irksome it is always open to Government to repudiate its obligations. This course is unlikely to be followed if only on the practical grounds that further borrowing would be extremely difficult.

Repayment involves the consideration that over a given period, long or short, repayments of principal must be added to current interest payments. If a substantial portion of the Debt is held externally then throughout the period extra surpluses would have to be earned in the balance of payments. This would probably necessitate policies which were disruptive of the natural flow of international trade.

To the extent that the Debt is held internally there will be a further redistribution of income from poorer to richer. Moreover, the effects would be strongly deflationary since the repeated Budget surpluses required would be more restrictive than the expansionary effects of the funds released.

The conclusion must be that the sheer size of the Debt today precludes any serious consideration of its total repayment. Reduction of the burden must be sought elsewhere.

9. Conversions. If economic conditions permit, it may be possible for Government to refinance (i.e. convert) debt incurred at high interest rates by borrowing afresh at lower rates.

In the twentieth century there have been two notably successful conversions. In 1932, in a period in which the prevailing economic conditions called for a policy of very low interest rates, £2,000 million War Loan was converted from 5 to 3½ per cent giving an annual saving to the tax-payer of £30 million, one-tenth of the total Debt charge at that time.

Similarly, in the period 1945-7, the Chancellor, who for economic reasons was pursuing a cheap money policy, forced down interest rates and achieved a number of conversions which resulted in a total annual saving of £38 million.

However, the inflationary conditions of modern times offer little prospect for conversion to lower interest rates. The opposite is in fact the case and in recent years the cost of servicing the Debt has been on a strongly rising trend.

10. The significance of Government interest receipts.

TABLE IV. CENTRAL GOVERNMENT PAYMENTS AND
RECEIPTS OF INTEREST 1965–75 (£m.)

	1965	1967	1969	1971	1973	1975
Debt interest payments	968	1,105	1,280	1,384	1,726	2,637
Interest and dividends from:						
Loans to local authorities	142	203	281	399	541	857
Loans to public corporations	313	414	602	736	889	1,147
Other	115	119	104	178	166	325
Interest payments *less* interest and dividend receipts	398	369	293	71	166	290

(*Source:National Income and Expenditure, 1976.*)

Table IV reflects the extent to which central Government has been involved in financing the capital account expenditures of a greatly expanded public sector. From a minimum commitment at the end of the Second World War, outstanding government loans to local authorities and nationalised industries had risen to £26,000 million by 1976. This substantial portion of the total may be viewed as reproductive in the sense that it is backed by income yielding tangible assets such as power stations and housing.

These loans to the public sector have been financed partly from budget surpluses and partly by central government borrowing from the private sector.

Certain trends will be observed. Firstly, the continuing rise in the Debt servicing charge was increasingly offset by interest receipts until 1971. The trend suggested that the Debt might ultimately become self-servicing. Secondly, even though the net charges upon the taxpayer rose to £290 million after 1971, it increased much less than the gross interest payments which almost doubled to £2,637 millions. The rise in the last figure reflects both a greater scale of Government borrowing and higher interest rates.

11. Inflation and devaluation. It may be noted in passing that inflation erodes both the *real* value of Debt holdings and the *real* burden of servicing it. When Debt is redeemed, payment is made in depreciated currency. For the purpose of meeting service charges a smaller proportion of real incomes is now required.

Secondly, when overseas investors have purchased sterling debt with currency converted at a given rate of exchange a devaluation leaves them with assets which are now worth less in terms of that currency.

THE NATIONAL LOANS FUND

12. The Budget judgment and the National Debt. Traditionally, the first precept of sound public finance was a balanced Budget. The principle of the private sector that income must always meet expenditure was equally applied in the public sector except in times of emergency.

Originating in 1694, the modern National Debt expanded during the eighteenth century as a result of wars which it proved impossible to finance from current tax revenue. In the intervals of peace, Chancellors were always concerned to find means of redeeming debt. The relative calm of the nineteenth century permitted some reduction by 1914 of the £850 million which had been outstanding at the end of the Napoleonic Wars. Two world wars then increased the Debt to £24,000 million. We can thus see that until 1945 deficits were incurred only in wartime or as a result of the miscalculation of the estimates.

After the war, having accepted the Keynesian technique for the management of demand, it was seen that in a deflationary situation it might be desirable deliberately to plan a deficit. Conversely, in an inflationary situation, a planned surplus would be indicated. We have seen in the preceding chapter the machinery which enables the Chancellor to arrive at his "judgment".

In 1977, with the reduction of inflation as the principal target of economic policy, the Chancellor was persuaded to plan a reduction of some £2,000 million in what had been since 1972 a burgeoning public sector deficit.

13. The complications of the long-term capital account. The Chancellor's task in planning a surplus or deficit with any accuracy has been made immensely more complicated by the extent to which the Exchequer has been involved in "below the line expenditure" to provide long-term capital to local authorities and nationalised industries.

When local authorities were unable or unwilling to obtain capital from the market they did so from the Exchequer through the Public Works Loans Board. From 1956 until April 1968, the nationalised industries sought all their investment requirements from the Exchequer.

An *ad hoc* system developed in which surpluses produced on current account were carried forward to the capital account (below the line). The investment needs of the public sector were then met and the Exchequer was left with a "net borrowing requirement". In short, the Chancellor borrowed from the market on behalf of the whole public sector.

NOTE: It therefore follows that when the Chancellor estimates the effect upon demand of a projected Budget surplus or deficit he will be concerned not simply with the impact of the current account of Central Government but rather with the combined current and capital accounts of the public sector as a whole.

14. Current account surpluses and capital account deficits in the 1960s. Some economists have levelled the criticism that inflationary trends in the 1960s were in part the product of an inappropriate presentation of the budget accounts. Record disinflationary surpluses overshadowed the size of the deficits incurred when the capital account was taken into consideration. The result was inadequate accounting control over total public sector spending.

The criticism continues that the impact of this overall public sector borrowing requirement would not necessarily have been inflationary had it been financed "legitimately" by borrowing from the private sector. The effect would have been neutral since increased public expenditure would be offset by reduced private spending.

However, the gilt-edged market was weak throughout the 1960s. The private sector was reluctant to lend and the borrowing requirement was repeatedly financed in part by the banking system. In effect, this implies that much public spending was financed by "printing money" (*see* 17 below).

15. Conclusion. The conclusion to the foregoing argument must be that a major element of the modern National Debt is attributable to the capital requirements of the public sector and that these must be managed wisely if public finance is to be an effective instrument of demand management.

In his 1967 Budget statement the Chancellor asked: "Is it necessarily the best arrangement that so much of the borrowing requirement of local authorities and public corporations is financed in the first instance by the Exchequer? The present arrangements have grown up as a series of *ad hoc* responses to particular situations over a long period of years. I think the time has come to take stock of the suitability of the present arrangements in the contemporary world and I have therefore put a review in hand."

The result of this review was the foundation, on the 1st April 1968, of the National Loans Fund.

16. The National Loans Fund. The Act which set up the Fund amended the law relating to Government borrowing and lending. It confined the Exchequer to the ordinary revenue and expenditure transactions of Central Government met from Parliamentary votes.

Government borrowing and lending for local authorities and nationalised industries would be dealt with separately through the medium of the Fund. Exchequer surpluses at the end of the year would be transferred to the Fund. Similarly, any Exchequer deficit would be met from the Fund.

The Treasury's borrowing powers which were previously covered by a variety of statutes were framed into a single set of provisions and all future Treasury borrowing was to be for the account of the Fund.

17. Appraisal. In the financial markets, public and private sectors must compete for control over the limited supply of real productive resources within the economy. During the 1970s, the *Public Sector Borrowing Requirement* (P.S.B.R.) has expanded in line with the growth of the public sector so that strains have been placed on those markets.

While the National Loans Fund Accounts provide better accounting control over public sector requirements and give a clearer picture for the development of macroeconomic policy, inflationary potential remains when public sector needs are financed by the banking system with a consequent monetary expansion.

This may happen in a number of ways.

(*a*) *Expansion of the note issue.* When due to existing inflation the Bank of England finds it necessary to increase the note circulation, the Issue Department is obliged to back new notes with newly acquired Government bonds. Inadvertently, Government borrowing and spending are literally financed by printing new money.

(*b*) *Exchange Equalisation Account.* (*See* 3(*a*) above.) When the reserves are used to purchase sterling which is then lent to Government by investment in Government Debt, in effect monetarily passive gold is translated into active new purchasing power.

(*c*) *Purchasing of gilts by the banks.* When banks lend to public or private sectors they increase the volume of credit. This results in an expansion of *bank deposit money* (*see* VII, 7 and VIII, 32).

(*d*) *Purchases of Treasury bills by the banking system.* In the first instance Treasury bill finance means borrowing from the banks with a consequent expansion of the money supply (*see* VIII, 32). There is, however, a second round effect. With more Treasury bills the banks have more liquid assets upon which to expand their lending by methods which will be considered in VIII.

If we accept the monetarist view that inflation is rooted in excessive monetary growth (*see* IV, **10**) then there are three implications. Firstly that there must be strict control over the rate of growth of the money supply. To achieve this, the P.S.B.R. must be reduced and the extent of bank borrowing carefully regulated. Finally, the growth of public spending itself must be strictly controlled.

However, even if this view is accepted there remain great difficulties, firstly in arriving at a precise definition of the money supply and secondly in devising effective methods for controlling its growth. These problems will be examined in the following two chapters.

PROGRESS TEST 6

1. Define the nature of the National Debt. **(1)**
2. Describe the basic structure of the Debt. **(2)**
3. Who owns the Debt? **(3)**
4. Compare the real burdens of the internally and externally held portions of the Debt. **(4, 5)**
5. In managing the Debt, what principles will the Bank of England observe? **(7)**
6. What possibilities exist for an active attempt to reduce the burden of the Debt? **(8, 9, 11)**
7. Why might the Debt ultimately become self-servicing? **(10)**
8. What is the significance of capital spending to accurate budgetary control? **(13)**
9. What is the National Loans Fund? **(16)**
10. What is the significance of the Public Sector Borrowing Requirement to the money supply? **(17)**

PART TWO

THE MONETARY SYSTEM

CHAPTER VII

The Functions,
Characteristics and Evolution of Money

THE FUNCTIONS OF MONEY

1. A fully planned economy without money. Provided that society is willing to surrender all individual choice to State-planning agencies it is possible to operate an economy without money. This has been demonstrated, for example, in the early days of the Soviet Union. The State determines the relative quantities of different lines of production while distribution is effected by a system of rationing which accords with prevailing notions of social justice. The weakness of such a system lies on the side of distribution once the economy has been raised above subsistence level. What principles of social justice, for example, would govern the allocation of grand pianos or croquet mallets?

2. A free economy without money. In a free economy the only alternative to the use of money is a system of barter such as that which largely prevailed in medieval England. There are, however, three major disadvantages:

(*a*) *Individual wants rarely coincide.* "Rather than there being a coincidence of wants there is likely to be a want of coincidence." It is unlikely that the baker's need for a pair of shoes will be timed to coincide with the shoemaker's need for a loaf of bread.

(*b*) *Adjustment of quantities of goods bartered.* It is unlikely that the shoemaker will want simultaneously the number of loaves of bread for which a pair of shoes would exchange.

(*c*) *Multiple exchange ratios.* It is necessary to establish separate exchange ratios between any one item and all other goods which enter into trade. There is no common denominator.

While barter may work in a simple society, it is clear that it would be inoperable in an advanced industrial economy practising a high degree of specialisation. What now becomes necessary is a "medium of exchange".

3. The functions of money. From the foregoing argument it may be deduced that money has certain functions:

(*a*) *A medium of exchange.* The most important function of money is to serve as the one universally acceptable denominator against which all men are willing to exchange their goods and services. It acts as the lubricant which promotes the smooth functioning of a market economy based upon division of labour not only between trades but also between processes. From this central function of money stem four others.

(*b*) *Extension of individual choice.* The distribution difficulty of the fully planned economy is overcome when the individual works for units of purchasing power which he can use at his discretion.

(*c*) *Standard unit of account.* Money cannot properly be said to be a measure of value since, unlike measures of weight or size, its own value varies. However, it does overcome the difficulty of multiple exchange ratios encountered in the barter system. It is the common denominator to which all trade items may be related.

(*d*) *A store of value.* Individual saving in an economy without money implies the setting aside of goods for future use. The self-evident disadvantage is that many goods are perishable and services cannot be stored. The use of money, however, enables purchasing power to be stored for use at a date determined by the individual.

It should be noted, nevertheless, that money fulfils this function imperfectly inasmuch as its purchasing power varies. The depreciation in the value of money since 1945 is not compensated by the interest paid on bank deposits after allowance has been made for the taxation of unearned income.

(*e*) *A means of deferred payment.* The extent to which money is capable of storing value gives it a final function. It is instrumental to credit transactions. Without money, present borrowing of goods and services would imply repayment in kind. Money enables general purchasing power to be utilised now and repaid later.

It should be noted that inflation will favour the debtor inasmuch as he will repay money whose purchasing power is less. Conversely a deflationary situation will favour the creditor.

THE EVOLUTION AND CHARACTERISTICS OF MONEY

4. Commodity money. The earliest forms of money were commodities held in high regard by the societies which used them. At first sight it would therefore seem that a prime characteristic of money is its intrinsic desirability. However, we shall shortly see that this is not so. Nevertheless, it should be emphasised that a quality common to all money has been relative scarcity. If the scarcity is too great, too little value is attached to it for it to continue in this role.

Additionally, early forms of commodity money enjoyed one or more other advantages, e.g. in the eastern Mediterranean, olive oil was easily divisible; in western Europe, iron was durable. The most universally acceptable of all commodity moneys, however, came to be gold. It had the foregoing qualities and was also portable. Second only to gold was silver. Initially, quantities of these metals were weighed in order to make payment, but from these it was only a short step to a standard coin of known weight and fineness guaranteed by the imprint of the State.

5. Paper money. Modern deposit banking began to develop in Britain for the first time in the sixteenth and seventeenth centuries in the hands of London goldsmiths. It was their practice to issue "warehouse receipts" for gold deposited with them and these receipts circulated freely as money, guaranteed by the good name of the goldsmith. In the 1680s, Francis Childs is credited with the introduction of the first true banknotes, receipts for gold but in standard denominations.

However, paper was seen only as a claim upon real money, gold, until 1931. The Bank of England's promise to pay the bearer on demand was a guarantee of immediate convertibility and apart from two major periods, 1797–1821 and 1914–25, this convertibility was maintained.

During the nineteenth century, it is doubtful, except in periods of national emergency, whether inconvertible paper money would have circulated freely. In the periods 1815–21 and 1918–25 there was considerable public agitation for the restoration of convertibility, but in 1931 the link between paper and gold was finally severed. Paper appeared for the first time in its own right as true money. This leads us to an important conclusion about the nature of money. Its principal characteristic is not its intrinsic desirability but its "acceptability." Paradoxically, this acceptability can be explained only by a general confidence that everyone will accept it. This confidence will be governed by the degree of political and economic stability. For example, where there is hyper-inflation, it is likely that paper money will cease to circulate and there will be a reversion to commodity money. This was partially demonstrated in post-1945 Germany when American cigarettes circulated as money. Our attention is therefore redirected to the first characteristic of money which has been noted. If it is to be acceptable, there must be a relative scarcity.

6. Limitation of the supply of paper money. When the sixteenth-century goldsmiths first issued receipts for gold deposits there was naturally a strict relationship between the quantity of gold and the paper circulated. However, as public confidence developed in the goldsmith's ability to pay he felt safe in increasing the amount of paper, ensuring only that he maintained an adequate ratio to gold to enable him to meet day-to-day claims for conversion. The danger of this practice was a loss of public confidence which would lead to a run on the bank with all note-holders anxious to convert paper to gold. Many small banks were forced out of business in this way. The 1844 Bank Charter Act aimed to exclude this danger. The sole right of note issue was gradually to be vested in the Bank of England. The Bank was to be permitted a small "fiduciary issue" of £14 million only partially backed by gold. Every note issued in excess of this amount had to be fully covered. England was placed firmly on the gold standard and had in consequence an inflexible money supply.

The Currency and Banknotes Act of 1913 introduced for the first time Treasury notes in denominations of £1 and 10 shillings. (The smallest denomination banknote had been and remained £5.) During the period 1914–18 the Treasury note issue was increased without gold cover and a considerable inflation resulted. Deflationary policies after 1920 sought to restore full convertibility and a large number of Treasury notes were withdrawn. The Gold Standard Act of 1925 established partial convertibility (gold could be purchased from the Issue Department in minimum quantities of 400 Troy ounces) but by 1928 it became apparent that further deflation of the note issue was undesirable. With many Treasury notes still in circulation it was decided to substitute for them £1 and 10 shilling Bank of England notes. This required legislation to permit a corresponding increase in the Bank's

fiduciary issue and the Currency and Banknotes Act of 1928, was
enacted. The fiduciary issue was established at £260 million but
could be increased with Treasury approval over a maximum
period of two years. After that the approval of Parliament had to
be sought. Subsequently, the Currency and Banknotes Act of
1954 confirmed the general position. The fiduciary issue was set
at £1,575 million and could only be increased with Treasury consent and with the ultimate approval of Parliament. In practice
such approval has come to be a formality.

NOTE: The legal position governing the note issue is thus de-
termined by the Acts of 1844, 1928 and 1954. The Bank of
England retains the power to increase its notes against gold
cover but since no notes have been backed in this way since
August, 1970 this power is of no real significance. In practice,
the Bank of England authorities in conjunction with the
Treasury determine whether an increase is desirable and
Parliamentary approval is given automatically.

7. Bank deposit money. (*See* also VIII, **32.**) The final stage in the
evolution of money is to be seen in its appearance as a bank deposit, a figure on a ledger which can be transferred through the
instrument of the cheque. Cheques were known in seventeenth-
century England but their use was given considerable stimulus by
the 1844 Bank Charter Act. It will be recalled that this Act
rigidly limited the money supply and this in a period of rapid industrial and commercial expansion. Growth might well have been
hampered by this restriction had it not been for an increasing
willingness to settle business transactions with the cheque.

It should be noted, however, that it is not the cheque itself
which is money but the deposit upon which it is drawn. The
cheque will of course be valid only if such a deposit exists and the
payee may not know this to be the case. Nevertheless, the cheque
would appear to be increasingly acceptable, the majority of
transactions involving payment of any size being settled in this
way. In recent years the banks have attempted to extend their
business by popularising current accounts. Many wage and salary
payments are made either by cheque or bank transfer while the
consumer, assisted by his banker's card (an instrument which
certifies any cheque up to a value of £30 or £50), has made ever-
greater use of his cheque-book even for relatively small payments.
Moreover, the increased use of credit cards, credit accounts and
hire purchase accounts which are settled regularly by cheque or

banker's order suggests that cash will continue to play a proportionately smaller part and will finally become the "small change" of the monetary system.

8. The difficulty of a precise definition of the money supply. It has been shown that conventionally money has come to be defined as coin, notes and bank deposits. However, should deposits of *all* types with *all* financial institutions be included within this definition? In recent years there has been a good deal of discussion of this question.

In 1970 the Bank of England concluded that it is possible to select different types of deposits to form various totals which can each be described as the stock of money. "There are, however, no clear rules for deciding which of these totals is most appropriate: there can be alternative definitions of the stock of money, encompassing a wider or narrower set of components."

9. Three Bank of England definitions. In 1978, Bank calculations of the money stock conform to three definitions, M1, sterling M3 and M3 (*see* Table V).

(*a*) *M1.* This is the narrow definition consisting of notes and coin in circulation with the public plus sterling sight deposits held by the private sector only.

(*b*) *Sterling M3.* This is made up of notes and coin in circulation with the public together with *all* sterling deposits (including certificates of deposit) held by U.K. residents in both the public and private sectors.

(*c*) *M3.* The third definition equals sterling M3 plus all deposits held by U.K. residents in other currencies.

In all three definitions deposits are confined to those with institutions included in the U.K. banking sector.

TABLE V.   MONEY STOCK, OCTOBER 1977

		£m.
	M1	21,503
Sterling	M3	42,828
	M3	46,816

(*Source: B.E.Q.B. December 1977.*)

PROGRESS TEST 7

1. Why may money be viewed as essential to an advanced economy? (1–3)

2. Explain why "acceptability" is the most important characteristic of money. (5)

3. What legislation today limits the quantity of banknotes? (6)

4. What was the significance of the Bank Charter Act, 1844? (6)

5. How did the Bank Charter Act stimulate the use of the cheque? (7)

6. What is "bank deposit money"? (7)

7. Compare the relative importance of banknotes and bank deposit money. (7)

8. Give three statistical definitions of the money stock. (9)

CHAPTER VIII

The Commercial Banks

STRUCTURE OF BRITISH BANKING

1. Classification. Over the past 400 years the British banking system has developed as one of the most highly specialised financial centres in the world. It has created a complex and sophisticated market for both short-term and long-term finance on an international scale, a business which is of value not only to Britain as a source of overseas earnings but also to overseas countries as a source of investment funds and trade credit. The system may be classified under six main headings.

(*a*) *The central bank.* At the centre of the system stands the Bank of England. It fulfils a unique role to which attention is given in the following chapter.

(*b*) *The commercial banks* are sometimes referred to as the "joint-stock banks." They are for the most part limited liability companies, subject to the appropriate company law and operated for the profit of their shareholders. They include:

(*i*) The London clearing banks.

(*ii*) The Scottish and Northern Irish banks.

(*iii*) British overseas and foreign banks with London offices.

(*c*) *The discount houses.* The London Discount Market Association comprises eleven houses. They have a specialised function in the provision of short-term finance.

(*d*) *The merchant banks.* Used loosely, this term is often applied to a variety of financial institutions. In a specific sense it includes:

(*i*) *Accepting houses.* The basic business is the "acceptance credit" through which a considerable part of Britain's overseas trade is financed.

(*ii*) *Issuing houses.* They are concerned with raising credit for borrowers at home and abroad and, where appropriate, organising a market in bonds and shares against which funds are raised.

(*e*) *The savings banks.* Independently operated savings banks where small savings could be deposited to earn a rate of interest arose in Britain in the early nineteenth century. To afford greater security to depositors, legislation in 1817 brought them under the supervision of the National Debt Commissioners. Management remained in the hands of local trustees—hence Trustee Savings Banks.

In order to bring savings facilities within reach of the whole community legislation in 1861 led to the foundation of the Post Office Savings Bank, now known as the National Savings Bank.

(*f*) *The National Giro.* The National Giro was set up in 1969 in the belief that by providing facilities for current account payments it would very quickly be in a position to compete on even terms with the commercial banks.

2. Evolution of the London clearing banks. It has been observed that in Britain the first indigenous banking was developed in the sixteenth and seventeenth centuries by goldsmiths who issued paper money against the security of gold deposits (*see* VII, 5). They also established rudimentary current accounts, cheque and bill-discounting facilities. An Act of 1707 imposed certain legal restrictions which delayed the development of joint-stock banking in England except for the Bank of England itself. Scotland did not suffer this legal impediment and joint-stock banking developed on a sound basis at an earlier date.

The result was a system of banking based upon private partnership which persisted until 1826. In that year the Country Bankers Act permitted the formation of joint-stock banks *with* note-issuing powers outside a sixty-five mile radius of London. In 1833 a further Act allowed joint-stock banks *without* note-issuing powers within that radius. The Bank Charter Act of 1844 denied all new banks the power to issue notes but the development of the cheque diminished the significance of this restriction. An Act of 1862 extended the privilege of limited liability to banking companies and the last obstacle to the growth of large-scale joint-stock banking was removed.

The following sixty years were a period of expansion, take-overs and amalgamations in which was established a national system of branch banking. In 1919, the formation of the British Bankers' Association promoted consultation and co-operation between its fifty-six members. Included in this membership were fourteen English, five Scottish and three Northern Ireland commercial banks.

A large part of British banking business is concentrated in the six members of the London Bankers' Clearing House (*see* VIII, 7). Until 1968 there were eleven which included Midland Bank Ltd.; Barclays Bank Ltd.; Lloyds Bank Ltd.; Westminster Bank Ltd.; National Provincial Bank Ltd.; District Bank Ltd.; Martins Bank Ltd.; Williams Deacon's Bank Ltd.; National Bank Ltd.; Coutts & Co.; Glyn Mills & Co. Mergers have caused the gradual loss of a separate identity of Martins following its fusion with Barclays and of District following its amalgamation with National Provincial and Westminster to form the National Westminster. Williams Deacon's merged with Glyn Mills to form Williams and Glyn's.

3. Scottish banks. Scottish banking business is concentrated in four banks with head offices and some 1,700 branches in Scotland. These banks retain the power of note issue which, apart from a small fiduciary issue, is made against the cover of Bank of England notes. The advantage is largely a matter of advertisement.

4. Northern Irish banks. There are three native banks with head offices and some 500 branches in Northern Ireland. Like the Scottish banks they issue their own notes. Additionally, a number of other banks with head offices in Dublin, Cork and London have branches in Northern Ireland.

5. British overseas banks. There are thirty-two members of the British Overseas Banks Association with head offices in London or the Commonwealth and branches overseas. The Association comprises four groups: African, Australasian, Canadian and Eastern. They act as exchange-dealers and finance monetary transactions between Britain and these areas and between third parties. They also employ funds in London primarily in the money market. They therefore provide a mechanism whereby British short-term investment funds can be rapidly employed in all parts of the world and conversely foreign funds employed in Britain. The bulk of their London deposit liabilities do in fact originate overseas.

6. Foreign banks. By far the most important are the American banks which due to increased U.S. investment in Europe have experienced a dramatic expansion of their business. At the end of 1971 deposits totalled £13,134 million. In a similar way other foreign banks by virtue of their trading connections and special knowledge are able to provide for their own nationals a unique service in London. In 1977 their sterling deposits amounted to £5,805 million.

A number of these banks fulfil all the functions of the domestic banks but by unwritten agreement do not attempt to compete with them.

7. Functions of the clearing banks. The description "London clearing banks" is applied to the six members of the London Bankers' Clearing House, the place where their representatives meet to settle inter-bank indebtedness. These banks account for the greater part of the normal commercial banking business of England and Wales although in the last decade there has been a considerable expansion of the business of the non-clearing banks.

8. Deposits. The basic clearing bank service from which all others stem is the provision of facilities for current and time deposit accounts.

(*a*) *Current accounts.* In October 1977 current accounts totalled £12,733 million covering personal and business deposits. The banks are enabled to exercise their principal function, the transfer of money, through the use of the current account in conjunction with:

(*i*) *The cheque system.* A cheque is an instruction to a bank to make payment of a specified sum to a third party.

(*ii*) *Bank Giro credit.* The expense of separate cheques and postages can be avoided by the completion of Bank Giro credit forms in favour of a number of payees and payment to the bank of the total amount either in cash or with a single cheque.

(*iii*) *The standing order.* This method of money transfer is designed for regular payments of fixed amount, e.g. mortgage or hire-purchase instalments. It is a standing instruction to the bank to pay a certain sum regularly upon a specified date.

(*iv*) *Direct debit.* A second method of automatic payment is the direct debit which differs from the standing order in which the "payer" gives his bank the necessary standing instruction. In this case it is the "payee" who originates the payment.

(*b*) *Deposit accounts and certificate of deposit.* In October 1977 they totalled £13,881 million. They differ from current accounts in two respects:

(*i*) *Interest.* These accounts yield interest.

A.E.—6

(*ii*) *Limitation of withdrawal.* Funds may be withdrawn only after an agreed period of notice has been given. In practice there is often flexibility in the application of this rule.

9. Advances. The second most important banking service and the one which is most profitable to the banks themselves is the provision of personal and business overdraft facilities against security. This security may take the form of something tangible and marketable, e.g. share certificates, savings certificates, title-deeds, insurance policies. Sometimes the proven integrity, business ability and prospects of the borrower are sufficient.

Rates of interest until September 1971 were geared to a formula, normally a fixed margin above Bank Rate subject to a minimum. The majority of customers paid 1 to 2 per cent above Bank Rate, the biggest and most credit-worthy about ½ per cent. Since 1971 the banks have pursued independent policies in respect of interest rates.

The provision of working capital for industry and commerce is based upon the assumption that the loan will be self-liquidating, i.e. as the firm's income grows, so it is enabled to repay the loan which has made its activities possible. Traditionally, the banks have financed agriculture with short-term advances of a seasonal nature. In industry, banks may be prepared to make longer term loans for, say, two to three years for the purchase of machinery and buildings. In commerce there has been in the last decade a considerable expansion in the finance of export contracts.

Advances in October 1977 stood at £14,310 million.

10. Security facilities. Bank strong-rooms are available to customers for the safe-keeping of valuables and night-safe facilities allow customers to deposit money overnight after banking hours for payment into their accounts the following morning.

11. Investment-advice and services. Banks will give advice on the investment of savings and through their own stockbrokers will make purchases and sales, their charges being paid out of the normal broking commission. Arrangements can be made for dividends to be paid directly into bank accounts or for the banks to detach coupons from bearer bonds and present them for payment. They will also act for their customers in applying for allotments arising from fresh capital issues and pay calls as they are made.

12. Income tax services. Most banks will advise or undertake to act on behalf of individuals in the preparation of income-tax returns, the checking of coding and notices of assessments and the making of claims for tax overpaid.

13. Executor and trustee services. Most banks have either an executor and trustee department or an affiliated company to deal with this branch of business. A bank may be nominated as an executor and, if necessary, a trustee of an estate after death. The advantages are professional expertise in handling a variety of assets, complete impartiality and continuity of administration.

14. Foreign travel. The banks will provide their customers with foreign currency, travellers' cheques which can be encashed at corresponding banks overseas or, for larger sums, letters of credit, any part of which the traveller can draw upon as required.

15. Remitting money abroad. Individuals may remit money abroad by two methods:

(*a*) *Bank draft.* This is a banker's cheque, often expressed in sterling but made payable in a foreign currency. The customer pays his bank in sterling at the current rate of exchange. The cheque will be honoured upon presentation at the foreign bank.

(*b*) *Cable transfer.* A credit is cabled by the payer's bank to the payee's bank.

16. Export finance. The larger commercial banks have special departments which specialise in the finance of foreign trade. They are assisted by banks affiliated to them overseas, or alternatively have arrangements with foreign banks which act as correspondents.

In the seller's market of the immediate post-war years international indebtedness was often settled on the basis of "cash on delivery" or even "cash with order". Increasing competition between the industrial nations has meant that price and quality are not always the deciding factors. The credit terms which the exporter is able to offer will often be decisive in winning an order. The banks have been encouraged, even in periods of domestic credit restraint, to afford short-, medium- and longer-term export finance.

17. Short-term finance. The most usual method of settlement for exported goods is the "bill of exchange". The exporter draws a bill on the overseas buyer, attaches shipping documents to it and hands it to his own bank for collection. The documents are then forwarded to a bank in the buyer's country and handed over against payment or acceptance, the proceeds then being transmitted to the exporter through the two banks. The bill may be payable at sight or at a fixed future date, normally a maximum of six months forward. In the latter case the drawee "accepts" the bill, i.e. agrees to pay when the bill is due. In both cases, however, the exporter must wait before the proceeds are credited to his account. The banks can help either by purchasing the bill or by making an advance against its security, the exporter's working capital thereby being immediately received. An interest charge and a collection commission are charged.

Bank finance is given against approved bills, approval being contingent upon:

(*a*) The financial standing of the drawee.

(*b*) Absence of restrictions upon money transfers from the country in which payment is to be made.

(*c*) The bill having a maximum of six months to run to maturity.

If the above conditions are not satisfied the banks may still provide finance if the Export Credits Guarantee Department provides suitable cover.

18. Export Credits Guarantee Department. This department of the Department of Trade provides extensive insurance cover against the risk of default by the foreign buyer whether his failure to pay results from insolvency or delay or from the political risk of exchange control restrictions being imposed in the buyer's country. The Department operates on commercial principles and charges an insurance premium.

19. Medium-term finance. This is offered by the banks to assist exporters in granting credit terms in excess of two years. Terms for each transaction are calculated on an individual basis but all are subject to the availability of E.C.G.D. cover.

20. Long-term finance. This is available from individual banks or banks in consortium for sums in excess of £2 million where repayment is spread over five to fifteen years. Such a loan would again be underwritten by the E.C.G.D. The unusual feature of such long-term finance is that it is provided by the banks direct to the overseas buyer. The British exporter can therefore be paid on a cash basis.

21. The economic importance of bank lending. It should be stressed that, while the wide range of financial services described are of great importance to the smooth running of the economy, it is bank lending which is of central interest to economists because of its implications for the money supply.

THE STRUCTURE OF LONDON CLEARING BANK LOANS

22. London clearing banks, a composite balance sheet. Examination of the liabilities side of the balance sheet shown in Table VI gives a clear picture of the structure and the limitations placed upon bank lending.

The principal items in the balance sheet will now be selected for explanation and comment.

23. Sterling deposits. Sight deposits are the current accounts upon which cheques may be drawn and which form the kernel of the money supply, M1 (*see* **32** below). The other deposits are time deposits upon which interest is paid and which may also be included in the sterling M3 definition of the money stock.

24. The 12½ per cent reserve ratio. In determining the level of their lending, banks must steer a middle course between two conflicting considerations. On the one hand, they wish to maximise loans in order to increase their revenue. On the other hand, they must maintain a sufficient reserve of cash or liquid assets readily convertible to cash in order to meet day to day withdrawals.

Until 1971, the London clearing banks voluntarily observed two rules, an 8 per cent cash ratio and a 28 per cent liquidity ratio of total liquid assets to deposit liabilities.

In 1971, the Bank of England imposed a uniform and obligatory rule for *all* deposit banks. It established a minimum reserve ratio of 12½ per cent, *eligible reserve assets* to *eligible deposit liabilities*.

25. Eligible liabilities. These are defined as the *sterling* deposit liabilities of the banking system with the exception of those deposits originally made for a minimum period of two years. Added to this are net liabilities in currencies other than sterling.

From Table VI it will be seen that the eligible liabilities of the

TABLE VI. LONDON CLEARING BANKS. A COMPOSITE BALANCE SHEET, OCTOBER 1977 (£m.)

Liabilities		
Sterling deposits		
Sight deposits		12,733
Other		13,881
	Total	26,614
Other currency deposits		
	Total	5,450
Eligible Liabilities		22,080
Reserve ratio	13.3%	
Sterling assets		
Notes and coin		727
Reserve assets		
Balances with the Bank of England		356
Money at call		1,107
U.K. and Northern Ireland Treasury bills		460
Other bills		489
British Government stocks up to one year		526
	Total	2,938
Special and supplementary deposits		649
Market loans other than reserve assets		649
Bills other than reserve assets		305
Advances		
United Kingdom		14,310
Overseas		2,468
Investments		
British Government stocks over one year and undated		1,397
Other		968
Other currency assets		
Market loans and advances		5,518
Bills		18
Investments		167
Sterling and other currencies miscellaneous assets		5,097
Acceptances		182

(*Source: B.E.Q.B. December 1977.*)

London clearing banks in October 1977, stood at £22,080 millions while the reserve ratio of 13.3 per cent was above the permitted minimum.

26. Eligible reserve assets. These are more strictly defined than the previous and looser concept of liquid assets. However, they share the characteristic that if they are not cash already they can be readily converted to cash on the financial markets.

(*a*) *Balances with the Bank of England.* All the clearing banks maintain accounts at the Bank of England. There is an informal arrangement that these balances will not be allowed to fall below $1\frac{1}{2}$ per cent of eligible liabilities. Note that cash in bank tills no longer counts as a reserve asset.

(*b*) *Money at call.* This is very short money advanced primarily to the London discount houses (*see* **36, 37** below).

(*c*) *Treasury bills.* (*See* also VI, **2**(*b*).) The banks can improve their cash position by running down their Treasury bill holdings or may sell them outright on the London discount market.

(*d*) *Other bills.* These are commercial and local authority bills representing short-term lending. The former may be treated as reserve assets *up to a maximum of 2 per cent of total eligible liabilities*. Like Treasury bills they may be sold on the discount market.

(*e*) *British Government stocks up to one year.* Again the banks may reduce their holdings as stocks mature or they may sell them on the discount market.

27. Special and supplementary deposits. Special deposits appeared in the balance sheet for the first time in 1960. The Bank of England has the power to call upon the banks to deposit a specified sum in cash, thus reducing bank liquidity and the power to expand credit (*see* **32** below). Interest is paid at current Treasury bill rate.

Supplementary special deposits were introduced in 1973 (*see* IX, **38**). When banks do not succeed in restraining the growth of deposits ("bank deposit money") in line with current guidelines they are "fined" by being required to make cash deposits with the Bank at zero interest.

28. Market loans and bills other than reserve assets. These items comprise loans to other banks and to the private and public sectors in forms which do not qualify them as eligible reserve assets.

29. Investments. These are made up almost wholly of British Government securities, some Commonwealth Government and local authority bonds and some fixed interest securities of public companies. All of these securities are marketable and therefore in one sense liquid. However, they are illiquid to the extent that sale on the stock exchange before maturity may involve a capital loss. The bankers' portfolios are so arranged that a proportion of their investment matures each year and the greater part of it within ten years.

The banks do not aim to maintain any fixed percentage of investments, this being the residual item after the demand for advances, the most lucrative asset, has been satisfied.

30. Advances. These assets are the most illiquid, the most risky and the most profitable. A fairly substantial proportion of overdrafts may in normal circumstances be for personal or professional purposes but by far the greater part are for business purposes.

THE CLEARING BANKS AND THE SUPPLY OF MONEY

31. Significance of the London clearing banks. The difficulties of a precise definition of the money stock have already been observed (*see* VII, **9**). However, if the sterling M3 definition is adopted, in October 1977 the supply of money amounted to £42,828 million. Of this £6,939 million comprised notes and coin in circulation with the public. At the same time the eligible liabilities of the London clearing banks stood at £22,080 million, the principal constitutent of the money supply.

32. The creation of bank deposit money. To a very small extent new deposits are created when notes are deposited at the banks rather than remaining in circulation. *The greater part of the new deposits are, however, created at the initiative of the banks themselves.* This occurs whenever a bank makes a loan. Loans may be made to:

(*a*) *The public sector.* Loans to Government whether in the form of purchases of securities or Treasury bills or in advances to the discount houses for the financing of Treasury bills will all result in the creation of fresh deposits immediately the proceeds are spent; e.g. Government funds raised in this way may be used to pay a civil engineer for road construction work. They then appear as an addition to his bank account.

(b) *The private sector*. Similarly, advances to private customers or purchases of commercial bills result in an expansion of deposits when the proceeds are spent.

It will be noted that in neither case do the banks hand out notes over the counter. If they purchase bills or securities they do so with a cheque drawn upon themselves. If they grant an overdraft, the borrower uses his cheque-book to make payments from an account which now shows a debit balance. The banks can create deposits in this way up to the point where their reserve assets bear a minimum $12\frac{1}{2}$ per cent ratio to eligible deposit liabilities.

EXAMPLE

Liabilities		Assets
Deposits	Reserve assets	Investments & advances
£50	£12.50	£37.50

In this position the banks are considerably "under-lent" since they are holding a reserve ratio of 25 per cent. They have capacity to increase their lending under the heading of investments and advances.

Deposits	Reserve Assets	Investments & advances
£100	£12.50	£87.50

In the second position more "deposit or ledger money" has been created and deposit liabilities have risen to £100. The banks are now said to be "fully lent", since their reserves bear the minimum $12\frac{1}{2}$ per cent ratio to deposit liabilities.

33. Restrictions upon the creation of deposits. The clearing banks do not have unlimited power to create money as has been demonstrated in the preceding example. The reserve assets rule imposes one restriction. Other limitations arise from the availability of collateral security, the necessity for all banks to observe a common lending policy and, most important of all, the controls which are imposed by monetary policy (*see* XIX, **33–8**).

34. Availability of collateral security. For a loan transaction to be completed it is necessary for the borrower to provide satisfactory security to the banker. Share certificates, insurance policies and title-deeds are examples of such security although in practice there may be some flexibility in what individual bankers accept. However, since collateral securities are themselves limited in supply, this limitation must exercise some restrictive effect upon the creation of deposits.

35. A common lending policy. The banks must move broadly in line in determining the level at which they will lend. Since there are now four big banks the probability is that three-quarters of any loans made by one will be expressed in fresh deposits for customers of the other three and only one-quarter as fresh deposits for its own customers. If all four banks are lending at the same rate, then their deposits will grow in line and their inter-indebtedness at the clearing house will roughly cancel out.

If, however, one bank adopts a more liberal lending policy than the others it will find that its cash balances at the Bank of England are gradually depleted as it settles its greater indebtedness with the other banks. In order to maintain its liquidity it must now drop back into line and restrict its lending.

THE LONDON DISCOUNT MARKET

36. Composition. The market comprises eleven discount houses which form the London Discount Market Association, together with a number of other firms which are not members and whose discounting operations form only a part of their total business.

37. The role of the discount houses. Essentially they are intermediaries in the provision of short-term finance standing between original lenders and ultimate borrowers, between banks with cash shortages and those with surpluses and between the commercial banks and the Bank of England.

(*a*) *Original lenders and ultimate borrowers.* The houses borrow from a variety of sources but primarily the commercial banks and for the most part *at call*, i.e. very short term.

In general the banks have favoured this arrangement since it provides them with an asset which yields interest and yet is highly liquid. Loans can be recalled immediately.

The ability of the houses to repay is underwritten by the Bank of England. Since 1829 they have enjoyed the *unique* right to borrow or to re-discount certain securities at the Bank. The securities which the Bank of England currently deems acceptable for this purpose are today's *eligible reserve assets*. At the Bank they must pay M.L.R., the only institutions which ever do so.

The funds which the houses borrow from the banks are then used to discount (at a higher interest rate than that paid) a number of instruments including Treasury, local authority and commercial bills and short-dated Government stocks. In other words the houses are making short-term loans to finance trade and to meet the needs of central and local government.

(b) *Banks with shortages and banks with surpluses.* When a bank with a cash shortage recalls money from the market, before resorting to the Bank of England where they are obliged to pay the penally high minimum lending rate, the houses will attempt to make good the repaid loan by borrowing from a bank with a cash surplus.

(c) *Commercial banks and the Bank of England.* Since 1825, the banks have never found themselves in a position where they have been obliged to borrow from the Bank of England. They have been able to maintain adequate cash reserves by the mechanism described in (b) above.

Finally, it should be stated that the market plays a central role in the application of monetary policy. This will be considered in IX.

PROGRESS TEST 8

1. What types of bank are found in the U.K.? **(1)**

2. What do you understand by the expression "clearing banks"? **(2)**

3. In terms of business volume, how important are the banks in Scotland and Northern Ireland compared with the London clearing banks? **(2–4)**

4. Explain the principal function of the British overseas banks. **(5)**

5. Point out the most striking feature of the U.S. banks in London. **(6)**

6. List the principal services provided by the commercial banks. **(8–20)**

7. Why is the banks' interest in export finance of especial economic significance? **(16)**

8. Explain the function of the Export Credits Guarantee Department. **(18)**

9. List the assets of the London clearing banks and compare their importance in the balance sheet. **(22)**

10. Explain the importance of the reserve ratio. (24)

11. Why are advances the asset of greatest interest to the banks? (30)

12. Define the "money supply". (31)

13. Explain the way in which the banks themselves are able to create both their own assets and liabilities. (32)

14. Why are the banks unable to expand their assets and liabilities without limit? (33–5)

15. Who are the members of the London Discount Market Association? (36)

16. In what sense is the Discount Market an intermediary between the Bank of England and the commercial banks? (37)

CHAPTER IX

The Bank of England

HISTORY

1. Foundation. The Governor and Company of the Bank of England was incorporated in 1694 by an Act of Parliament which granted a Royal Charter. It was the result of pressure in the City for a larger institution which could offer greater security and lower interest rates than the existing private banks. The privilege of a Royal Charter was offered in return for a loan to the Government of £1,200,000 against an annuity of £100,000.

2. The early work of the Bank. In the eighteenth century, the Bank accepted deposits and made advances against security. It discounted approved bills of exchange and later undertook the circulation of Exchequer bills and the issue of Government securities. In 1751 it took over the management of the National Debt.

3. The Bank Charter Act, 1844. The unique position of the Bank was advanced a stage further by this Act which decreed that no new banks would have the power to issue notes while existing banks would have this power curtailed. The result was that in due course the Bank of England became the only note-issuing bank in England and Wales. The Act also granted a fiduciary issue to the Bank, all notes in excess of which had to be backed by gold.

It was also established that the Bank should be divided into two departments, the Issue Department and the Banking Department, the object being to enable the same institution to carry out the duties of a central note-issuing authority at the same time as it engaged in normal commercial banking. The two functions did not prove to be entirely complementary with the result that commercial activities have almost completely disappeared, being gradually replaced by central banking functions.

4. Growth of central banking functions. The establishment of the Exchange Equalisation Account in 1932 following the departure from the gold standard, the introduction of exchange control in

1939 and the great increase in Government expenditure through-out this century all added to the special responsibilities of the Bank. The position was formally acknowledged in 1946 with the Act of nationalisation.

5. The Bank of England Act, 1946. The Bank was taken out of private ownership and the capital stock vested in the Treasury. Power was expressly given to the Treasury to issue such directives to the Bank as seemed to accord with the public interest. In fact there has never been occasion to use this power since the Bank has simply continued its pre-nationalisation practice of meeting the Government's requirements in respect of monetary policy without resort to statutory intervention.

The Radcliffe Committee found that the Bank remained a separate entity but that through a number of committees continuous consultation with the Treasury was maintained, views and advice being exchanged and policy determined. It is this series of liaison bodies that we refer to as "the monetary authorities".

ADMINISTRATION OF THE BANK

6. The Court of Directors. The Crown appoints a governor, deputy governor and sixteen directors to the Court which controls the Bank. There may be four working or executive directors with the remainder in a part-time capacity drawn from banking, commerce, shipping, industry and the trade unions.

7. The committees. The policy body which examines the work of all the other committees is the Committee of Treasury made up of seven members of the Court including the governor and deputy governor.

The other standing committees are:

(*a*) *The Debden Committee* which supervises the Bank printing works at Debden.

(*b*) *The Audit Committee.*

(*c*) *The Committee to Consider the Securities of Certain Funds* which supervises the investment of the Banking Department.

(*d*) *The Committee on Bank Premises.*

(*e*) *The Staff Committee.*

(*f*) *The Charitable Appeals Committee.*

(*g*) *The Committee on Permanent Control of Expenditure.*

8. The departments. There are eight departments each subdivided into a number of offices covering various aspects of the Bank's work.

(a) *The Accountant's Department* maintains registers of stock on behalf of the U.K. Government, Commonwealth Governments, nationalised industries and some local authorities and issues dividend warrants.

(b) *The Cashier's Department* deals with the note issue, the Exchange Equalisation Account, and all banking operations. Under the last heading come dealings with the discount market and in securities.

(c) *The Economic Intelligence Department* is concerned with collating and interpreting financial and economic information.

(d) *The Overseas Department* is responsible for relations with foreign central banks and international financial bodies.

(e) *The Audit Department.*

(f) *The Secretary's Department.*

(g) *The Establishment Department.*

(h) *The Printing Works.*

THE BANK RETURN

9. Significance. Like the balance sheet of the commercial banks the Bank Return gives an insight into the operations of the Bank of England. For accounting purposes the twofold division into Issue Department and Banking Department has continued to be observed since 1844.

10. Issue Department (selected items), November 1977.

TABLE VII.   BANK RETURN, ISSUE DEPARTMENT

Liabilities		Assets	
Notes issued:	£m.		£m.
In circulation	7,338	Government debt	11
In Banking Depart-ment	12	Other Government securities	6,479
		Other assets including coin other than gold	860
Total	£7,350	Total	£7,350

(*Source: B.E.Q.B.*)

11. Issue Department liabilities. It will be observed that liabilities consist entirely of notes, either in circulation or in reserve with the Banking Department.

12. Issue Department assets. Assets are made up of:

(*a*) *Government debt.* Direct lending by the Bank to Government which ceased in 1844 but continued to be shown as a separate item in the Bank Return.

(*b*) *Other Government securities.* This is by far the most important group of assets and any increase in the note issue implies an equivalent increase in Government securities. This is to say that whenever the note issue is expanded the Issue Department receives interest-bearing securities in exchange.

(*c*) *Other assets.* Included in this category are certain eligible bills and coin other than gold coin.

NOTE: It will be seen that the note issue is almost entirely fiduciary.

13. Banking Department (selected items), November 1977.

TABLE VIII.   BANK RETURN, BANKING DEPARTMENT

Liabilities	£m.	Assets	£m.
Capital	15	Government securities	1,709
Deposits:			
Public	20	Advances and other accounts	236
Bankers	292	Premises, equipment and other securities	154
Reserves and other accounts	613		
Special	1,171	Notes and coin	12
Total	£2,111	Total	£2,111

(*Source: B.E.Q.B.*)

14. Public deposits. These are the balances of the branches of Government and include the accounts of the Exchequer, the Paymaster-General, the Revenue Departments, the National Debt Commissioners and the National and Trustee Savings Banks.

It will be noted that the balance is relatively small. This is deliberately so since the accumulation of large public deposits in consequence, say, of substantial tax payments would correspondingly reduce bankers' deposits.

The reverse would be true when Government is making payments to society. Alternating shortages and excesses of cash would cause wide fluctuations in the short-term rate of interest and since the Government is the largest short-term borrower it desires an orderly and stable money market (*see* 25 below).

15. Bankers' deposits. The Bank of England is the bankers' bank and stands in much the same relationship to the clearing banks as the latter do to their customers. The clearing banks are enabled to make payments to each other or to the Exchequer by cheques drawn on their accounts and they can draw out the notes and coin that they require.

(*a*) *The clearing.* Net indebtedness between banks which can be settled only in cash is regulated through an adjustment in the bankers' balances at the Bank of England. Settlement at local clearings is carried out through the provincial branches of the Bank of England.

(*b*) *Cash and coin.* In the same way that the individual may draw notes or coin from his bank so the clearing banks can draw upon their accounts at the Bank of England. At holiday-times when the public's demand for cash rises, the banks are able to meet requirements by drawing upon these balances.

NOTE: We shall see later that bankers' deposits are important to the implementation of monetary policy. In the same way that the banks are able to vary the volume of their total deposits the Bank of England is in a position to vary the volume of bankers' deposits and therefore, at least theoretically, the credit which is related to them.

16. Reserves and other accounts. These include unallocated profits together with the accounts of overseas central banks maintained in London to assist in settling trade indebtedness, accounts of overseas Governments and the few remaining private accounts. The Bank of England does not compete with the commercial banks and will not therefore accept fresh private business. However, a number of old-established firms continue to enjoy the banking facilities which they have always had.

17. Special deposits. This item corresponds to the asset which appears in the combined balance sheet of the commercial banks.

It has been noted that the banks can be called upon to deposit a percentage of their own total deposits with the Bank of England as a means of reducing their liquidity and hence restricting their power to create deposits.

18. Government securities. Included here are Treasury bills and longer-dated securities (bonds) and Ways and Means Advances to the Exchequer to cover a temporary need for funds. This occurs normally when at the end of the day the Exchequer balances are run down and the Government needs to borrow only until the following day. Since July 1971, Treasury bills discounted for customers appear under this heading.

19. Advances and other accounts. These fall into two groups:

(*a*) *Private customers*. Advances on private accounts.

(*b*) *Discount market*. The Bank discounts bills for the discount market and also makes advances against bills as collateral security. In so doing it carries out its function as "lender of last resort". If for any reason the commercial banks recall money from the market (money at call and short notice) the discount houses in order to meet their obligations may now be "forced into the Bank" to borrow at minimum lending rate. Since this rate is in excess of discount rates they are put under penalty and there will be a restriction of business until the market can get out of the Bank.

If the Bank wishes to avoid this situation it will operate "at the back door", acquiring bills approaching maturity from the commercial banks and enabling them again to increase their lending to the discount houses.

These operations are vital to the control of the monetary system and further consideration will be given to them (*see* **36** below).

20. Premises, equipment and other securities. These are non-Government securities and include commercial bills acquired from time to time in order to test their quality and discourage the circulation of bills of which the Bank does not approve. Also included are shares and debentures in certain institutions established in the 1930s to stimulate industrial activity and in the 1940s to promote post-war industrial and commercial reconstruction. Since July 1971, premises and equipment have been added to this heading.

21. Notes and coin. It will be observed that this item is insufficient to cover the total balances of the commercial banks held with the Bank of England. If therefore there is an unduly high demand for cash by the banks consequent upon an increased demand by the general public the Bank of England's reserves will be depleted. If it falls below a certain level, the machinery will be set in motion for an increase in the fiduciary issue (*see* VII, 6). This level is known as the "proportion", the ratio between cash reserves and total assets, and is somewhat similar to the cash ratio of the commercial banks.

THE BANK OF ENGLAND'S DOMESTIC BUSINESS

22. The bankers' bank. It has been noted that the commercial bankers maintain cash balances with the Bank of England in order to facilitate the operation of the clearing and from which they replenish their supplies of notes and coin.

Beyond routine banking business exists a close relationship maintained by constant contacts through organisations such as the Committee of London Clearing Bankers and the British Bankers' Association. There are regular meetings between the governor and deputy governor of the Bank and the chairman and deputy chairman of the Committee of London Clearing Bankers as well as meetings at a lower level between bank executives and Bank of England senior officials. Both operational and policy matters are discussed. In this way the Bank becomes the channel of communication between Government and the banking system and the means whereby the Chancellor can make his wishes known without resort to the statutory powers which exist but which have never been used.

The Bank of England Act 1946 gave power to the Bank to request information from and make recommendations to bankers. If authorised by the Treasury it also empowered the Bank to issue directions to any banker for the purpose of securing that effect is given to any such request or recommendation. The evidence would, however, seem to cast doubt upon the effectiveness of this clause.

23. Banker to the discount houses. The eleven discount houses which make up the London Discount Market Association all maintain working balances at the Bank but unlike the clearing banks enjoy the unique privilege of being allowed to borrow.

Each house maintains a Loan Account at the Discount Office of the Bank of England where, if it is unable to meet its commitments, it can always raise cash either by rediscounting approved bills or by borrowing against eligible security. The Bank, however, dictates its own terms, specifically with reference to the interest charged which is known as "minimum lending rate". Since this is in excess of "Treasury bill rate" (the rate at which the market discounts Treasury bills) and well in excess of "money rate" (the rate at which the market borrows from the clearing banks to finance its operations), the discount houses will use the Bank only as "the lender of last resort".

Nevertheless, this borrowing facility is vital to the functioning of the monetary system. The clearing banks are enabled to maintain minimal cash reserves in the certain knowledge that when necessary money can be recalled from the discount houses which in turn will always be able to repay by resorting to the Bank of England.

24. Banker to the Government. The Bank's unique position among financial institutions stems from its historic relationship with Government.

Of first importance is the Exchequer account, the Government's central bank balance which together with certain subsidiary accounts is held at the Bank of England. The Bank also arranges to meet the Government's borrowing requirements either through Ways and Means Advances or through short-term securities (Treasury bills) and long-term bonds whether for cash or conversion.

25. Treasury bills. The Treasury offers a certain quantity of Treasury bills for sale by tender every Friday. These bills are normally for ninety-one days and do not yield any set rate of interest. Instead, offers are made at a price less than redemption value, i.e. the bills are discounted. It is the Bank of England which opens the tenders, makes the allotments, issues the bills and credits the proceeds to the Exchequer account. Bills are allotted to the highest bidders among applications from the discount houses; the Bank of England itself, acting on behalf of foreign central banks; the London branches of overseas banks and British banks acting on behalf of institutional investors. (By agreement with the discount houses the clearing banks do not compete on their own behalf at the weekly tender but make their purchases of

bills from the discount houses after the bills have run at least a
week.)

The Bank of England also pays bills as they mature.

It has been observed earlier (*see* **14** above) that the Bank seeks
to avoid alternating shortages and excesses of cash in the money
market which would cause fluctuations in short-term interest
rates. To this end it operates almost daily in the market, putting
cash out by buying Treasury bills or taking cash in by selling.
This is one aspect of the Bank's "open market operations" and is
carried out through a firm of discount brokers known as "the
special buyer". The Bank does not itself deal directly with the
market.

26. Issues of stock. The Bank also carries out continuous open
market operations in long-term securities. It advises the Government on new issues and conversions, publishes prospectuses, receives applications and allots the bonds.

On the day that a new issue is made, it is not anticipated that
the public will take up the whole amount. Arrangements are
therefore made for the balance to be bought by the "departments", which effectively means the Issue Department of the
Bank. These bonds are then gradually released to the market
through the "Government broker", a firm of stockbrokers acting
on behalf of the Bank.

The Bank is also a regular buyer of the stock which next
matures so that on the redemption date the number of bonds remaining in the hands of the public is considerably reduced.

It therefore follows that whether the Bank is releasing a new
issue or redeeming or refinancing existing debt, cash movements
between the public and private sectors are smoothed out over a
period of months.

Through these open market operations the Bank seeks to
establish an orderly gilt-edged market which is consistent with
the wise management of the National Debt. If security prices are
falling (i.e. interest rates rising) the Bank may intervene more
actively as a buyer in order to check the trend. Similarly, as a
seller, if the Bank has always "on tap" at least one medium- and
one long-dated stock, the rate at which it releases them to the
market will have a major influence upon the price and therefore
the yield of gilt-edged securities.

THE BANK OF ENGLAND'S EXTERNAL BUSINESS

27. Five tasks. There are five tasks which the Bank must perform in its dealings outside the U.K.

   (*a*) The operation of the Exchange Equalisation Account.
   (*b*) The management of foreign exchange control.
   (*c*) Monetary relations with the sterling area.
   (*d*) Monetary relations with foreign central banks.
   (*e*) Participation in international financial institutions.

28. The Exchange Equalisation Account. After the gold standard was abandoned in 1931 there no longer existed a common denominator which would automatically relate the exchange values of two paper currencies. In order to avoid the fluctuations which would have resulted from the determination of exchange rates solely by market forces the Finance Act of 1932 set up the Exchange Equalisation Account. Gold was transferred from the Issue Department and these funds, placed under the control of the Treasury, were to be utilised in stabilising the foreign exchange markets.

An excess supply of sterling which resulted in a depreciation in its exchange value was checked by the purchase of sterling with gold or foreign currencies. Conversely, an appreciation in the exchange rate was checked by the sale of sterling for gold or foreign currencies.

In 1939, the balance of the gold held by the Issue Department was transferred to the Account which ever since has been the sole depository of the nation's gold and foreign currency reserves.

The Finance Act of 1946 widened the scope of the Account to include the conservation or disposition in the national interest of the means of making payments abroad.

The Bank of England manages the Account in accordance with the terms of Britain's membership of the International Monetary Fund. Currently this means that the exchange rate of sterling must be held within the limits of $2.54 and $2.66.

NOTE: When the Bank enters the foreign exchange markets to buy sterling with gold or foreign currencies the proceeds are lent to the Exchequer against "tap" Treasury bills. Conversely, when sterling is sold it becomes necessary to call in loans, with the result that the Exchequer has to borrow from other sources.

29. Foreign exchange control. Exchange control was introduced in 1939 and given a peacetime form in the Exchange Control Act of 1947. The Treasury was given extensive powers of control over the conversion of sterling to foreign currencies and over the disposal of the foreign currency receipts of U.K. residents.

Control policy varies and is agreed between the Treasury and the Bank of England and administered by the latter.

Some 120 banks have been appointed authorised dealers in foreign exchange and they are allowed a certain latitude according to the policy in force to deal freely with applications for foreign currencies.

30. The sterling area. Sterling has two important international roles:

(a) *A world trading currency.* A considerable part of world trade is invoiced and financed in sterling and many overseas banks maintain trading balances in London.

(b) *A world reserve currency.* Many countries find it convenient to hold reserves in sterling in London where it earns a rate of interest rather than in gold. Those countries which hold the bulk of their reserves in this way are members of "the sterling area".

Close liaison on operational and policy matters is necessary between the Bank of England and the monetary authorities of sterling area countries. These include gold and foreign currency sales within the area in order that members may make payments to countries outside the area. They also include discussion of the management of the overseas sterling countries' holdings of British Government securities.

31. Foreign central banks. The Bank of England provides banking services, e.g. the management of sterling holdings, for many foreign central banks. These banks provide reciprocal services.

In recent years this relationship has developed beyond a narrow banking connection to the point where there are regular exchanges of views and information. The link is especially strong with the U.S. Federal Reserve System, the Bank of Canada and the European central banks.

32. International financial institutions. The Bank of England takes an active part in the work of a number of international bodies and in some cases provides the representative of the U.K.

(*a*) *Bank for International Settlements.* The Bank of England as the country's central bank is a member in its own right. Post-war, the B.I.S. has been primarily concerned with the acceptance from European central banks of short-term deposits of gold and dollars and the granting of short-term credits.

(*b*) *The International Monetary Fund* (*see* XII, **31–41**). The Bank works in conjunction with the Treasury in making preparations for I.M.F. proceedings.

The Bank also makes a substantial contribution to the works of:

(*c*) *The International Bank for Reconstruction and Development* (*see* XII, **50**).

(*d*) *The Organisation for Economic Co-operation and Development* (*see* X, **41**).

THE BANK OF ENGLAND AND THE IMPLEMENTATION OF MONETARY POLICY

33. Traditional monetary policy. It has been observed previously (*see* IV, **2**) that classical monetary policy centred upon the regulatory effect of moving interest rates upon the demand for and the supply of credit. In practice, this had meant variations in Bank rate which were "made effective" by supporting operations in Government debt.

During the 1930s the power of monetary policy to achieve its objectives was questioned (*see* IV, **2**(*b*)) and Bank rate remained static from 1931 to 1951. When in 1951 monetary policy was re-activated experiments were made with additional weapons of credit control. By 1971, methods had been evolved which placed the twin instruments of Bank rate and open market operations in a different perspective.

34. The Bank of England's minimum lending rate (M.L.R.). In the course of some 250 years traditional Bank rate had acquired a number of functions.

(*a*) *The "prime rate".* It was the rate to which bank deposit and lending rates were directly linked.

(*b*) *An indicator of the Chancellor's intentions.* Particularly during the 1960s, variations in the rate were viewed as a signal of the Government's assessment of the state of the economy and of future economic policy. From an international standpoint, if for some reason short-term foreign funds were being switched out of sterling investment bringing pressure on the exchange rate then it was hoped that a more attractive interest rate would encourage their retention. Additionally, it indicated to foreign sterling holders and to businessmen at home that the Government intended to take a firm hold on inflationary pressures. This, it was reasoned, would improve confidence.

(c) *The minimum lending rate to the discount houses.* Most significantly, Bank rate was defined as the minimum rate at which the Bank of England would re-discount eligible securities for the discount houses. In the event that the houses were obliged to repay money at call borrowed from the banks they would be "forced into the Bank of England" where they would pay a rate of interest in excess of the rates at which they were discounting. In short, they now made a loss. It followed that if Bank rate rose bill rates would not lag far behind.

By 1972 these functions had been largely overtaken by events. The implementation in 1971 of the Bank's proposals for *Competition and Credit Control* led to the commercial banks adopting their own independent base rates to which their other rates were now linked.

Secondly, while from an external point of view Bank rate was still important in checking the outflow of "hot money", as an economic signal it was increasingly displaced by explicit Government statements. The third and most important function was proving on occasion to be ineffective. During 1972, there developed a situation in which the market could *theoretically* borrow at Bank rate, a supposedly penal rate while the *actual* market rate for money lay above. Moreover, the Bank had developed techniques for influencing bill rates *directly* (*see* 36).

Consequently, on the 9th October 1972, Bank rate was replaced by *minimum lending rate*, defined as the minimum rate at which the Bank would re-discount securities for the discount houses. It differed in being the product rather than the cause of market rates and was calculated by taking the last Treasury bill rate, adding $\frac{1}{2}$ per cent and rounding up to the nearest quarter point.

In practice market forces induced repeated shifts in M.L.R. which often conflicted with the interest rates desired by the authorities. On such occasions the Bank suspended the formula and dictated M.L.R. as it had done with Bank rate. The position was regularised on 25th May 1978 when the Bank announced that henceforth it would once again administer the rate (still called M.L.R.) every Thursday.

35. Open market operations in gilt-edged securities. It should first be noted that in its operations in the gilt-edged market, the Bank may find that its monetary policy objectives conflict with those of its Debt management policy. For example, if the Bank finds it necessary to borrow large sums of money by the sale of gilts, this will depress capital values and force up interest rates (*see* IV, **2**(*b*)). High interest rates may not be appropriate to current monetary policy. Equally, it may be the case that the Bank places the desirability of Debt servicing at low interest rates above the need for high interest rates called for by monetary policy. During the 1960s this proved in fact to be the case. The Bank gave preference to its Debt management responsibilities and was consequently inhibited in using market operations for monetary purposes.

In 1971, the Bank indicated its willingness to see interest rates rise. Priority would now be given to monetary objectives and open market operations in gilts conducted in the traditional way.

When the Bank goes to the open market to purchase Government securities from the general public it must pay with cheques drawn upon itself. When these cheques are paid into the commercial banks, the Bank of England will have an adverse balance at the Clearing House. This can be settled only by crediting the cash balances of the commercial banks, i.e. bankers' deposits will increase. We have seen that these deposits are treated as part of banks' reserve assets. Since these have now been enlarged the banks will be able to pursue a more liberal lending policy and deposits will grow.

Conversely, when the Bank enters the market to sell, cheques drawn on the commercial banks in favour of the Bank of England will result in a reduction of bankers' deposits and a curtailment of their ability to lend. The immediate effect will be the recall of money from the discount market in order to make good cash balances. The discount houses will now be compelled to borrow from the Bank of England where minimum lending rate is now made effective. Since the houses are making a loss on this borrowing they will be obliged to curtail their lending in order to repay as soon as possible. Credit will be scarce and consequently dear.

36. Open market operations in Treasury bills. The Bank may also operate in the market in Treasury bills in a way which can influence short-term interest rates directly.

On the assumption that the Bank has some flexibility in

borrowing internally, i.e. from Government departments, it may regulate the supply of bills to the market in a way which will produce the interest rates which it desires. Not only is this possible at the Friday tender but also in the type of day to day dealings on the market in which the Bank has engaged since 1971. Whereas previously it had agreed not to try to influence rates in this way subsequently it has done so.

It should also be noted that Treasury bills are one of the reserve assets upon which the banking system can base the expansion of credit. It follows that one aspect of monetary policy will be the regulation of the supply of these assets, since the greater the proportion of short-term Government borrowing the more liquid the banking system and the greater the danger of an inflationary monetary expansion. During the 1970s there has in fact been a considerable expansion of the Treasury bill issue.

One way of dealing with this excessive liquidity is by calls for special deposits.

37. Special deposits. The scheme was first introduced in 1960. From time to time the banks may be called upon to make special deposits with the Bank of England. They are calculated as a percentage of total bank deposits, cannot be treated as part of the cash balances (and hence reserve assets) but do yield interest, in normal circumstances the current Treasury bill rate.

The object of the special deposit scheme was to restrict the liquidity of the banks, thereby putting a brake upon lending where the traditional instruments of monetary policy had failed.

The evidence of the 1960s suggests that this scheme did not prove as effective as had been hoped. Nevertheless, it was retained in the new monetary policy of 1971.

38. Supplementary special deposits. The basis of the 1971 policy was a strictly defined and universally applicable reserve ratio against which open market operations and the special deposits scheme could be used to contain bank liquidity. With the power to create credit limited, flexible interest rates could not be left to regulate the demand for money and its allocation between different uses.

The policy did not have the potency which had been expected. The banks found it possible by a variety of means to "manufacture" their own reserve assets and thus their capacity for creating credit.

The existing instruments were therefore augmented in 1973 with a *supplementary special deposit scheme* ("*the corset*"). The scheme was suspended in 1975 and reinstated in November, 1976.

The approach is different in that an attempt is made to regulate the liabilities side of the balance sheet directly rather than bringing pressure to bear upon bank assets. These liabilities of course represent "bank deposit money" (*see* VIII, 32).

The banks are obliged to restrain the rate of growth of their *Interest Bearing Eligible Liabilities* (I.B.E.L.s) to a specified percentage. If they exceed this rate they are "fined" by being required to deposit up to 50 per cent of the excess growth in cash at zero interest.

Even this approach has not been without its difficulties. By, for example, offering more free services, banks may persuade their customers away from deposit accounts and into current accounts which are not subject to the same constraints. Equally, they may direct such deposits into other interest bearing financial assets such as Treasury bills and short dated local government securities.

39. Problems of current monetary policy. A number of problems emerge from our discussion of money so far.

(*a*) *Should the thrust of monetary policy rest upon the control of the money supply or the manipulation of interest rates?* It has been observed that traditional monetary policy rested upon the power of a moving Bank rate to regulate monetary demand. Modern monetarists assert that this is to approach the problem from the wrong direction. It is impossible to peg interest rates at a level different from "the natural rate" for the same reasons that it is impossible to peg the level of unemployment at anything other than the natural or market rate. This rate will be determined by the demand for loans and the availability of credit, which when granted generates an expansion of "bank deposit money". If emphasis is placed upon the supply side, upon control of the availability of credit then the interest rate will be the product of monetary policy rather than its principal criterion.

(*b*) *What is money?* If it is conceded that emphasis should be placed upon controlling the rate of growth of the money supply, there remains the problem of a precise definition of money (*see* VII, 9).

(*c*) *Debt management and the interest rate.* When a restrictive monetary policy results in rising interest rates this conflicts with the Bank's concern to minimise the cost of Government borrowing.

(*d*) *International capital flows.* Short-term foreign investment capital ("hot money") is sensitive to differences in interest rates in the world's financial centres. Domestic rates must therefore be broadly in line with international rates if destabilising "hot money" flows are to be avoided.

(*e*) *Should there be a discretionary monetary policy?* It was shown in IV, **12**(*b*) that monetarists argue that so little is known of the precise relationship between the rate of monetary growth and aggregate demand that no attempt should be made at "fine tuning the economy".

(*f*) *Which instruments of control are effective?* Our experience of monetary policy since 1951 shows that there are major difficulties in prescribing effective instruments of monetary control (*see* **33–8** above).

PROGRESS TEST 9

1. Why may the Bank of England be described as a "central bank"? **(1–5)**

2. Describe the organisation of the Bank. **(6–8)**

3. What is the nature of the assets which back the note issue? **(12)**

4. Why are public deposits at the Bank surprisingly small? **(14)**

5. What essential purpose do Bankers' deposits serve? **(15)**

6. What are "Special deposits"? **(17)**

7. Explain the phrase "lender of last resort". **(19)**

8. What is the "proportion"? **(21)**

9. List the three key rates of interest in the money market. **(23)**

10. How are Treasury bills issued? **(25)**

11. Who is the "special buyer"? **(25)**

12. How does the Bank attempt to establish an orderly gilt-edged market? **(26)**

13. What is the Exchange Equalisation Account? **(28)**

14. Describe the two international roles of sterling. **(30)**

15. Define minimum lending rate. **(34)**

16. Explain the use of open market operations in making minimum lending rate effective. **(35)**

17. What problem inhibits the Bank in employing open market operations to pursue its monetary policy? (35)

18. How effective has the Special deposit scheme been? (37)

19. Explain the operation of the Supplementary Special Deposit scheme. (38)

20. Outline the principal problem areas of modern monetary policy. (39)

PART THREE

INTERNATIONAL TRADE AND PAYMENTS

CHAPTER X

The Liberalisation of World Trade

THE THEORETICAL CASE FOR FREE TRADE

1. The theory of comparative costs. The gains to be derived from international trade are explained by the theory of comparative costs. This theory is best developed in stages, the first of which is the proposition that the immediate cause of international trade lies in absolute differences between domestic and foreign prices.

2. Absolute differences in international prices. Given a rate of exchange between the currencies of two countries it is possible to make direct price comparisons. When price differences exceed transportation costs between these countries it is clearly profitable for them to engage in trade. However, this is not the end of the argument, for we must now discover the reason for these price differences.

3. Absolute differences in international costs. International price differences imply absolute international differences in production costs since long-run prices, whatever the degree of competition or monopoly, must at least cover long-run costs.

So far the theory seems to make the obvious suggestion that trade between two countries will be profitable when each specialises in the production of those goods for which it has the lowest costs of production. This is not the whole story, however, for trade may still take place in two commodities between two countries and to their mutual benefit even when one country has an absolute advantage in the production of both goods provided that each country has dissimilar cost ratios. This proposition is the core of the theory of comparative cost.

4. Dissimilar cost ratios. The principle may be illustrated by two simple arithmetical examples. Assume in each case trade between two countries only, the U.S.A. and the U.K., and in only two goods, wheat and textiles.

EXAMPLE 1. *The U.S.A. having lower production costs in wheat, the U.K. in textiles.*

Let us assume that in the U.S.A. 10 units of resources (land, labour and capital) will produce either 10 tonnes of wheat or 5 metres of cloth and that in the U.K. 10 units of resources will produce either 10 metres of cloth or 5 tonnes of wheat. While in this example neither country has an absolute advantage in the production of both goods each has a comparative advantage in the production of one.

If we further assume that the U.S.A. has 300 resource units and the U.K. 200 and that each divides its production evenly between wheat and textiles, total output will be as follows:

TABLE IX.   EXAMPLE OF PRODUCTION FIGURES
BEFORE TRADE

	Resource units	Metres of cloth	Tonnes of wheat
U.S.A.	300	75	150
U.K.	200	100	50
Total	500	175	200

Let each country now specialise completely in that commodity in which it enjoys a comparative advantage and the result will be as follows:

TABLE X.   PRODUCTION FIGURES AFTER SPECIALISATION

	Resource units	Metres of cloth	Tonnes of wheat
U.S.A.	300	—	300
U.K.	200	200	—
Total	500	200	300

As a result of specialisation, the total output of the two countries has been maximised and trade will take place to their mutual advantage at any exchange rate within the limits determined by their respective cost ratios, i.e. 5 metres of cloth: 10 tonnes of wheat and 5 tonnes of wheat: 10 metres of cloth. At the limits trade may still take place although all the benefit will be enjoyed by one or the other country.

EXAMPLE 2. *The U.S.A. having lower production costs in both wheat and textiles.*

More significantly trade may still be mutually advantageous even though the U.S.A. has an absolute advantage in the production of both wheat and textiles.

Let us now assume that in the U.S.A. 10 units of resources will produce 10 tonnes of wheat or 9 metres of cloth and that in the U.K. the same quantity of resources will yield only 4 tonnes of wheat or 8 metres of cloth. Again assuming the U.S.A. to have 300 resource units and the U.K. 200, each dividing their resources equally between the two goods, the result will be as follows:

TABLE XI.   PRODUCTION FIGURES BEFORE TRADE,
ONE COUNTRY HAVING AN ABSOLUTE ADVANTAGE

	Resource units	Metres of cloth	Tonnes of wheat
U.S.A.	300	135	150
U.K.	200	80	40
Total	500	215	190

If there is now complete specialisation in the products for which each has a comparative advantage the result will be:

TABLE XII.   PRODUCTION FIGURES AFTER TRADE, EACH
COUNTRY HAVING A COMPARATIVE ADVANTAGE

	Resource units	Metres of cloth	Tonnes of wheat
U.S.A.	300	—	300
U.K.	200	160	—
Total	500	160	300

The effect of complete specialisation has been a substantial increase in total wheat production but a fall in the production of cloth. The U.K. even when devoting all its resources to this activity is unable to achieve the previous figures. For this reason specialisation in the U.S.A. will not be complete and resources will still be directed to cloth production:

TABLE XIII.   PRODUCTION FIGURES INCREASED EVEN WITH INCOMPLETE SPECIALISATION

	Resource units	Metres of cloth	Tonnes of wheat
U.S.A.	300	81	210
U.K.	200	160	—
Total	500	241	210

Let us assume that 30 per cent of her resources are so used. In this position total output of both cloth and wheat has been increased as a result of specialisation. Again, at any exchange rate within the limits set by their respective cost ratios each is able to enjoy a higher consumption of both cloth and wheat.

5. Significance of comparative costs. From the foregoing discussion it will be seen that it is differences in "comparative" not "absolute" costs which provide the basis for international trade and that impediments to such trade serve to restrict the growth of total output and rising world living standards.

However, the benefits of increased world output will not be evenly distributed between countries but will depend upon "the terms of trade."

6. The terms of trade. The terms of trade between two countries are dictated by the elasticity of each country's demand for imports relative to the elasticity of the supply of the other country's exports.

In Table X above if U.S. demand for textiles is relatively stronger than the U.K. demand for wheat then the terms of trade will move in favour of the U.K. A world price for wheat will be established at an exchange ratio approximating to 10 tonnes of wheat: 5 metres of cloth. If the terms of trade move against the U.K. the world price of textiles is falling and the new exchange ratio will be closer to 5 tonnes of wheat: 10 metres of cloth.

In the inter-war period the terms of trade moved against the primary producing countries in favour of the manufacturing countries since the world price of raw materials and foodstuffs fell more steeply than the world price of manufactures. To this extent the hardships of industrial depression were somewhat mitigated. After 1945 the sharp upturn in the demand of the manufacturing countries for raw materials moved the terms of trade in favour of the primary producers, until 1955. Thereafter, the movement was again generally in favour of the industrial countries.

THE EMPIRICAL ARGUMENT FOR FREE TRADE

7. Great Britain and the free traders. At the close of the Napoleonic Wars British commerce lay strangled by a complex web of import and export duties. Almost every item which entered into trade was subject to taxes upon which Government depended for the greater part of its revenue.

On the other hand British industry had no rival anywhere else in the world and felt in no need of protective customs duties. Rapid industrialisation had built up enormous production potential which required the safety-valve of wider overseas markets. It was argued that lower import duties would reduce the price of food and raw materials. The result would be lower wage and production costs. Moreover, if Britain led the way in lowering duties the foreigner might be induced to follow.

The consequence of these pressures was the great British free trade movement beginning in the 1820s when Huskisson initiated a reduction of duties. The process was continued by Peel and completed by Gladstone. By the 1860s all protective duties had been abolished. There remained only a few "countervailing customs duties" (i.e. duties on imports which correspond to internal excise duties).

8. The results of free trade. The full effects of free trading policies can be observed in the extremely rapid expansion of British overseas trade in the years 1850–70. (It should, however, be noted that there also existed other favourable circumstances.)

APPROXIMATE VALUE OF EXPORTS (£m.)

1850	1854	1860	1870
71	97	135	250

Moreover, as had been hoped, other European nations began to emulate Britain's example in reducing tariffs (e.g. Holland, Portugal, Switzerland, Germany, Austria and most notably France as a result of the Cobden Commercial Treaty, 1860).

The last quarter of the century, although a period of depression and falling prices, saw a continued expansion in the volume of British exports.

9. Reaction to free trade. Until 1870 the strength of her industry enabled Britain to enjoy a virtual monopoly of exported manufactures throughout the world. Thereafter, her competitors began to gather strength, their developing industry increasingly sheltered by rising tariffs. In 1880 Germany raised duties and was shortly followed by France. In 1890 the effects of the McKinley Tariff in the U.S.A. were especially severe for U.K. exports. The Dingley Tariff of 1897 finally committed the U.S.A. to a policy of protection and in 1902 Germany followed suit.

At this stage it may be argued that protection was invaluable to the newly developing industrial countries since it assisted them to narrow Britain's lead and, in some industries, to overhaul her. In any event the total volume of world trade continued to expand and by 1914 there had developed an intricate pattern of international specialisation.

10. Economic nationalism, 1920–39. After a short-lived boom the world economy sank into depression. Four years of war had disrupted the pattern of international trade. Old customers had turned to alternative suppliers or had developed domestic sources. Throughout the industrial world unemployment figures rose and international payments were unbalanced. In the prevailing climate of political and economic uncertainty nations everywhere sought self-sufficiency. Reverting to an earlier ideal they believed that only in economic independence could national security be achieved. This thinking made itself manifest in high protective tariffs which aimed hopefully to conserve the domestic market for domestic industry, thus guaranteeing some measure of employment.

11. The consequences for international trade. Attempts by one country to penalise the exports of another could only lead to retaliatory action, to the detriment of both. The volume of world trade therefore shrank. The decline was accelerated by the practice, adopted increasingly after the 1929–31 slump, of bilateral trading agreements which replaced the normal multilateral basis of world trade and payments. (Bilateral trade requires each country to balance its payments separately with all its trading partners. The total volume is therefore dictated by the country with the lower imports. Multilateral trade enables a country with a deficit in one part of the world to finance it with a surplus earned elsewhere. Total trade is maximised.)

12. Britain's return to protection. While Britain remained wedded to the ideal of free trade long after her competitors had taken refuge in protection the slump brought some of her major industries to the verge of collapse. Under mounting pressure from manufacturers the Government agreed to afford a degree of protection to the home market and in 1932 the Import Duties Act was passed. Free trade was now a dead letter.

13. Conclusion. In international economic relationships as in domestic affairs, the Second World War provided a radically new approach. It was appreciated that there would need to be a high degree of co-operation between nations if the pre-war stagnation of world trade was not to be repeated.

The objective was to be a balanced expansion of international trade which would lead to rising world living standards. Instrumental to this ulterior goal would be three subsidiary aims:

(a) The gradual reduction and final abolition of protective duties and quotas throughout the world (see **19–32** below).

(b) International co-operation to improve the means of financing world trade (see XII, **31–41**).

(c) The promotion of investment by the advanced countries in the developing countries in order that the latter might play a fuller part in an expanding world economy (see XII, **49–52**).

While it is true to say that the validity of the general principle of free trade has now been universally accepted there remain certain reservations.

THE CASE FOR PROTECTION

14. Political and strategic reasons. Government economic policies are by no means based solely upon objective economic considerations. Political or social pressures may be such that a Government finds itself impelled to afford protection to a particu-

lar sector of the economy. In the U.S.A. powerful sectional interests have frequently been successful in persuading Government in
this way to reduce the intensity of foreign competition.

Again, for strategic reasons a country may feel it necessary to
develop domestic sources of supply if it believes that complete
dependence upon an overseas source may leave it exposed to un-
welcome foreign pressures.

In a more extreme way, when there exists the possibility of
military confrontation there will be no inclination to assist the
opponent's economy by engaging in trade, e.g. until June 1971
there was a complete embargo by the U.S.A. on all trade with
China.

In short there may be, at least in the short term, a perfectly
valid case for restricting foreign trade based upon factors which
override purely economic considerations.

15. Assistance for infant industries. Possibly the only sound economic argument in favour of protection is that which claims that
it is necessary to give short-term assistance to new industry in
order that it may establish itself.

This argument will be particularly valid where there is initially
an investment of a high proportion of capital. At first output will
be small and unit costs very high. As output expands and the
economies of scale are enjoyed, so unit costs fall and the industry
becomes more internationally competitive. At this stage it is then
desirable that the protective duty should be removed and that the
industry should stand on its own feet. The difficulty is that once
interests have become entrenched there is likely to be considerable
resistance to the removal of the duty.

Moreover, there is always a considerable possibility that an industry will be encouraged which has no real chance of survival in
competitive conditions.

16. Correction of the balance of payments. It may be argued that
where there is an adverse balance of payments it is legitimate to
restrict the volume of imports and to encourage domestic im-
port-displacing industry. However, pre-war experience suggests
that such action invites retaliation from the country against whose
exports there is discrimination. The problem then escalates.

The General Agreement on Tariffs and Trade (*see* **24**(*b*) below)
exceptionally permits this practice but only after the fullest international consultation.

17. Protection against "dumping." It may occur that a foreign producer is able to practise "discriminating monopoly." He produces on a large scale in order to gain the advantage of low unit costs but restricts supply to his home market in order to secure a high price. He then disposes of the surplus overseas at very low prices, if necessary below total unit cost. The British steel market was exposed to such "unfair competition" from the German steel cartel in the 1920s producing, inevitably, a demand for protection which was finally acceded to in 1932.

18. Protection of vested interests. In old-established industries there may be built up a vast stock of fixed capital which will seem of great value to the owners but may in due course become obsolescent. Similarly, the workers in these industries will acquire specialist skills, in which they too have a vested interest.

If such an industry is now faced with a new foreign competitor whose production costs and selling prices are infinitely lower there will be a demand for protection against "unfair" foreign competition. Such was the appeal of the Lancashire cotton industry when faced with competition from Japan and Hong Kong where wage rates were relatively much lower.

A too simplistic economic answer to such an appeal would be that cheap imports could only be of benefit to the U.K. economy as a whole and that it would be better to divert the factors of production currently devoted to cotton manufacture to some other activity commanding a higher return. However, factors of production in the form of mills, textile machinery, skilled spinners and weavers are relatively immobile. They cannot suddenly be translated into, for example, a motor assembly plant.

Thus, if the running down of an industry is generally agreed to be desirable it may also be conceded that in the short term a degree of protection is necessary to ease the difficulties of reallocating resources.

THE GENERAL AGREEMENT ON TARIFFS AND TRADE (G.A.T.T.)

19. The goal of global multilateral trade. It has been observed that during the Second World War a good deal of thought was directed towards the creation of a liberal, multilateral system of world trade. Close co-operation was envisaged in the field of international trade relations, payments and investment. Wartime planning produced the most striking results in respect of payments and investment with the setting up of the International Monetary Fund and the International Bank for Reconstruction and Development. Co-operation in respect of trade was somewhat delayed.

After the war, it quickly became apparent that the original objective was overly ambitious and, faced with Communist expansion, attention was concentrated upon promoting European co-operation and reconstruction to meet this threat. In the 1950s and 1960s therefore the most notable achievements in liberalising trade have been regional in nature and have been centred upon Europe (see 34(b), (c) below).

20. The abortive International Trade Organisation (I.T.O.). The end of excessively ambitious international planning was marked by the failure of the U.S. Congress in 1950 to ratify the treaty setting up an International Trade Organisation. The I.T.O. Charter had been signed by fifty-four countries in March 1948 and covered a very wide range of topics including not only trade but also employment, cartels, economic development and state trading.

The failure of the I.T.O. might have signalled the end of any global attack on tariffs but for the almost accidental birth of G.A.T.T.

21. Nature of G.A.T.T. In 1947 an international conference met in Geneva to consider a draft charter for I.T.O. As a sign of good faith the U.S.A. also engaged immediately in negotiations with twenty-two other countries which resulted in commitments on 45,000 different rates of duty embodied within principles laid down by a "General Agreement on Tariffs and Trade." On 1st January 1948, G.A.T.T. began its life when eight of the contracting countries made effective the concessions negotiated in Geneva. At this stage G.A.T.T. was viewed simply as a provisional arrangement which would lapse once the I.T.O. was established. In the event it has remained the principal instrument for achieving tariff reductions on a global scale.

It should be noted that technically G.A.T.T., unlike the I.M.F. or the I.B.R.D., is not an organisation but a treaty and that the signatories are not strictly speaking "members" but "contracting parties". However, it does have a permanent secretariat located in Switzerland and since 1953 an informal court to consider disputes.

22. The basic principles of G.A.T.T. The Agreement comprises thirty-eight Articles and many annexes and schedules covering the thousands of concessions which have subsequently been negotiated.

There are, however, four basic principles:

(*a*) *Most favoured nation treatment* (*mfn*). This first rule requires that any concession made to one signatory must be made equally to all.

(*b*) *A binding commitment* to observe all concessions already negotiated.

(*c*) *A general prohibition against quantitative restrictions* (quotas).

(*d*) *Developing countries.* Special provisions in respect of the trade of the developing countries.

Articles not concerned with these general principles relate to exceptions to the rules and to other commercial measures whose effect may be to impede trade.

23. Tariff obligations. The signatories are obliged to accord mfn treatment to each other in respect of duties, customs regulations and internal taxes and regulations.

The exceptions to this general rule are:

(*a*) *An existing well-known tariff preference*, e.g. Commonwealth preference.

(*b*) *A full customs union or a free trade area*, e.g. E.E.C., E.F.T.A.

Once negotiated, concessions must be observed except where it can be demonstrated that as a result imports have risen so steeply as to constitute a threat to domestic producers.

24. Quantitative restrictions. While there is a general prohibition of quota restrictions, among the several exceptions to the rule the four most important are in respect of:

(*a*) *Agriculture.* Quotas may be imposed upon agricultural imports when it can be shown that they are necessary for the implementation of Government policies on marketing and production control.

(*b*) *Balance of payments.* When a country's monetary reserves are in jeopardy quotas may be applied but may be continued only in close consultation with the other signatories.

(c) *National security.* Trade may be directly controlled when national security is at issue.

(d) *Developing countries.* Developing countries are permitted to impose non-discriminatory import restrictions as a means of fostering infant industry.

In all cases where quotas are permitted they must be applied in accordance with the mfn principle.

25. Specific measures to assist developing countries. A new Part IV headed "Trade and Development" was added to the Agreement in 1965 and comprises three Articles which oblige the advanced countries:

(a) *To give high priority to the reduction and elimination of restrictions on those goods which are of especial interest to the developing countries.*

(b) *To refrain from introducing all new restrictions on such products.*

(c) *To give favourable internal tax treatment to the primary products of the developing countries.*

The developing countries are equally obliged under Part IV to take similar action in respect of the trade of those countries less developed than themselves.

26. Operational procedures. The signatories of G.A.T.T. meet annually and also at special tariff conferences. Between meetings an Intersessional Committee prepares agendas while working parties report on specific topics. The existence of a permanent secretariat adds continually to the work of G.A.T.T. and enables it to behave more like genuine international organisations.

The work falls into three categories:

(a) The elimination of quota restrictions.
(b) The regulation of disputes.
(c) The reduction of tariffs.

27. Elimination of quota restrictions. For as long as a chronic imbalance remained in payments between the U.S.A. and the rest of the world the majority of signatories took advantage of the balance of payments exception to the general prohibition of quotas. In 1958, the U.S.A. for the first time moved into deficit and the Western European countries were able both to restore the convertibility of currencies and the following year at the Tokyo session of G.A.T.T. to reaffirm their intention to abandon the balance of payments escape clause as soon as possible. Subsequently, all the major trading nations gave up the quantitative restrictions which had been justified on these grounds.

The remaining major problems in this area related to restrictions upon agricultural products in which progress has been disappointingly slow.

Countries which still make use of the balance of payments exception are required to hold periodical consultations with G.A.T.T. as a means of exerting pressure upon them. Discussions are also mandatory when new restrictions are to be imposed.

NOTE: When in 1964 Britain imposed a 15 per cent import surcharge as a measure to correct the balance of payments the rules were violated since although it is permissible to employ quantitative restrictions for this purpose an increased tariff may not be so employed. In consultation with G.A.T.T. considerable pressure was exerted for the early removal of this surcharge.

28. Regulation of disputes. It is in this little publicised area that G.A.T.T. has enjoyed some of its most notable successes. Previously trade disputes often went unresolved for many years, souring international relations and normally ending in success for the stronger party.

G.A.T.T. has improved matters by providing a world forum before which grievances can be aired and also a formal complaints procedure. Many disputes have been resolved bilaterally, probably assisted by the knowledge that G.A.T.T. stands in the background, e.g. the U.K. Government was persuaded to repeal a restriction upon the manufacture of pure Virginia cigarettes when the U.S.A. protested that this violated the General Agreement.

If the dispute is not settled by the parties concerned an appeal may be made to the collective membership. A report is drafted and recommendations made. If these recommendations are not observed the complainant country may be authorised to suspend certain of its trade obligations to the other country *but* only to a degree which will not escalate the dispute, e.g. the 1962 "chicken war." The E.E.C. increased rates of duty on poultry imports which were mainly from the U.S.A. The dispute was unresolved and upon appeal to G.A.T.T. it was calculated that U.S. exports had suffered by $26 million in 1963. The U.S.A. was then authorised to reduce concessions to E.E.C. by an amount which would have a similar effect on the Community's trade. Duties were raised on brandy, trucks and other imports by an amount which affected E.E.C. trade by a sum estimated at $25.4 million.

Although in this case the dispute was not settled the main point is that retaliation was limited and there was no further escalation of the problem.

29. Reduction of tariffs. The major achievement of G.A.T.T. has been a series of six tariff conferences (the last being the "Kennedy Round"), at which reductions have been effected on more than 60,000 rates of duty covering more than half the world's trade.

In each new agreement the mfn principle is applied. Before each conference the participants prepare a list of products on which they are prepared to negotiate. Countries are then paired on the "chief supplier" principle, i.e. one country negotiates on those products which are chiefly supplied by a second country. The negotiations result in a large number of bilateral agreements which are then incorporated in a single master agreement to which each country appends a signature. All the signatories then enjoy all the concessions which have been made at that conference. A set of bilateral agreements have been in this way made multilateral in effect.

The advantage of this system lies primarily in the time saved and difficulties avoided were a similar volume of concessions to be negotiated independently by separate trade agreements. Moreover, conferences provide an atmosphere in which countries are disposed to be generous since while negotiating they know that they are about to receive many more benefits from other negotiations taking place concurrently.

30. The Kennedy Round. As duties have been lowered negotiations have become tougher and more protracted, the Kennedy Round lasting from May 1964 to June 1967. At this conference the procedure was somewhat different. Instead of negotiations being based upon specific products it was felt that more rapid progress would be made by linear reductions of all national tariffs with minimal lists of excepted goods. In the case of the U.S.A. the Administration had authority to halve the tariff with only ten excepted products and to abolish all duties which did not exceed 5 per cent. The results although not as spectacular as had been hoped were nevertheless most notable.

The major industrial countries reduced tariffs on imports valued at $26 billion in 1964. Some 70 per cent of the reductions were of the order of 50 per cent or more. In the U.K. cuts on industrial imports averaged 38 per cent. The major benefits to U.K. exports have resulted from the reductions made by the E.E.C., U.S.A. and Japan while the same countries have been the principal beneficiaries of the U.K. cuts.

Although progress at this conference was essentially limited to manufactured goods and to tariff restrictions on trade, it is generally agreed that both the scope and scale of the cuts achieved were infinitely more significant than those resulting from any previous negotiations and that for many manufactured products duties will cease to be a restriction to trade.

31. The Tokyo Round. A ministerial meeting of G.A.T.T. was held in Tokyo in September, 1973 and attended by 83 contracting members. They formally launched international negotiations intended to produce agreement on a new set of general tariff cuts and reductions in other barriers to world trade.

That little progress has subsequently been made is in no small part due to the effect upon world trading arrangements of the instability of exchange rates throughout the 1970s (*see* XII, 42–7).

32. Appraisal of G.A.T.T. In the first place it must be acknowledged that G.A.T.T. has provided a context for orderly international trade negotiations without historical parallel. In its thirty years of existence it has achieved a massive reduction of the obstacles to trade throughout the world.

On the other hand its success has been largely confined to trade in manufactured goods. Relatively little progress has been made in respect of agricultural products. This failure has given rise to some scepticism in the developing countries and the likelihood of continuing pressure through U.N.C.T.A.D. for a revision of G.A.T.T.'s rules in a way more favourable to those countries.

NOTE: United Nations Conference on Trade and Development (U.N.C.T.A.D.), first convened in 1964, is supposed to meet every three years.

33. Organisation for Trade Co-operation (O.T.C.). A weakness of the G.A.T.T. arrangements is that they are provisional and may be dissolved at any time. An attempt to rectify this difficulty was made in 1955 when the signatories negotiated an Organisation for Trade Co-operation, which was to be a permanent world organisation to administer G.A.T.T. Due to the opposition of protectionist interests, primarily in the U.S.A., this agreement has never been ratified.

34. Regional co-operation. Co-existent with G.A.T.T., which is concerned with the liberalisation of trade on a global basis, there exist a number of regional arrangements which have been established for a diversity of political and economic reasons. The most important are:

(a) The Sterling Area (*see* **35–39** below).
(b) The European Economic Community (*see* **40–49** below).
(c) The European Free Trade Area (*see* **50** below).

STERLING AREA

35. Origin. In the second half of the nineteenth century a large part of all international trade payments were made through London and in sterling. This practice is explained by the following reasons:

(a) *Britain observed a full gold standard.* Sterling was freely convertible to gold and no restriction was placed upon the import or export of gold. The world consequently had full confidence in sterling as a form of international money.

(b) *The London money market* was a highly sophisticated mechanism without parallel elsewhere which permitted the profitable deployment of short-term funds from all over the world for the primary purpose of financing international trade.

(c) *The London capital market* was also highly evolved and dealt in the securities of the entire world. It was the principal international source of long-term investment capital.

(d) *Britain was the world's chief importer* and very many overseas countries were enabled to enjoy substantial sterling earnings. Rather than hold these earnings in gold reserves in their own countries it paid to put them to profitable use in the London money and capital markets.

36. The sterling area of the 1930s. When Britain abandoned the gold standard in 1931 many countries ceased to hold their reserves in sterling, because of the uncertainty of the exchange rate of the pound relative to gold and the dollar. London therefore declined as the world's financial centre. Nevertheless, for the other reasons mentioned above (**35**(*b*), (*c*) and (*d*)) some countries continued to link their currencies to sterling.

37. Characteristics of the modern sterling area. From 1939 until 1958, when sterling convertibility was restored, the main characteristics of the area were:

(a) *The centralisation of gold and dollar reserves in London.* The external earnings of the area were pooled and external payments made from this pool.

(b) *Free convertibility of all sterling area currencies with each other.*

(c) *Membership based on the Commonwealth countries (except Canada), Iraq, Iceland, Ireland and Burma.*

(d) *Exchange controls* which restricted the convertibility of sterling area currencies.

(e) *Tariff and quota restrictions* which discriminated against countries outside the area.

Today the last two features have been dropped and membership has further declined so that it remains essentially a number of Commonwealth countries together with the British possessions.

38. The sterling balances. While each member retains independent control over its trade and payments, it pegs the exchange rate of its currency to sterling and holds its reserves in the form of bank deposits, Treasury bills and other U.K. Government securities in London. These are the sterling balances and are temporary in nature since they will be reduced either by the purchase of U.K. exports or by conversion to foreign currencies for the purpose of making payment outside the area.

In principle they represent short- or long-term lending to the U.K. Government initiated by central banks which acquire sterling holdings from their own nationals in exchange for domestic currency.

Sterling balances may also be held by countries outside the area which acquire them for normal trade and financial purposes and by international organisations such as the I.M.F.

39. Prospects. In the decade following the war the sterling area contributed to the liberalisation of world trade and payments by providing a stable multilateral system for its members. Subsequently, this function was largely superseded by the development of a world system which has permitted the restoration of currency convertibility and which has served directly to promote freer trading relations.

Moreover, Britain's greater participation in European economic affairs and her subsequent entry into the Common Market almost certainly spell the end of a system which in its time has served a very useful purpose.

EUROPEAN ECONOMIC COMMUNITY (E.E.C.)

40. Organisation for European Economic Co-operation (O.E.E.C.). O.E.E.C. was established in 1948 and comprised sixteen countries. Its initial task was the administration of Marshall Aid (American assistance to Europe) in the Joint European Recovery Programme. It then developed as an organisation for general economic co-operation whose major achievement lay in the progressive removal of quantitative restrictions upon European trade assisted by a system of multilateral payments, the European Payments Union. (When in 1958 ten European countries adopted global convertibility of their currencies on current account, the E.P.U. lost its function and was brought to a close.)

41. Organisation for Economic Co-operation and Development (O.E.C.D.). By the close of the 1950s Europe had made considerable progress in the liberalisation of trade and payments, but simultaneously increasing economic interdependence between Europe and North America had brought the need for fresh forms of co-operation. Therefore, in 1961, O.E.E.C. was replaced by O.E.C.D. (To O.E.E.C.'s membership of Austria, Belgium, Denmark, France, Germany, Greece, Iceland, Ireland, Italy, Luxembourg, the Netherlands, Norway, Portugal, Sweden, Switzerland, Turkey and the U.K. were added Canada, Spain and the U.S.A. and, in 1965, Japan.)

Through a series of committees O.E.C.D. seeks to promote co-operation in a wide variety of economic fields and aims at the development of the whole free world. In this respect it is more outward looking than O.E.E.C. which was concerned only with the development of Europe.

42. European Coal and Steel Community. In the early 1950s strong arguments were being advanced in Europe for much closer economic integration than was possible under the auspices of O.E.E.C. If Europe was to compete with the continental economies of the U.S.A. and the Soviet Union then industrial rationalisation was necessary across frontiers. A single mass European market would enable the economies of scale to be exploited to the full.

The first fruit of this thinking was the establishment in 1952 of the European Coal and Steel Community (E.C.S.C.). All restrictions on trade in coal, steel and iron-ore between Belgium, the Netherlands, Luxembourg, France, Germany and Italy were abolished while a common tariff on these commodities was adopted against countries outside the group.

43. Treaty establishing the European Economic Community (Treaty of Rome), 1957. In 1955, the members of the E.C.S.C. decided to enlarge the scope of their agreement to cover the whole of their economies. Negotiations led to the signing of the Treaty of Rome on 25th March 1957 and its implementation from 1st January 1958. (Simultaneously a separate treaty set up a European Atomic Energy Community, Euratom).

The treaty is a complex document comprising more than 200 Articles. The objectives may be classified in the following way:

(*a*) *The creation of a full customs union* with free trade in industrial and agricultural products (*see* **44–45** below).

(*b*) *The creation of a common market in labour, enterprise and capital* (*see* **46** below). The free movement of people businesses, and capital.

(*c*) *The ultimate integration of national economies into a single European economy* (*see* **47** below).

(*d*) *Political union* (*see* **48** below).

44. A full customs union. There are two aspects to the creation of a full customs union. Firstly, the abolition of all restrictions upon trade within the group and, secondly, the adoption by the union of a common external tariff and commercial policy.

The treaty envisaged a transitional period of between twelve and fifteen years. In the event progress was more rapid than anticipated and all tariff and quota restrictions (other than in exceptional circumstances) were finally abolished on 1st July 1968.

While the establishment of free trade in industrial products had brought rapid benefits and raised relatively few problems, free trade in agricultural products presented many more difficulties.

45. A common agricultural policy (C.A.P.). The basic problem derives from a technological revolution in European farming methods which is rapidly raising productivity, tending to depress prices and cause vast numbers of farmers to leave the land. Already the Community is fully self-sufficient in pork, sugar, potatoes, vegetables, milk and butter and almost self-sufficient in cheese, poultry, veal, beef, wheat and feed grains. On occasion the output of some commodities outstrips demand. The difficulty has therefore been to establish free trade in these goods and at the same time secure the economic position of the Community's farmers.

The structure of the common agricultural policy is based upon four factors:

(a) *Target price*. This is the base price established by reference to the region of the Community with the least adequate supplies. Subsidies are then paid as necessary to enable farmers to achieve the target price.

(b) *Intervention price*. This is the guaranteed minimum selling price at which the Community will purchase all surpluses. It stands at a given percentage below target price.

(c) *Threshold price*. This provides the basis for calculating the variable import levy. Having allowed for the transportation and marketing costs of imports it is the price necessary to bring the price of these imports into line with the target price. In short, imports from outside the Community are not permitted to compete with any price advantage.

(d) *Variable import levy*. This is constantly recalculated and is equivalent to the difference between the world price of the commodity and the Community's threshold price.

EXAMPLE

	Per tonne of wheat	
	$	$
Target price		96.00
Intervention price		88.00
Threshold price		
Target price	96.00	
Less Marketing/transport costs	4.00	92.00
Variable import levy		
Threshold price	92.00	
Less World price	56.00	36.00

Two important aspects of this policy should be noted. In the first place the Community operates no production controls to eliminate possible surpluses. Secondly, the variable import levy serves to make countries outside the Community the residual suppliers of those products which the Community cannot itself produce in their entirety.

46. A common market in labour, capital and enterprise. Already free movement of individuals in search of work is permitted within the Nine and social legislation and labour law are being harmonised so that all workers enjoy the same rights and protection.

Firms also are able to move freely, to expand throughout the union or to participate in mergers. Progress is also being made on the elimination of restrictions which impede the rationalisation of service industries, insurance, banking, law, medicine.

47. The full integration of national economies. Free trade is only the first step in the creation of a wholly effective customs union. Beyond this lies the harmonisation of many aspects of the social and economic life of the uniting countries. It is necessary to develop a common approach to monopolies and mergers, transportation and energy, fiscal and monetary policy, prices and incomes and to social security services to name but a few areas in which differences must be eliminated.

The progress made by E.E.C. in this direction has been quite substantial in those matters specifically covered by the Treaty of Rome but hesitant in matters dependent upon negotiation by the Council of Ministers. The field in which least success has been achieved is that of monetary and fiscal policy since these are subjects which lie at the heart of national sovereignty. Integration here seems to depend upon simultaneous progress towards some form of political union.

48. Political union. Since the Second World War many Europeans have seen political union as the ultimate goal. Early attempts to achieve this objective directly were too ambitious and attention therefore turned to economic union as a first step.

In 1961 the six countries reaffirmed that the ultimate objective of E.E.C. was to achieve a formal political union. However, a gulf has remained between the French concept of a loose confederation of sovereign states and the broadly agreed aim of the remaining five of a supranational federal government. At the present time therefore political integration would seem to be a distant, if desirable, goal.

49. E.E.C. institutions. There are four basic institutions:

(a) *The Commission* represents the Community itself as distinct from the member states. It is a nine-member executive body which administers Community policies and proposes fresh ones to the Council of Ministers.

(b) *Council of Ministers.* The Council comprises nine members, one from each country. It makes the final decision on policy proposals made by the Commission and it is therefore through this instrument that national governments are able to influence the evolution of the Community.

(c) *Court of Justice.* The Court is the sole arbiter of the legality of actions taken by the Commission and the Council and its decisions have the force of law throughout the Community.

(d) *European Parliament.* This body has little real power save for its right to remove the Commission upon a vote of censure.

BRITAIN AND THE EUROPEAN COMMUNITIES

50. European Free Trade Area (E.F.T.A.). In the mid 1950s Britain was unprepared for obligations as far reaching as those implied by the Rome Treaty. Her trade was global rather than focused upon Europe and the Community's common external tariff seemed to threaten old-established relations, particularly those with the Commonwealth. Moreover, the implications of political union seemed unacceptable to a country which had never really visualised itself as an integral part of Europe.

Britain therefore engaged in negotiations to establish a broad free trading area based upon the membership of O.E.E.C. and of which the newly established E.E.C. would be a part. This attempt broke down in 1958, whereupon attention was directed to securing the co-operation of other European countries. In 1960 the Stockholm Convention set up the European Free Trade Area comprising the U.K., Norway, Sweden, Denmark, Portugal, Switzerland and Austria.

The main provision was that tariff and quantitative restrictions upon trade in industrial products should be progressively removed. This differed from the E.E.C. arrangements in that there was no provision for a common external tariff. Each member was completely free to determine its own trade policies with the rest of the world.

51. U.K. applications to join E.E.C. By the early 1960s opinion in Britain was beginning to shift. The rapid economic expansion in

Europe resulting from the creation of E.E.C. could now be observed. Moreover, despite the growing obstacle of the Community's common external tariff this was the segment of the U.K.'s overseas trade which was expanding most rapidly.

Consequently, in 1961 Britain opened negotiations to enter the Community. This was followed in 1962 by the remaining members of E.F.T.A. expressing a willingness to join or become associate members. In 1963 negotiations were abruptly halted when France unilaterally vetoed British entry.

In May 1967, a second application for full membership was lodged. In December of the same year the Council of Ministers failed to reach unanimous agreement on the British application which was nevertheless kept on record and reconsidered over the following two years. Finally, at the end of 1969 it was agreed to open negotiations with the U.K. and other candidate countries as soon as the necessary preparatory work could be completed.

52. The basis of the U.K. application. The reasons for the U.K.'s application and the basic issues for negotiation are to be found in a 1967 White Paper (Cmnd. 3269) and in a statement by the Foreign Secretary on 4th July 1967.

(*a*) *From the economic point of view* the White Paper spoke of "the long-term potential for Europe, and therefore for Britain, of the creation of a single market of approaching 300 million people with all the scope and incentive which this will provide for British industry, and of the enormous possibilities which an integrated strategy for technology on a truly continental scale, can create."

(*b*) *From the political point of view* the White Paper pointed out that whatever the economic arguments "the Government's purpose derives above all from our recognition that Europe is now faced with the opportunity of a great move forward in political unity and that we can—and indeed we must—play our full part in it . . . Together we can ensure that Europe plays in world affairs the part which the Europe of today is not at present playing."

(*c*) *The fundamental issues for negotiation* were said by the Foreign Secretary to include the inequitable burden upon Britain of E.E.C.'s existing financial arrangements for agriculture; the need for a transitional period; the need to make provision for the interests of the developing countries particularly those dependent on the Commonwealth Sugar Agreement; the need to make provision for New Zealand's dairy products.

53. Accession and renegotiation. On the 1st January, 1973, the U.K. acceded to the Treaty of Rome and was joined by Denmark and Eire. "The Six" became "the Nine".

There were, however, many in both Labour and Conservative parties who were not sympathetic to membership. They continued to stress what they believed to be the economic disadvantages to Britain, particularly the ultimate loss of independence to manage the economy with purely national objectives.

The incoming Labour Government therefore undertook to renegotiate the terms of British membership. Four basic reasons were advanced.

(*a*) *The burden of the Community budget.* It was argued that Britain enjoyed only 14 per cent of the Community's Gross Domestic Product but contributed 24 per cent of the budget. When the negotiations were concluded at a summit meeting in Dublin in March 1975, this problem had been remedied with a new mechanism which automatically corrected "disproportionate contributions".

(*b*) *The common agricultural policy was particularly onerous for Britain.* It was made clear that Britain was making no attempt to change the terms of the Treaty of Rome, only to improve the application of certain clauses. The C.A.P., it was said, limited access to world markets and encouraged the production of surpluses, particularly in respect of certain products such as beef and butter. It kept selling prices unnecessarily high and was too inflexible since it did not differentiate in its treatment of the problems of different areas of the Community.

Some concessions were made to the British point of view.

(*c*) *The constraints upon trade relations with the Commonwealth and the Third World.* The common tariff had an adverse effect upon trade in agricultural products which was neither in the interests of the producing countries nor of the consuming countries in E.E.C. Little progress seems to have been made in dealing with this complaint, except in respect of the specific case of New Zealand. At the conclusion of Britain's five-year transitional period at the end of 1977 concessions were made for the access of New Zealand dairy produce for a three-year period.

(*d*) *Regional policy.* Britain argued for a measure of independence which would otherwise have been denied, in dealing with her severe regional problems by a variety of methods which amounted to subsidisation. This implied "unfair competition" with parallel industries in Europe. Advantage has been taken of the concessions which were made.

The Government considered that the renegotiations had been successful and recommended that the U.K.'s membership of E.E.C. should continue.

54. The referendum. During 1975 a powerful campaign was mounted by the supporters and the opponents of British membership to determine finally whether the U.K. should remain in the Community. A referendum in June produced an overwhelming response in favour.

PROGRESS TEST 10

1. Explain the theory of comparative costs.   (1–5)

2. What do you understand by "the terms of trade"?   (6)

3. What benefit did the U.K. derive from free trade in the nineteenth century?   (8)

4. Explain the phrase "economic nationalism".   (10)

5. What effect did the economic nationalism of the 1930s have upon international trade?   (11)

6. List the reasons which might validly be offered in support of protection.   (14–18)

7. What was I.T.O.?   (20)

8. Single out the main features of G.A.T.T.   (22)

9. What is the mfn principle?   (22(a))

10. What exceptions are there to the general prohibition of quotas?   (24)

11. Give an example of G.A.T.T.'s success in reducing the strain of international trade disputes.   (28)

12. Outline the results of the Kennedy Round.   (30)

13. What is the Tokyo round?   (31)

14. Describe the origins of the sterling area.   (35)

15. What are the principal features of the modern sterling area?   (37)

16. What are the sterling balances?   (38)

17. Describe the evolution of O.E.C.D.   (40–41)

18. What are the main features of the Treaty of Rome?   (43)

19. Distinguish between a customs union and a free trade area.   (44, 50)

20. Describe the operation of the C.A.P.   (45)

21. What are the main institutions of E.E.C.?   (49)

22. What was the Stockholm Convention?   (50)

23. Outline the basis of Britain's re-negotiation of E.E.C. membership.   (53)

CHAPTER XI

The U.K. Balance of Payments

THE BALANCE OF PAYMENTS ACCOUNTS

1. Concept of the balance of payments. The balance of payments accounts of the U.K. include all transactions between U.K. residents and non-residents, transactions being registered when the ownership of goods or assets changes or when services are rendered.

The accounts are set out in sterling values although clearly every transaction involves a foreign currency. Conversions are made simply by applying current rates of exchange.

The term "U.K. residents" includes all individuals residing permanently in the U.K., business undertakings located in the U.K. (but excluding their foreign branches) and U.K. central and local government authorities and agencies.

At the outset, the point should be stressed that international payments must balance. For any deficit resulting from an adverse trading balance there must be a compensatory monetary movement, i.e. a running down of national reserves, or alternatively an increase in overseas borrowing.

2. Compilation of the accounts. The accounts are to be found in a number of official publications. In the spring of each year, a White Paper gives *Preliminary Estimates* for the preceding year. These figures are finalised in a Pink Book, *United Kingdom Balance of Payments Accounts* which appears in the autumn. Estimates of the current position are published in *Economic Trends* and in the *Bank of England Quarterly Bulletin*.

The concept that international payments must balance can be demonstrated through a presentation based upon five major headings (*see* Table XIV).

(a) *Current account.*
(b) *Investment and other capital flows.*
(c) *Balancing item.*
(d) *Total currency flow.*
(e) *Official financing.*

TABLE XIV. SUMMARY BALANCE OF PAYMENTS, 1971–6 (£m.)

	1971	1972	1973	1974	1975	1976
Current Account						
Visible trade	+280	−702	−2,353	−5,194	−3,203	−3,571
Invisibles	+778	+808	+1,444	+1,657	+1,556	+2,344
Current balance	+1,058	+106	−909	−3,537	−1,647	−1,227
Currency flow and official financing						
Current balance	+1,058	+106	−909	−3,537	−1,647	−1,227
Investment and other capital flows	+1,816	−688	+49	+1,684	+203	−2,819
Balancing item	+272	−683	+148	+282	−21	+418
Total currency flow	+3,146	−1,265	−771	−1,646	−1,465	−3,628
Allocation of special drawing rights	+125	+124	—	—	—	—
Total	+3,271	−1,141	−771	−1,646	−1,465	−3,628
Financed as follows						
I.M.F.	−554	−415	—	—	—	+1,018
Other monetary authorities	−1,263	+864	—	—	—	−34
H.M. Government	—	—	—	+644	+423	—
Public sector under E.C.S.	+82	—	+999	+1,107	+387	+1,791
Official reserves (drawings on +/additions to—)	−1,536	+692	−228	−105	+655	+853
Total official financing	−3,271	+1,141	+771	+1,646	+1,465	+3,628

(*Source: B.E.Q.B. December 1977.*)

3. Current account. The current account comprises two main categories:

(*a*) *Visible trade.* The principal payments and receipts are in respect of imported and exported goods. *The Overseas Trade Statistics of the United Kingdom* provide the basis for the balance of payments figures subject to certain adjustments in respect of valuation and coverage. The most important adjustment is the deduction of freight and insurance from the valuation of imports since these values appear elsewhere under the heading of "Invisible trade".

(*b*) *Invisible trade.* This includes:

(*i*) *Government.* All U.K. Government current expenditure and receipts not appropriate to visible or other invisible trade transactions.

(*ii*) *Transport: shipping.* U.K. payments and receipts in respect of freight, time charter hire, port disbursements and passage money.

(*iii*) *Transport: civil aviation.* Receipts in respect of all non-resident transactions with British airlines and payments in respect of resident transactions with overseas airlines.

(*iv*) *Travel.* All personal expenditure by U.K. residents abroad and by non-residents in the U.K.

(*v*) *Other services.* Among miscellaneous service transactions are included receipts and payments for financial services, royalties, commissions and education.

(*vi*) *Interest profits and dividends.* All investment income remitted from and to the U.K. in respect of profits and dividends together with profits remitted or retained for reinvestment. In the public sector are balanced payments and receipts on inter-government loans and on the debit side payments on overseas holdings of U.K. Government, local authority and public corporation securities together with the interest due on official currency liabilities.

(*vii*) *Private transfers.* Remittance to and from the U.K. of migrants' funds, gifts and legacies.

4. Investment and other capital flows. These fall under the headings:

(*a*) *Official long-term capital.* Inter-government loans by the U.K. and repaid to the U.K. and to the U.K. and repaid by the U.K. together with subscriptions to certain international organisations, e.g. International Development Association.

(b) *Overseas investment in U.K. public sector*. U.K. Government stocks, local authority securities and mortgages, public corporation issues and borrowing by public corporations and local authorities from foreign banks.

(c) *Overseas investment in U.K. private sector*. Direct investments by foreign companies with U.K. branches and portfolio investment in U.K. company shares.

(d) *U.K. private investment overseas*. Both direct and portfolio investment.

(e) *Overseas currency borrowing or lending (net) by U.K. banks.*

(f) *Import credits excluding trade credit between related firms.*

(g) *Export credits excluding trade credit between related firms.*

(h) *Overseas exchange reserves in sterling.*

(i) *Other external banking and money market liabilities in sterling.*

(j) *Other short-term flows.*

5. The balancing item. This is the amount necessary to arrive at a balance and represents the net total of errors and omissions throughout the accounts.

The value of the balancing item will be such that total payments will equal total receipts for the balance of payments considered in its entirety. When the item is positive, if we assume the figure for total investments and other capital flows to be correct an unrecorded net export is signified. If we regard the current account as correct an unrecorded net reduction in assets has occurred (i.e. U.K. foreign assets have diminished or foreign U.K. assets increased). The opposite conclusions will apply when the balancing item is negative.

In the short term the item is more likely to be the product of unrecorded capital flows but in the longer term is not amenable to reliable analysis.

6. Total currency flow. This is the net currency flow resulting from all external transactions. It includes the current balance, total investment and capital flows and the balancing item.

7. Official financing. This means increases or decreases in the country's reserves or official borrowing drawn or repaid. They reflect the total currency flow together with the allocation of Special Drawing Rights and the payment of gold subscriptions to the International Monetary Fund.

When the total currency flow is positive, i.e. in favour of the

U.K., there will be a corresponding increase in the reserves or net repayments of overseas borrowing or a combination of both.

This heading covers the balance of loan transactions with the I.M.F. and other overseas monetary authorities and the drawings on or additions to the official reserves.

8. Relationship of current account and investment and capital flows. It has been observed that the accounts as a whole must balance. If, however, we consider the current account alone it is highly unlikely that in practice a balance will be struck. When payments exceed receipts a current account deficit has arisen and when receipts exceed payments there is a current account surplus.

An immediate conclusion might be that investment and capital flows will be induced by the result achieved in the current account. A deficit may be financed by short- or long-term borrowing which implies a corresponding charge upon the investment and capital-flow sector of the accounts. Similarly, a current account surplus implies a corresponding outward capital flow.

However, it would be erroneous to assume that investment and capital flows are determined solely in this way since many capital transactions occur quite independently and without any reference to the current balance, e.g. a Government decision to grant an overseas loan. In simple terms, a decision to invest overseas does not take account of whether the country has earned a sufficient surplus on its current account to finance that investment. It may occur that even with a current deficit there is still a substantial outward movement of investment capital which will add further to the total deficit. This was notably the case in 1964 when a capital account deficit of £370 million was added to a current deficit of £399 million.

When this is the case the total deficit (or surplus) will be matched by a change in the reserves or in short-term borrowing from the I.M.F. and foreign central banks. This change appears under the heading of "Official financing".

ANALYSIS OF THE ACCOUNTS

9. Current account, 1966–76.
In only very few years since the eighteenth century has the visible trade balance been positive but this has normally been compensated by a surplus on invisible trade to give an overall surplus on current account.

TABLE XV.   CURRENT ACCOUNT, 1966–76 (£m.)

	1966	1968	1970	1972	1974	1976
Visible trade						
Exports (f.o.b.)	5,182	6,273	7,885	9,449	16,538	25,416
Imports (f.o.b.)	5,255	6,916	7,882	10,151	21,732	28,987
Visible balance	−73	−643	+3	−702	−5,194	−3,571
Invisibles						
Government services and transfers (net)	−470	−466	−480	−561	−858	−1,546
Private services and transfers (net)	+209	+478	+576	+835	+1,209	+2,581
Interest, profits and dividends:						
Public sector	−160	−235	−264	−143	−355	−652
Private sector	+549	+560	+796	+677	+1,661	+1,961
Invisible balance	+128	+337	+628	+808	+1,657	+2,344
Current balance	+55	−306	+631	+106	−3,537	−1,227

(*Source: U.K. Balance of Payments Accounts.*)

On the invisible account the recurrent deficit in the public sector in respect of services, transfers and interest payments is usually outweighed by the surplus enjoyed in the private sector (*see* Table XV).

10. Trends in visible trade. In the period 1913–45 the volume of British exports declined irregularly and over the whole period 1913–76 increased by only about 35 per cent. (At current values the increase was sixfold.) The visible trade account remained in deficit and its traditional relationship to the invisible account was unchanged (*see* Table XVI).

TABLE XVI.   VISIBLE AND INVISIBLE BALANCES, SELECTED PERIODS 1913–76

	1913	1927–29	1937–38	1952–54	1964	1967	1976
Visibles	−134	−373	−388	−242	−537	−552	−3,571
Invisibles	+340	+480	+355	+384	+138	+255	+2,344

(*Sources: Abstract of British Historical Statistics* (C.U.P., 1962); *U.K. Balance of Payments* (H.M.S.O.).)

The second trend which we may note is in respect of the U.K.'s share of world export trade in manufactures (which account for about 85 per cent of our visible exports). The decline which had originated in the 1870s but was interrupted in the period 1939–50 continued during the 1950s. In the middle of that decade the U.K.'s share of world markets stood at about 20 per cent. By the late 1960s it had fallen to 11 per cent and continued to decline in the 1970s. The immediate explanation of the decline since 1950 lies in the economic recovery from a standing start of the industrial nations of the world, particularly Germany and Japan, and their subsequent growth rates which greatly exceeded that of the U.K. A lower growth is not of itself particularly significant but taken in conjunction with the U.K.'s recurrent difficulties on current account requires some explanation upon which to base remedial policies.

Certain factors bear upon Britain's competitiveness in international trade and clearly play their part in explaining the post-1955 decline in her share of world markets.

11. Competitive factors in international trade. In the first place it may be noted that during the 1950s and 1960s U.K. prices rose on average twice as fast as those of our major industrial competitors. Until the 1967 devaluation this was clearly a factor which served to diminish the international competitiveness of British goods. The extent to which uncompetitive prices may be viewed as the cause of Britain's declining share of world markets depends upon assumptions made about the elasticity of demand for exports. Early econometric studies suggested that relative prices were comparatively unimportant. Later studies, however, conclude that the elasticity of demand is much greater than was originally believed. At present, the view generally held is that while price is one very important factor there are others.

There then emerges a list of criticisms which have periodically been aimed at British exporters since the nineteenth century:

(a) *Absence of aggressive marketing.*

(b) *Failure to research effectively the requirements of local markets.*

(c) *Unwillingness to vary basic designs to cater for local tastes.*

(d) *Poor after-sales service.*

(e) *Poor quality.*

(f) *Uncompetitive credit terms.*

(g) *Deliveries—long dated, unreliable and late.*

The validity of these criticisms is not amenable to testing by econometric techniques but it is generally agreed that they exert considerable influence.

Finally it must be recognised that the volume of exports depends not only upon the conditions of demand but also upon the conditions of supply. If the economy is being run at a high level of demand then exports are likely to be diverted to home consumption, attracted by the easier market conditions. Manufacturers require more than the assurance of politicians that "exporting is fun".

12. Imports. The visible trade balance depends of course not only upon the receipts from exports but also upon the cost of imports. The first observation therefore is that when aggregate domestic demand is managed at a high level not only are exports diverted to home consumption but an increase in the volume of imports is also encouraged.

Comparison of the rate of increase of imports and exports during the 1960s at first sight seems reassuring (*see* Table XVII).

It will be observed that with the exceptions of the years 1963–64, 1966–67 and 1967–68, the value of exports grew more rapidly than the value of imports. The figures, however, disguise

TABLE XVII.   ANNUAL INCREASE IN IMPORTS/EXPORTS,
1961–70 (£m.)

	1961–2	1962–3	1963–4	1964–5	1965–6	1966–7	1967–8	1968–9	1969–70
Imports	53	272	641	46	206	419	1,242	286	680
Exports	102	293	184	311	405	−60	1,151	788	824

(*Source: U.K. Balance of Payments.*)

the fact that the volume of imports was growing more rapidly than the volume of exports. This discrepancy between the value and volume growth rate of imports and exports was explained by a continuing movement of the terms of trade in favour of the U.K.

Secondly, it will be noticed that from 1961 to the crisis year of 1964 and again from 1964 to the devaluation year of 1967 the rate of increase of imports far exceeded the rate of increase of exports. Subsequently, imports responded to devaluation in 1968–9 but the trend was re-established in 1969–70 with imports expanding at a far more rapid rate than exports.

It is accepted that since the U.K. is highly dependent upon imported foods and raw materials economic expansion will be related to an increase in such imports. However, since 1950 the growth rate of these items has diminished relative to the growth rate of imported manufactures.

TABLE XVIII.   ANNUAL INCREASE IN IMPORTS/EXPORTS,
1971–6 (£m.)

	1971–2	1972–3	1973–4	1974–5	1975–6
Imports	1,370	4,317	7,264	932	6,323
Exports	588	2,666	4,423	2,923	5,955

(*Source: U.K. Balance of Payments.*)

Table XVIII shows that the more rapid growth of imports over exports continued into the 1970s. In the middle years of the period this could be attributed to the reflationary stimulus of 1972–3 aimed at inducing more rapid growth. The substantial rise in the value of both imports and exports in 1973–4 was in part the consequence of the downward float of the sterling exchange rate. The huge increase in the value of imports was however, primarily due to the 25 per cent deterioration in Britain's terms of trade during the period 1971–4. A simultaneous boom in Japan, Western Europe and the U.S.A. sharply increased world

demand for foodstuffs and primary products and prices accelerated. It was, however, the fourfold increase in the price of oil
between 1973 and 1974 which made the biggest impact, placing an
additional £2,000 million upon Britain's import bill. The fall in
the rate of increase of both imports and exports in 1974–5 is evidence of the effect of world recession upon international trade,
while recovery is reflected in the turnround of the figures for
1975–6. It will be observed that in that year exports were beginning to close up on imports. This more optimistic trend was continued throughout 1977.

13. Invisible trade. Examination of current account transactions
shown in Table XV and the annual average surpluses shown in
Table XIX reveals the importance of invisible trade to the balance of payments. This has long been the position. In the 1930s
net earnings on invisible account paid for approximately one-
third of U.K. visible imports. At the outbreak of war invisible
receipts stood at 44 per cent of total receipts while payments
represented 18 per cent of total payments.

In the immediate post-war years the relative importance of invisibles declined but by the late 1960s had been restored to the
position where they produced 38 per cent of total export earnings
and accounted for 32 per cent of total payments. Since the invisible account consistently produced a surplus it is clear that it
made a major contribution to the current account surpluses of
the 1950s and to a reduction of the deficits in the 1960s and 1970s.

TABLE XIX.   AVERAGE SURPLUSES ON INVISIBLE ACCOUNT,
CYCLICAL PERIODS, 1952–74 (£m.)

	1952–55	1956–60	1961–64	1965–67	1968–70	1971–74
Average surplus net	327	230	173	181	514	1,172
Average Government account deficit	99	210	378	460	470	677
Average surplus less Government account	426	440	551	641	984	1,849

(*Source: U.K. Balance of Payments.*)

14. Government account. Reference to Table XIX shows the
significance of Government overseas expenditure to the invisible

account and hence to the current account and the total balance of payments position. There was a rapid escalation of the net deficit until the period 1961–4. Thereafter the rate of increase was checked and appears finally to have been contained after allowing for inflation.

The Government account divides into services and transfers. The first category includes military and diplomatic expenditure. Military-support costs consistently account for well over half the deficit. Transfers include military and economic aid programmes and subscriptions to international organisations.

Whether or not their burden upon the balance of payments is deemed tolerable rests upon the political view of the role which Britain should play in world affairs.

15. Private services and transfers. The accounts show five categories:

(*a*) *Transport: shipping.* The post-war period saw a continuous deterioration in this account with deficits being returned in the 1960s. The trend was reversed in 1967 only to relapse into deficit again in 1970. During the 1970s it has hovered around the break even point.

The sums involved are by far the largest items in the invisible accounts but the net flows are relatively small.

A number of factors bear upon the U.K.'s weakened position as a maritime power:

(*i*) *Unfair competition* from countries which subsidise their shipping lines for strategic or prestige reasons.

(*ii*) *The rapid increase in world tonnage.* Britain's share shows a relative decline.

(*iii*) *Imports are carried increasingly in foreign ships* and since these tend to be bulk cargoes the freight charges are higher than the export cargoes carried in British ships.

(*b*) *Transport: civil aviation.* In the past decade both sides of the account have grown quite rapidly but in step, to give a consistent and stable small surplus.

(*c*) *Travel.* This part of the accounts has always shown a fairly substantial deficit and it would seem that until recent years Britain has not viewed the tourist industry as a potential major exporter. During the 1970s the surplus has continued to expand.

(*d*) *Other services.* This category is a major contributor to the net surplus and includes a variety of items such as banking and financial services, royalties, commissions and education.

(e) *Private transfers.* This category normally shows a deficit which has ranged from a low point of £14 million in 1963 to a high point of £96 million in 1968. In 1970 the figure was £72 million. Subsequently, higher figures reflect inflation.

16. Interest, profits and dividends: private sector. Prior to 1914 Britain was the world's principal overseas investor, the income from her investments making an ever-growing contribution to the total of invisible exports. In the inter-war period the rate of investment slackened and during the Second World War a substantial portion of her holdings were liquidated to finance imports.

After the war investment abroad was resumed with cumulative benefits for the balance of payments since the net surplus on this item currently makes by far the biggest contribution to the total surplus on the invisible account (*see* Table XX).

TABLE XX. INTEREST, PROFITS AND DIVIDENDS:
PRIVATE SECTOR NET SURPLUSES, 1965–76

1965	1966	1967	1968	1969	1970	1971	1972	1973	1974	1975	1976
576	549	549	560	793	796	709	677	1,523	1,661	1,417	1,961

There is, however, one important new feature in the accounts of the 1960s and 1970s. During this period the rate of foreign investment in the U.K. has grown substantially with a corresponding rise on the debit side of the account. Until 1968 the rate of growth of debits in fact exceeded that of credits. This clearly has significance for exchange-control restrictions upon outward capital movements which, while they may be justifiable in the short run to correct an adverse balance of payments, in the long run must serve to erode the net surpluses on profits and dividends.

17. Interest, profits and dividends: public sector. Substantial deficits under this heading constitute a major offset to the surpluses in the private sector (*see* Table XXI).

TABLE XXI. INTEREST, PROFITS AND DIVIDENDS:
PUBLIC SECTOR NET DEFICITS, 1971–76 (£m.)

1971	1972	1973	1974	1975	1976
−204	−143	−200	−355	−517	−652

Very large debit items arise in respect of overseas holdings of U.K. Government securities, interest paid on official currency liabilities and charges paid on I.M.F. drawings.

18. Investment and other capital flows. The twelve items which make up investment and other capital flows are shown in Table XXII.

(*a*) *Official long-term capital.* Lending, chiefly at favourable rates to developing countries continued to exceed repayments at a stable level.

(*b*) *Public sector.* This item excludes foreign currency borrowing by the public sector under the exchange cover scheme whereby Government guarantees the loan at an agreed rate of exchange. Such borrowing is shown as a financing item.

(*c*) *Private sector.* Overseas investment in British industry continued at high levels totalling £9,525 million for the period.

(*d*) *U.K. private investment overseas.* Overseas investment showed a sharp upturn in 1976 and throughout the period amounted to £8,753 million. This was, however, £772 million less than the sum invested in the U.K. private sector by overseas investors (*see* **16** above).

(*e*) *Overseas currency borrowing and lending.* U.K. banks provide a source of international investment finance for both domestic and overseas residents. The decline in the figures towards the end of the period in some measure reflects world recession.

(*f*) *Exchange reserves in sterling.* These are "the sterling balances" representing the extent to which certain overseas countries prefer to invest a portion of their central monetary reserves and trading balances in income yielding financial assets. A comparison of the two items reveals the preference for short-term investments in banking and money market liabilities. The alternations between large sums flowing in (+) and flowing out (−) demonstrate the volatility of the market.

(*g*) *Import and export credit.* An import credit is the equivalent of an overseas exporter making an investment in the U.K. Conversely, an export credit represents a new overseas investment for the U.K. The rapid expansion of export credits throughout the period will be noted.

19. Total currency flow and official financing. When the balances on current and investment and other capital flow accounts are totalled and adjusted by means of the balancing item, a figure for

TABLE XXII. INVESTMENT AND OTHER CAPITAL FLOWS, 1971–6 (£m.)

	1971	1972	1973	1974	1975	1976
Investment and other capital flows						
Official long-term capital	−274	−255	−254	−276	−288	−158
Overseas investment in the U.K.:						
Public sector	+107	+120	+175	+252	+43	+203
Private sector	+1,052	+773	+1,652	+2,278	+1,719	+2,051
U.K. private investment overseas	−836	−1,383	−1,848	−1,149	−1,383	−2,154
Overseas currency borrowing or lending (net) by U.K. banks to finance:						
U.K. investment overseas	+280	+725	+595	+270	+320	+165
Other transactions	+191	−254	−70	−564	−85	−271
Exchange reserves in sterling						
British Government stocks	+55	+65	+74	−124	+7	+14
Banking and money market liabilities	+658	+222	+87	+1,534	−624	−1,421
Other external banking and money market liabilities in sterling	+709	−91	−7	+148	+550	+255
Import credit	+54	+198	+349	+172	+224	+242
Export credit	−287	−409	−552	−809	−570	−1,178
Other short-term flows	+107	−399	−152	−48	+290	−567
Total investment and other capital flows	+1,816	−688	+49	+1,684	+203	−2,819

(*Source: B.E.Q.B. December 1977.*)

the total currency flow for the year is established. To this is added any allocation of Special Drawing Rights by the I.M.F.

If the final figure is negative, official financing will involve overseas borrowing or drawing upon the reserves. When the figure is positive as it was in 1971 official financing implies a repayment of existing short-term loans from foreign central banks and the I.M.F. or an addition to the reserves.

EQUILIBRIUM IN THE BALANCE OF PAYMENTS

20. The concept of equilibrium. While international payments must always balance they need not necessarily be in equilibrium. By "long-term equilibrium" is understood a situation in which, at any given rate of exchange, the average current account surplus taken over a period of years is sufficient to finance all net external capital transactions (investment, foreign aid and debt repayment) together with any necessary expansion of official reserves to cover increased liabilities. Further, this equilibrium will be genuine only when it has been achieved without recourse to the management of domestic demand at a level inconsistent with full employment and without dependence upon trade and payment restrictions inconsistent with a country's obligations to G.A.T.T. and the I.M.F.

It should be stressed that disequilibrium will occur not only when a country consistently experiences an adverse balance of payments but also when it recurrently produces large surpluses, e.g. this has repeatedly been the case in post-war Germany.

21. Disequilibrium in the U.K. balance of payments: the origin. While the U.K. balance of payments was never very strong during the 1950s it has been argued that the year 1958–9 marked a positive turning-point after which there was a steady deterioration until 1967, significant of a fundamental disequilibrium.

Throughout the 1950s there had been a gradual reduction of the restrictions upon foreign trade and payments which during and immediately after the war had served to limit the volume of imports and restrict the export of capital. In this way the balance of payments had been protected. In 1958 sterling was made freely convertible to gold or dollars for all non-resident holders in respect of current account transactions. In 1958–9 the residual import restrictions which had been designed to conserve foreign exchange were finally removed. Apart from a normal customs tariff which had in any case been lowered as a result of G.A.T.T. the U.K. had now adopted a comparatively liberal system of trade and payments. It was now inevitable that in any expansionary phase, with domestic demand running at a higher level, imports would boom. In the event between 1956 and 1960 total imports rose by 23 per cent and manufactures upon which restrictions had been most stringent by some 56 per cent.

22. Disequilibrium, 1961–4. It has been observed (*see* 111, 12) that during the 1950s the major goal of Government economic policy had been full employment but that in the 1960s attention became increasingly directed to more rapid growth. Whereas in the preceding period (1956–60) the annual average growth of Gross Domestic Product was only 2.4 per cent, in the period 1961–4 it increased to 3.6 per cent. With demand now functioning at a higher level the balance of payments was subjected to stress and two sterling crises (in 1961 and 1964) resulted.

Due to expansion of imports the visible trade balance worsened in 1961 to £153 million, recovered marginally in 1962 and 1963 with figures of −£104 million and −£80 million, only to plummet in 1964 to −£537 million. On the invisible account moreover the Government deficit was increasing more rapidly than the private-sector surplus, while one aspect of the latter was in fact declining. The net surplus on private services fell from £230 million in 1962 to £177 million in 1963 and £167 million in 1964.

While a net capital inflow relieved the pressure in 1961, subsequent capital account deficits of £98 million in 1962, £148 million in 1963 and £370 million in 1964 were clearly not being financed from the current balance. The cumulative deficit over the period on current and capital account was £740 million, largely financed by massive borrowing from the I.M.F. and a depletion of the reserves by £327 million.

23. Disequilibrium, 1965–7. In this period the balance of payments and the preservation of the exchange rate of sterling became a major target of economic policy. Stringent demand management slowed the growth rate to an average of 1.6 per cent per annum, initially with some result. The visible trade deficit shrank to £237 million in 1965 and £73 million in 1966, only to rocket to £552 million in 1967. The surplus on the invisible account could not match these figures. In fact the net yield from invisibles fell in 1966 by £32 million due primarily to a substantial rise in the

Government account deficit and a fall in the net surplus from profits and dividends.

The result was that although the current account deficit was reduced to £77 million in 1965 and converted to a surplus of £55 million in 1966, in 1967 a deficit of £297 million was returned. It is perfectly clear that the current account was not able to support the net outward flow of investment which totalled £462 million.

If a comparison is made with the preceding period in terms of the old "basic balance" (i.e. current account plus capital account), the cumulative deficit, ignoring the balancing item, had deteriorated from £740 million to £781 million despite Government remedial policies. The position was further aggravated by a diminution of the sterling balances over the period by £431 million, and by other adverse monetary movements.

Official financing during this time amounted net to £165 million drawn from the I.M.F., £1,095 million borrowed from other monetary authorities, £165 million drawn from the reserves and £520 million transferred to the reserves upon the liquidation of the U.S. dollar portfolio.

24. Deflation or devaluation. From the foregoing discussion it would seem conclusive that a fundamental disequilibrium existed in the U.K. balance of payments from 1959 to 1967. In this situation the balance may be rectified by operating on:

(*a*) *The current account.* Broadly the intention will be to make domestic prices more internationally competitive either by deflation or devaluation. (Detailed consideration will be given to this subject in the following chapter.)

(*b*) *Investment and other capital flows.* Exchange control restrictions upon capital movements may be tightened.

In the event devaluation was forced upon the Government in November 1967 and although this was no voluntary act of policy it was hoped that it would provide in the long run the solution for the hitherto intractable balance of payments problem.

25. Impact of devaluation on the balance of payments. The immediate consequence of devaluation is to raise the price of a given quantity of imports and reduce the receipts from a given quantity of exports. It was not therefore surprising that in 1968 the current balance worsened to £306 million. The "basic balance", however, improved from the 1967 deficit of £418 million to £387 million

due primarily to a net inflow of official long-term capital and to
an increase in overseas investment in the U.K. public sector.

By 1969 the visible trade balance was responding to devaluation, exports expanding by £788 million and imports by £286
million, to reduce the deficit to £141 million. In 1970 exports continued their sharp upward trend, growing by £824 million while
imports disappointingly also rose sharply by £680 million. The
result was a highly unusual surplus on visible trade, albeit of only
£3 million.

The surplus on invisibles also improved dramatically, having
more than doubled from £255 million in 1967 to £628 million in
1970.

The net result was an improvement in the current balance to a
surplus of £631 million and in the "basic balance" to a surplus of
£338 million in 1970. Short-term capital movements were also
especially favourable to the U.K. balance of payments in 1970,
adding a further £161 million to the surplus.

The total currency inflow produced in the years of surplus,
1969 and 1970, amounted to £2,163 million. From this position
the authorities were enabled to repay £164 million of I.M.F.
drawings and £1,830 million of foreign central bank borrowing
and also to add £169 million to the reserves.

26. Deterioration in the balance of payments, 1971–4. The deterioration in the current account from a surplus of £1,058 million in 1971 to a deficit of £3,537 million in 1974 was unprecedented both in speed and scale. The 1974 current deficit in fact
amounted to almost 5 per cent of national income, about £1.50
per week per inhabitant. There were three basic reasons.

(a) *Stimulus to aggregate demand.* With unemployment exceeding one million for the first time since the 1930s, Government
felt impelled to reflate the economy and pursue growth policies as
the first priority. It recognised that an inevitable consequence
would be some imbalance in international payments but hoped to
offset this by permitting the sterling exchange rate to float downwards. This hope was not fulfilled. There was a big upsurge in imports and exports were diverted to the home market.

(b) *The downward float of sterling.* The immediate effect of a
depreciated exchange rate is to raise the cost of imports. Only in
the longer term when industry has had time to increase output
will exports respond to the price advantage which they now enjoy
in overseas markets. However, if domestic inflation keeps pace

with the rate of depreciation in the exchange rate this price advantage never materialises. This proved to be the case.

(c) *Adverse terms of trade.* The terms of trade signify a ratio between the export prices of one country relative to the export prices of another. During the early 1970s the terms of trade moved strongly in favour of the primary producing countries (*see* **12** above).

27. Improvement from 1974–7. Between 1974 and 1976 the current account gradually improved from a deficit of £3,537 million to one of £1,227 million. However, inflation continued at very high levels and the lack of foreign confidence in the ability of the U.K. Government to gain control of the situation was reflected in capital outflows of £2,819 million in 1976, primarily short-term deposits in the U.K. money market. Government was consequently left with a total deficit of £3,628 million to finance by borrowing from I.M.F. and other central monetary institutions.

As a condition of a further loan to finance the prospective 1977 deficit I.M.F. insisted upon strict control of the U.K. Public Sector Borrowing Requirement, the expansion of domestic credit and the rate of growth of the money supply. Implied was some belief in a monetary explanation of U.K. inflation.

In 1977, the economy responded to these measures with a gradual reduction in the rate of inflation. The current balance showed substantial improvement moving to a surplus of £399 million for the third quarter of the year. Significantly, this figure incorporated an improvement in the visible balance from a deficit of £930 million in the first quarter to one of only £50 million in the third quarter.

28. Prospects in 1978. The depressive effects of recession upon imports, the impact of stricter monetary control upon inflation, a depreciated sterling exchange rate and more favourable terms of trade all augur well for the immediate future. Supported by increasing revenues from North Sea oil, 1978 should see a comfortable payments surplus. Whether the position can then be stabilised depends upon the handling of the next boom. If domestic demand is permitted to race ahead then experience suggests a familiar sequence of events in which imports burgeon and overseas debts accumulate.

PROGRESS TEST 11

1. Why must international payments always balance? (1)
2. List the main items in the current account. (3)
3. What is the significance of the "balancing item"? (5)
4. What does a positive total currency flow indicate? (7)
5. How do current account items relate to investment and capital flows? (8)
6. Describe the general trend in the visible trade balance in the twentieth century. (10)
7. What criticisms have been levelled at British exporters in this century? (11)
8. Explain the significance of import trends in the 1960s. (12)
9. Explain the importance of invisible trade to the U.K. balance of payments. (13)
10. Compare the relative importance of the various items on the invisible account which fall under the heading "private services and transfers". (15)
11. What is the significance of restrictions upon outward capital movements for the balance of invisible trade? (16)
12. Compare the importance of "official long-term capital" with the other items which appear under the heading "Investment and other capital flows". (18)
13. Explain the "concept of equilibrium" in the balance of payments. (20)
14. What was the source of disequilibrium in the U.K. balance of payments at the end of the 1950s? (21)
15. Account for the 1964 sterling crisis. (22)
16. What were the effects of the 1967 devaluation upon the balance of payments? (25)
17. Explain the deterioration in the balance of payments, 1971–4. (26)
18. What brought about an improvement, 1974–7? (27)

CHAPTER XII

Foreign Exchange

THE DETERMINATION OF FOREIGN EXCHANGE RATES

1. The rate of exchange. The rate of exchange may be defined as the domestic money price of foreign currency purchased on the foreign exchange market. The rate varies daily and is derived from the domestic price quoted for bankers' bills of exchange transmitted by cable, the quickest means of international payment. This establishes the "base" rate. Other slower means of international payment, bankers' sight and time bills and trade sight and time bills are carried by airmail and sell at a discount from the base rate to take account of differing liquidity and risk factors.

In this way a pattern of exchange rates is established all of which are geared to the base rate which may be taken as the "key" rate of exchange.

Movements in the rates of exchange depend upon the structure of the foreign exchange market (*see* **2, 3, 4** below).

2. Variable exchange rates. In this situation exchange rates may be completely free to move in response to market forces. Such a foreign exchange system in fact approximates to the classical notion of perfect competition since any given foreign currency is a homogeneous product and the market comprises many buyers and sellers none of whom is able individually to influence the final price.

The demand for foreign currency originates in the debit items in the balance of payments while the supply derives from the credit items. It therefore follows that when demand increases relative to supply the price of foreign currency is forced upward, i.e. the exchange rate moves against the home country. The opposite will be the case when supply exceeds demand.

3. Stable exchange rate systems. Exchange rates have in practice rarely been left free to be determined by demand and supply. Stabilisation has been achieved in two ways:

(a) *Passive stabilisation.* This system is exemplified by the "gold standard" which functioned throughout the greater part of the nineteenth century and with interruptions to the 1930s. A country observes a full gold standard when its monetary unit is defined in terms of a fixed weight of gold, when the monetary authorities are prepared to buy and sell gold freely at this fixed ratio and when there are no restrictions placed upon the free international movement of gold.

In the situation where a number of countries observe this standard their currencies are linked by a common denominator and must therefore always exchange at this fixed rate.

(b) *Active stabilisation.* A genuine international gold standard has not functioned since the 1930s. Subsequently, foreign exchange markets have either been controlled directly or stabilised by official intervention. Intervention requires that the monetary authorities should have at their disposal both supplies of the domestic currency and reserves of gold and convertible foreign currencies. When the flow of domestic currency on to the world's foreign exchange markets is excessive the reserves are used to buy up the surplus in order to support the price (i.e. exchange rate) at the fixed level. Similarly, when the domestic currency is in *short* supply on the exchange markets the tendency for its price to rise will be forestalled when the monetary authorities sell domestic currency against gold or foreign currency.

4. Exchange control. In neither of the two preceding systems is any restriction placed upon private transactions in foreign exchange. Where the foreign exchange market is fully controlled all foreign currency earnings must be sold to the control authority at a given exchange rate and all purchases made from the authority at a given rate.

The supply of foreign currency earnings (i.e. the credit items in the balance of payments) is largely outside the control of the exchange authority except to the extent that exports or foreign loans can be encouraged. Supply is therefore taken as fixed and the authority turns its attention to restricting demand, usually by a system of licensed imports. Licences are allocated to individuals in a way which restricts the total volume of imports, and hence the demand for foreign exchange, to a level which equates with the supply of foreign currency earnings.

5. Balance of payments disequilibrium and foreign exchange rates. When there exists a fundamental disequilibrium in the balance of payments the effect upon exchange rates varies with the nature of the foreign exchange market.

(*a*) *Freely fluctuating rates.* When there is a recurrent deficit disequilibrium, there will be a continuing deterioration in the rate of exchange. Conversely, with a surplus disequilibrium the exchange rate will appreciate.

(*b*) *Stable rates.* Whether the rates of exchange are stabilised actively or passively the results will be the same. With a deficit disequilibrium there will be a continuing diminution in the reserves and/or an accumulation of foreign debt. A surplus disequilibrium will produce additions to the reserves and/or a reduction of foreign debt.

(*c*) *Exchange control.* The existence of exchange control is itself evidence of a "suppressed" disequilibrium. Were the demand for foreign currency free to rise the result would be an exchange rate lower than the one which currently pertains.

We shall now examine in some detail the adjustment of international payments disequilibrium under different systems of foreign exchange, making special reference to the historical experience of the U.K.

ADJUSTMENT OF PAYMENTS DISEQUILIBRIUM IN A PASSIVE STABLE RATE SYSTEM

6. The classical theory of adjustment. The oldest theory of international payments adjustment was propounded by the eighteenth-century writer David Hulme and refined by the British classical economists of the nineteenth century. It hinges on the concept of "the price-specie flow mechanism". An inflow of gold resulting from an excess of exports over imports will increase the domestic money supply and raise home prices. Conversely, the outflow of gold from abroad will reduce the foreign money supply and foreign prices. The response will be an expansion of imports and a reduction of exports to the point where international payments are automatically brought into equilibrium.

7. The gold standard. Prior to 1914 and during the second half of the 1920s the pound sterling was defined as 113 grains of gold and the U.S. dollar as 23.22 grains. Since the pound therefore represented 4.8665 times as much gold as the dollar, the so-called "mint parity" of the two currencies was £1: $4.8665. Any holder of 113 grains of gold could freely acquire £1 or $4.8665 from the

U.K. or U.S. monetary authorities respectively or alternatively exchange these sums against 113 grains of gold.

Any tendency for the exchange rate to move away from the mint parity was checked when importers, rather than accept an unfavourable rate, would withdraw and export gold in payment. However, a marginal movement of the exchange rate was possible within the limits set by the "gold points".

(a) *The gold export point* by adding the cost of freight, insurance and handling to the mint parity rate of exchange established the effective rate above which it paid the importer to make payment in gold.

(b) *The gold import point* by similarly subtracting shipment from the mint parity rate of exchange established the lowest rate which the foreign importer would accept rather than make payment in gold.

It therefore follows that on the gold standard any disequilibrium in international payments was compensated by gold movements which left the exchange rate undisturbed within the range of the two gold points.

8. Restoration of equilibrium. A gold standard implies a stringent control over a country's money supply. The 1844 Bank Charter Act permitted a small fiduciary issue in Britain but required that every other banknote should have full gold cover (*see* IX, 3).

Given an unfavourable balance of payments and a movement of the exchange rate to the gold export point, bullion now flowed out of the country. It followed that the volume of currency had now to be curtailed and the banking system was compelled to follow a policy of deflation. Bank Rate was raised and the Bank of England engaged in open market operations to reduce the cash reserves of the commercial banks which, in turn, were obliged to restrict credit in order to maintain their cash ratio (*see* IX, 36). In short, there was a contraction of the money supply in terms of both cash and bank deposits.

It was argued that these deflationary policies produced a decline in the domestic price level which encouraged exports and discouraged imports. Equilibrium in the balance of payments was restored automatically, albeit at the expense of a deflation over which there was no control.

Given a favourable balance of payments and an inflow of gold the course of events was reversed.

9. Advantages and disadvantages of the gold standard. Assuming the foregoing explanation to be an accurate account of the sequence of events on an international gold standard, certain advantages and disadvantages are apparent.

(*a*) *Advantages.* Internally it is impossible for inflation to be excessive since the money supply is strictly controlled. The domestic price level must therefore in the long run remain internationally competitive and the balance of payments can be left to adjust itself automatically.

(*b*) *Disadvantages.* Economic expansion may be impeded by a too inflexible and arbitrary restriction of the supply of money and credit. Moreover, the inevitable deflation or inflation which must accompany an outward or inward gold flow may be wholly at odds with internal economic needs, e.g. deflation in a situation of high unemployment.

By the 1930s a considerable body of opinion was disposed against a wholly arbitrary system in which gold was the master and a country was robbed of control over its economic fortunes.

10. The validity of the price-specie flow mechanism. Two main criticisms emerge which reduce the validity of the theory as conceived by the classical economists.

(*a*) *Quantity theory of money criticism.* The quantity theory assumes that a change in the money supply will bring about a proportionate change in the price level. However, the effect of a change depends upon the extent to which the volume of spending responds. A decrease in the quantity of money may be compensated by an increase in its velocity of circulation and vice versa. Therefore there can be no direct or certain response from prices to any given change in the money supply.

(*b*) *No allowance for income changes.* In the classical theory of perfect competition and continuing full employment there could be no change in spending which did not simultaneously produce a corresponding change in both prices and incomes. The classical economists saw that deflation (reduced spending) subsequent to an adverse balance of payments reduced the purchasing power (i.e. income) of the deficit country since exports were now made at lower prices. However, the view was that the reduction of income was the incidental accompaniment of the reduction in prices, the latter being the key to international payments adjustment. It was not seen that there could be an autonomous change

in income unrelated to price change which would itself contribute
to adjustment.

11. Income change and the balance of payments. Modern theory
places a great deal of emphasis upon the notion that income
changes play a major role in the long-run adjustment of international payments.

Where there exists a recurrent disequilibrium at stable exchange
rates and the deficit country is forced to deflate, prices may or
may not respond. What is certain is that at lower levels of spending national income will decline, thus inducing a fall in home consumption. The volume of imports will be reduced and goods
released from home use for export.

At the same time the income of the surplus country will be inflated with unpredictable consequences for the price level. However, at the higher income level further imports will be attracted
and exports diverted to home use.

Nevertheless, it is to be expected that at the same time prices
will be falling in the deficit country and rising in the surplus
country.

The two sets of circumstances will combine to reduce both
deficit and surplus and establish an equilibrium.

12. Variations on the gold standard. In 1914 the gold standard
was suspended but fixed rates of exchange maintained. After the
war exchange rates between many currencies were permitted to
fluctuate and settle at whatever level the market determined. In
the resulting chaos many monetary authorities were convinced of
the desirability of a return to the gold standard. This course was
followed by Austria (1922), Germany (1924), Britain (1925),
France (1928).

(a) *The gold bullion standard.* Britain did not readopt a full gold
standard as it had functioned before 1914. It was more a gold
bullion standard. Bank of England paper was convertible but
only into gold bars in minimum quantities of 400 ounces, about
£1,560. While gold was once more used in settlement of international payments it was no longer circulated internally.

(b) *The gold exchange standard.* This technique enables a
country to link its currency to gold without in fact holding gold
reserves of its own. Instead, it holds its reserves in the currency of
a country observing the gold standard and thus enjoys the advantage of interest receipts on these deposits.

13. Abandonment of the gold standard. For a number of reasons the world was obliged to abandon an international gold standard in the years between 1931 and 1936.

(a) *Failure to observe gold standard obligations.* It has been noted that an automatic consequence of payments disequilibrium will be a degree of inflation in the surplus country and of deflation in the deficit country. During the period of the restored gold standard no country was prepared fully to accept these consequences. In deficit countries such as the U.K. it would have been necessary to permit severe deflation even in the prevailing conditions of industrial depression and rising unemployment. In surplus countries such as the U.S.A. which was receiving huge quantities of gold there was an unwillingness to accept an inflation which might jeopardise exports. The inward flow of gold was therefore stabilised.

(b) *"Hot money."* Before 1914 most capital movements were for the purpose of long-term investment. After the war a huge volume of short-term money shifted from one country to another in search of refuge from depreciation. These movements added instability to the balance of international payments.

(c) *Overvaluation of sterling.* In 1925 the mint parity of sterling was re-established at its 1914 level. In view of the great inflation which had occurred in Britain during the war this rate clearly overvalued the pound. The degree of deflation required to reduce the U.K. price level to a point which made the exchange rate realistic proved impossible of attainment. There followed inevitably a fundamental disequilibrium in the balance of payments which produced a steady drain upon the gold reserves. Following an adverse balance of £100 million, Britain in 1931 was compelled to leave the gold standard. Since sterling was a key reserve and trading currency other countries were obliged to follow suit.

EXCHANGE CONTROL SYSTEMS

14. Origins. Exchange controls were first adopted by many Governments during the First World War as a means of safeguarding those imports vital to the economy. After the war controls were abandoned until the international financial crisis of 1931. Failure of confidence in the ability of one nation after another to honour its short-term international obligations led to massive withdrawals of funds from these countries which were checked only by the reimposition of exchange controls.

In due course confidence in sterling was affected but instead of adopting controls the U.K. reacted first by abandoning the gold standard and allowing the pound to depreciate and then, in 1932, stabilising at a lower parity with the aid of the Exchange Equalisation Account.

By 1935 a clear pattern had emerged in which Germany and the countries of south-east Europe together with Brazil, Argentina and Chile practised stringent exchange controls. The currencies of the rest of the world remained freely convertible.

15. Extension of exchange controls. During the Second World War tight controls were imposed by all countries. After the war while other direct economic controls were dismantled exchange control was retained. By 1958 there were only eleven fully convertible currencies. After 1958 a general easing of international payment difficulties enabled many more countries to revert either to full or partial convertibility. While it is true that exchange controls have not yet been completely eliminated they no longer have the restrictive effect on trade and payments that they had during the post-war years. The exception is in the case of some developing countries where they are used as a major instrument of economic policy.

16. Purposes of an exchange-control system. An exchange-control system will have one or more of the following purposes:

(a) *Correction of a balance of payments disequilibrium.* Since 1945, exchange controls have been, and still are, imposed to correct a disequilibrium which springs from massive capital outflows. For example, half the 1964 U.K. deficit sprang from capital account transactions and controls over these were subsequently tightened.

Current account deficits may be corrected in this way where countries are unwilling to deflate or devalue. However, after 1958, all the world's major trading nations agreed to abandon controls over current account transactions.

(b) *Instrument of economic planning.* We have seen in Part One that in private-enterprise economies Governments seek to implement national economic plans by indirect methods, notably fiscal and monetary policy. Since the achievement of objectives such as full employment or more rapid growth may set up inflationary pressures which induce a balance of payments disequilibrium, exchange controls may be adopted as a short-term planning expedient.

(c) *Source of revenue*. In this case the exchange-control authority arbitrarily sets the price at which it will purchase foreign exchange below that at which it will sell, thus leaving itself a profit margin. Today this objective is mainly restricted to the developing countries.

(d) *Protection*. Like a customs tariff exchange controls may be used to protect domestic industry.

17. Types of system. Exchange-control systems may vary considerably in detail but all will fall into one or other of two categories:

(a) *Single-rate systems*. The exchange-control authority has the sole right to buy and sell foreign currency but does so at one official rate. In this case the price mechanism plays no part in allocating currency between competing importers. The system must therefore be supported by import licences which determine who shall be entitled to foreign currency.

(b) *Multi-rate systems*. There is one official buying rate and one or more selling rates. In this case the price mechanism serves partially to allocate the supply of foreign currency and there need be less reliance on supporting trade controls.

18. Disadvantage of exchange control. The major criticism of any system of exchange control is that by rendering a currency inconvertible it disrupts multilateral settlements which enable a country to offset a deficit in one sector of its trading with a surplus earned elsewhere.

Let us suppose that Peru has traditionally a deficit in its trade with Chile, which has normally been financed by a surplus in its trade with the U.S.A., i.e. dollar earnings have been converted to Chilean pesos. If the U.S.A. now adopts exchange control which makes the dollar inconvertible then Peru must balance its payments bilaterally with Chile.

To do so it must reduce its imports (probably by adopting its own exchange controls) to the detriment of Chile and itself. Peru is still left with dollars which can only be utilised in the U.S.A. for the purchase of imports which it might otherwise not wish to take.

In short, the volume of world trade is reduced and the natural pattern distorted. The advantages of international specialisation are lost.

ADJUSTMENT OF PAYMENTS DISEQUILIBRIUM IN VARIABLE EXCHANGE RATE SYSTEMS

19. Variants. Variable exchange rate systems may be of many types ranging from a position in which the rate is determined solely by market forces to the other extreme of an "adjustable peg". The operation of the latter is exemplified by the U.K. Exchange Equalisation Account and has been described earlier under the heading of "active stabilisation" (*see* 3(*b*)). (The adjustable peg may be considered a variant of either the stable or fluctuating rate systems since it combines both principles.)

Between the two extremes lie a number of *floating rate* systems which display varying degrees of flexibility. However, all the variants share the common principle that the exchange rate moves continuously or occasionally.

20. Adjustment through freely fluctuating exchange rates. When the exchange rate is permitted to move freely and without limit the risk of foreign exchange dealing is intensified. Dealers are unwilling to hold bills of exchange and therefore when exporters supply them in exchange for domestic cash they must be sold immediately to importers who wish to make payment in foreign currency.

An increase in the supply of foreign bills will force down their price (i.e. improve the rate of exchange) until there is an increase in demand from importers wishing to settle accounts abroad. If this demand continues to increase the price of bills of exchange will be forced up (i.e. the exchange rate deteriorates). In this way imports and exports continuously offset each other at varying exchange ratios. There can consequently be no disequilibrium in the balance of payments and therefore no need for compensatory short-term capital movements. It follows that gold and foreign currency reserves are not required.

21. Adjustment of disequilibrium in an adjustable-peg system. This is the system to which the major trading nations of the world adhered from 1945 to 1972. In the short run exchange rates are pegged and adjustment takes place as in a stable rate system. In the long run adjustment is assisted by planned and limited variations in the exchange rate.

In the case of a recurrent deficit disequilibrium a planned devaluation will be effected and in the case of a surplus disequilibrium there will be a planned revaluation.

The problem then arises of selecting the right exchange rate to establish equilibrium. One solution is to allow the market temporary freedom to establish a rate in response to the forces of demand and supply. This was done in the U.K. in 1931 and to a limited degree in Germany in 1971. Equilibrium achieved, the rate is then stabilised. However, this approach is seldom favoured since it unleashes the possibility of large speculative capital movements out of a currency which is depreciating or into a currency which is appreciating. These movements will only serve to exacerbate the disequilibrium.

It is possible nevertheless to make a theoretical approach to the problem through the "Doctrine of Purchasing Power Parity".

22. Doctrine of purchasing power parity. In the 1920s Gustav Cassel argued that the equilibrium rate of exchange between two currencies should reflect the ratio between their respective domestic purchasing powers. For example, if the purchasing power of $1 in the U.S.A. is a half of the purchasing power of £1 in the U.K., the equilibrium rate of exchange is $2:£1.

Unfortunately, this theoretical approach is beset with difficulties:

(a) *Problem of comparing purchasing power.* It is clearly difficult if not impossible to compare the purchasing power of, say, the pound sterling and the Congolese franc when assortments of goods are purchased in the two countries.

(b) *Inadequate coverage.* The theory in any case only utilises the merchandise price level to determine purchasing power parities, thus excluding the service and capital transactions which also influence the exchange rate.

(c) *Autonomous influences on the rate of exchange.* It is possible that a change in a buyer's tastes or income may act independently upon the exchange rate without any change in comparative price levels.

We may conclude therefore that while this theory is useful in drawing attention to the effect upon the exchanges of differing national rates of inflation or deflation it is of little value in determining an equilibrium rate of exchange.

23. Determining the equilibrium rate in practice. In the absence of any accurate technique reliance has to be placed upon a mixture of economic analysis and guesswork. The test of a genuine new equilibrium rate is whether it reverses those tendencies which have produced a disequilibrium in the first place. In the case of a deficit disequilibrium economic analysis will attempt to establish the degree of devaluation necessary to improve the balance of individual items in the accounts. For example, an assessment of demand and supply elasticities of imports and exports must be made in order to predict the response of these items to a given depreciation in the exchange rate.

24. The effectiveness of devaluation. The effectiveness of devaluation in remedying a fundamental payments disequilibrium depends upon the relative elasticities of demand and supply in respect of foreign exchange. If both are highly elastic then the new more unfavourable exchange rate will induce a greatly increased supply of foreign exchange at the same time as demand is greatly curtailed. The devaluation will have been extremely effective. The opposite will be the case when elasticities are low and a much greater devaluation may be necessary to eliminate even a small deficit.

25. Elasticity of demand for foreign exchange. This depends primarily upon the elasticity of domestic demand for imports. Elasticity will tend to be high where luxury consumer goods and expensive capital equipment constitute a large part of total imports and low when foodstuffs, raw materials and semi-manufactures are the principal elements. The ease of substitution of home-produced goods for imports will also affect the degree of elasticity.

When import supply is wholly elastic (i.e. when the supply can be varied at constant price) then the elasticity of demand for imports wholly determines the elasticity of demand for foreign exchange.

In this case, when the elasticity of demand for imports is greater than zero, devaluation will produce a reduction in the volume of imports and consequently of the demand for foreign exchange. From the side of demand devaluation has proved effective.

26. Elasticity of supply of foreign exchange. The principal determining factor is the elasticity of foreign demand for domestic exports. When export supply is perfectly elastic, i.e. the domestic price remains unchanged after devaluation, then the elasticity of demand for exports wholly determines foreign exchange supply elasticity.

When export demand elasticity has a value of 1 (unit elasticity) a 10 per cent devaluation will produce a 10 per cent increase in the volume of exports and total foreign exchange receipts will therefore remain constant, i.e. the supply elasticity of foreign exchange is zero and the effect of devaluation is zero.

When export demand elasticity has a value greater than 1, a 10 per cent devaluation will produce an increase in the volume of exports in excess of 10 per cent and total foreign exchange receipts will be enlarged, i.e. the supply elasticity of foreign exchange is greater than zero and devaluation will have been effective.

When export demand elasticity has a value below one then a 10 per cent devaluation will not be matched by an equivalent increase in the volume of imports and total foreign exchange receipts will decline. The deficit has been enlarged.

27. Import and export supply elasticities. In the preceding two paragraphs it was assumed that the supply of imports and exports was wholly elastic, i.e. that the "foreign currency" price of imports and the "domestic" price of exports remained unchanged after devaluation. In that case the demand elasticities for imports and exports were the sole determinants of the effectiveness of devaluation. Allowance must now be made for this unrealistic assumption.

In the extreme (and hypothetical) case of perfectly inelastic supply of both imports and exports, by definition there can be no variation in the quantity supplied. A 10 per cent devaluation can have no effect upon the volume of domestic exports but domestic prices will be forced up by 10 per cent as foreign buyers compete to retain their share of the fixed supply. Similarly, foreign exporters, unable to curtail their output, will compete to retain their market in the devaluing country by cutting their prices by 10 per cent. The effect of devaluation is therefore neutral.

On the other hand when the supply elasticity of imports is high then devaluation will have the effect of increasing domestic import prices and it may be expected that imports will contract provided that import demand elasticity is also high.

When the supply elasticity of exports is high then exports will expand at lower foreign exchange prices provided that export demand elasticity is also high.

On the other hand when demand elasticities are low it is preferable that supply elasticities should also be low since the lack of any great response to devaluation in the demand for imports and exports will be compensated by a relatively small fall in foreign exchange export prices and a relatively small rise in domestic import prices.

28. The theoretical case for freely fluctuating rates. The argument in favour of fluctuating exchange rates derives largely from observation of the drawbacks inherent in exchange rates which are too inflexible. When rates are pegged it is expected that a deficit will be adjusted by a deflationary movement of domestic incomes and prices and that, hopefully, output and employment will be undisturbed by lower price and wage levels. In practice oligopolistic industries and powerful trade unions are able to resist the downward pressure on prices and wages, so that the reduced expenditure engendered by deflation manifests itself in declining output and rising unemployment. Since Governments are committed both to growth and full employment they are likely to frustrate deflation by adopting compensatory fiscal and monetary policies. The balance of payments therefore remains in deficit disequilibrium.

Within these limiting circumstances it is unlikely that long-run adjustment can be achieved in a stable rate system without recourse to direct controls on trade and payments. Since these run counter to the world's declared intention to liberalise trade and payments the only alternative is to adopt a system of fluctuating exchange rates. Governments are then free to pursue their own policies for growth and full employment in the knowledge that the external balance of payments is self-regulating.

29. The case against fluctuating rates. Criticism of fluctuating rates is again based upon observation of the difficulties which arose during the early 1920s and again in the 1930s when fixed exchange rates were abandoned. These were periods of great uncertainty which saw violent movements in the exchanges accompanied by massive flows of speculative capital (hot money) and deleterious effects upon trade.

This argument is countered by the suggestion that it confuses cause with effect, that violent exchange rate fluctuations were a product of an instability which sprang from other deep-rooted causes.

A further standard argument against a fluctuating rate system is that it increases the risks of (and therefore deters) international trade. Apart from accepting the normal business risks of their own trade, importers and exporters must also accept the risk of adverse movements in the exchanges.

Against this argument it is claimed that the development of forward exchange markets which may be associated with a fluctuating rate system enables the trader to hedge foreign exchange risks.

Finally, it is claimed that a stable rate system enforces a monetary discipline which makes hyper-inflation impossible. On the other hand, it is argued, a fluctuating rate system leaves a country permanently exposed to this danger.

30. The case for and against an adjustable-peg system. It has already been noted that this was the system, sponsored by the International Monetary Fund, through which the world's major trading nations sought to achieve international payments equilibrium.

The intention is to enjoy the combined advantages of stable and fluctuating rate systems while eliminating their disadvantages. Short-term stability is achieved by supporting operations on the exchange markets, in the case of the U.K., through the medium of the Exchange Equalisation Account. If in the long term a fundamental surplus or deficit disequilibrium develops at the existing exchange rate, then provision is made for an adjustment upward or downward to a new peg.

In practice the weakness of this system proved twofold. In the first place there is the difficulty of determining the appropriate degree of rate variation (*see* **16–18** above). Secondly, for political and prestige reasons, and in the case of a key currency country such as the U.K. the implications for overseas holders of sterling, a decision to devalue is likely to be postponed in the hope that internal economic measures will rectify the disequilibrium. In the event the decision is likely to be put off until overseas credit is exhausted and the reserves are disappearing. At this point it becomes universally apparent that devaluation is imminent with a resulting capital flight which puts the reserves under further pressure and makes devaluation inevitable. Such proved to be the case in the U.K. devaluation of 1967.

INTERNATIONAL MONETARY FUND (I.M.F.)

31. Objectives. The Articles of Agreement of the International Monetary Fund (I.M.F.) were signed at a 1944 conference in Bretton Woods, New Hampshire, by forty-four nations. The agreement was implemented in March 1947.

The objectives set out in Article I are fivefold:

(*a*) *International monetary co-operation*, through a permanent institution.

(*b*) *Balanced expansion of world trade*. This is the key objective since the other purposes are means to this end.

(*c*) *Exchange stability*. The maintenance of orderly exchange relations and the avoidance of competitive devaluations.

(*d*) *Multilateral payments*. The elimination of exchange restrictions and the promotion of multilateral payments on current account.

(*e*) *Short-term credit*. In order to add confidence to trading relations, the provision of short-term credit in the event of a temporary balance of payments disequilibrium experienced by a member.

32. The I.M.F.'s resources and their significance. There are today more than 100 members each of which contributes to the I.M.F. a quota, calculated in U.S. dollars and related to its G.N.P. Of this quota 25 per cent is paid in gold (the gold tranche) and the remainder in its own currency.

The size of the quota is important in that it determines:

(*a*) *The voting power* of each member's Executive Director.

(*b*) *The extent of a member's drawing rights*.

33. Drawing rights. Technically the I.M.F. does not grant loans but authorises a member to purchase with its own currency the currency of another member, i.e. it has the right to draw foreign currency from the Fund subject to certain conditions. These stipulate that the Fund must not previously have declared the desired currency to be scarce nor the drawer to be ineligible and that drawings should not exceed 25 per cent of a member's quota in any one year or a total of 20 per cent. It follows that as a member exercises its drawing rights so the Fund's holding of that country's currency rises. It can be seen therefore that strictly this is not a loan although the drawing country is expected to redeem the Fund's excess holding of its currency in gold or other acceptable currency normally within three to five years.

It should be stressed therefore that the Fund provides only short-term finance to enable a country to meet a temporary disequilibrium in its payments. The Fund's resources must continue to rotate if they are to carry out their function as an international reserve.

34. The Bretton Woods exchange rate policy. Upon joining a member declared a par value for its currency in terms of the U.S. dollar.

All exchange transactions with other members were then carried out within 1 per cent of this parity (*see* 44(*c*) below). If a member wished to vary this rate it could do so only after consultation with the I.M.F. and then only to correct a fundamental disequilibrium in its payments.

In this way the I.M.F. rules sought to ensure short-term stability of the exchanges which allowed for long-term adjustments, i.e. this was an adjustable-peg system.

35. Prohibition of exchange control. Article VIII prohibits the application of exchange-control restrictions on current account transactions. On the other hand Article VI permits controls over capital movements.

There are two exceptions to the general prohibition:

(*a*) *Scarce currencies.* If the Fund is unable to supply a particular currency and has declared it to be scarce then controls may be imposed on transactions in that currency. This was the case with the U.S. dollar until 1958 due to a continuing U.S. surplus disequilibrium.

(*b*) *Existing controls may be retained.* Article XIV permits a country to retain controls over current account payments which existed when it became a member. This was viewed simply as a post-war transitional measure but in the event it was not until 1961 that Western Europe was able to adopt Article VIII. Where advantage is still taken of Article XIV members are obliged to consult annually with I.M.F. in order to justify the continued retention of controls.

36. Appraisal of the I.M.F.'s operations. From the foregoing discussion it can be seen that the I.M.F. has aimed to promote the expansion of world trade by improving the means for international settlement in two ways:

(*a*) Stabilising the foreign exchange markets.

(*b*) Providing short-term compensatory finance.

37. Stabilising the foreign exchange markets. The intention at Bretton Woods was to establish a system which combined the advantages of a gold standard with those of a fluctuating rate system. What was desired in the exchanges was short-run stability with long-run flexibility since it was considered inevitable that periodically there would have to be a realignment of exchange rates. A devaluation or revaluation would, however, be carried out in an orderly way and only after international consultation.

In the event until 1971 the goal of stability was achieved but at the expense of an almost total inflexibility of the exchanges in the long run. For a variety of reasons Governments proved unwilling to depart from a rate of exchange once it had been established. The result was continuing disequilibrium in the payments of a number of countries over protracted periods, e.g. the U.K. 1959–67, the U.S.A. 1958–71.

38. Short-term compensatory finance. In this respect the intention was to guarantee the convertibility of currencies by supporting national reserves with the resources of the I.M.F. A country with a deficit disequilibrium would be able to obtain short-term finance while it adopted remedial internal policies which would not include resort to exchange control. However, such an objective would only be achieved in a world in which there was a substantial degree of equilibrium overall and no persistent maladjustments such as the dollar shortage. For this reason throughout the 1950s the world was compelled to rely upon exchange controls, and only when the U.S.A. moved into deficit did it become possible to achieve convertibility. At the same time the Fund's reserves began to be employed in the way which had been anticipated.

However, the return to convertibility brought another problem, the massive movement of speculative capital between the world's financial centres which has had a highly unstabilising effect upon the balance of international payments. This factor placed the Fund's resources under strain and led to the "General Arrangements to Borrow".

39. General Arrangements to Borrow (G.A.B.). Since 1962 the I.M.F. resources have had support from the "Group of Ten" (E.E.C. (the original Six), U.S.A., U.K., Sweden and Japan).

Additionally, there have been developed "swap arrangements" between central banks whereby each agrees to make balances available to the others for specified periods of time. In the late 1960s the U.K. made much use of these facilities.

40. World liquidity problem. Apart from the strain placed upon national reserves and the resources of the Fund by speculative capital movements it became increasingly clear in the 1960s that the rapid expansion of world trade called for additions to the international money supply. Throughout the post-war period there has been a steady decline in the ratio of official reserves of gold and foreign exchange to world imports from about 80 per cent in the late 1940s to about 30 per cent at the end of the 1960s. This decline was partially offset by the conditional reserves of the I.M.F. drawing rights, the G.A.B. and the swap arrangements. However, since the last two devices were purely *ad hoc* measures it was felt there should be a more positive and formal attempt to raise the level of international reserves. Consequently, in April 1968, the I.M.F. published its plan for "Special Drawing Rights".

41. Special Drawing Rights (S.D.R.s). The simplest way to envisage the scheme is to see the S.D.R.s as "international paper money" which all countries will accept in settlement of debt.

Technically they take the form of an automatic right to receive foreign currency by transferring one's S.D.R.s to another country designated by the Fund. The basic obligation of each member is to provide his own currency upon the Fund's request up to a total of three times his own allocation of S.D.R.s.

There is a very broad requirement for drawing countries to reconstitute their position but the repayment terms are very liberal. In due course this requirement may well be reconsidered.

Individual allocations are related to members' basic quotas and total distributions planned for quinquennial periods. The scheme was activated in 1970 since when there have been two distributions.

THE FOREIGN EXCHANGE CRISIS OF 1971

42. Persistent U.S. disequilibrium. It has previously been noted that in 1958 the U.S. balance of payments moved into a deficit which has subsequently remained unchanged due primarily to overseas military and aid commitments. For the post-war dollar shortage there was consequently substituted a dollar glut which periodically expressed itself in pressure on the dollar exchange rate. In due course this situation led the U.S.A. in 1968 to restrict the convertibility of dollars into gold. Gold from the reserves would now be sold at the official price of $35 only *to central banks*. Parallel to this official gold market there developed a free market with a substantially higher price which gave a truer reflection of the dollar's real international value.

43. Dollar crisis, 1971. In August large sales of surplus dollars by European central banks produced such a heavy drain of U.S. gold reserves that convertibility was now *entirely* suspended. Pressure on dollar exchange rates throughout the world then caused the emergency closure of exchange markets. When dealings were resumed the price of the dollar in terms of all other major currencies had fallen substantially away from the previous parities.

The U.S. monetary authorities were then subjected to considerable pressure from their world trading partners to accept an *official* devaluation against gold in order that markets might be quickly stabilised. Rather than accept a course of action which would depreciate the dollar uniformly against *all* other countries, the U.S. authorities preferred that certain of her major trade competitors, notably Japan and the West European nations, should *revalue* individually and in varying degrees against the dollar. This solution was not acceptable to those countries since they feared that such revaluations might weaken the competitiveness of their export prices and so have adverse effects upon their trade.

In this impasse exchange rates were permitted to float with central banks intervening only to forestall an excessive appreciation of their own currencies. The U.S.A. meanwhile took action to protect her balance of payments by imposing a 10 per cent import surcharge. Over the following four months fears were expressed that possible retaliatory trade and currency restrictions coupled with the existing exchange rate instability were leading to a downturn in trade and conceivably a world depression.

44. Group of Ten meeting, December 1971. After long preliminary negotiations the finance ministers of the Group of Ten met in late December at the Smithsonian Institute, Washington and arrived at a *temporary* solution to which the I.M.F. gave its support. This subsequently became known as the Smithsonian agreement. The compromise involved:

(a) *Concessions by the U.S.A.* The U.S.A. agreed to devalue gold from $35 per fine ounce to $38, i.e. a devaluation of 8.57 per cent. Since the dollar remains wholly inconvertible the measurement against gold has only numerical significance. Gold provides a useful yardstick. At the same time the import surcharge was abandoned.

(b) *Concessions by the Group of Ten.* The other members of the Group of Ten agreed to revalue against the dollar by varying amounts. At one end of the scale the Japanese yen and the German mark appreciated by 16.9 and 13.5 per cent respectively. At the other extreme, Italy and Sweden appreciated by only 7.5 per cent. Roughly in the middle, the U.K. and France revalued by 8.57 per cent, precisely the same as the increase in the dollar price of gold; i.e. while revaluing against the dollar they maintained their existing parities with gold.

(c) *Wider margins.* To give the exchanges greater flexibility and monetary authorities a stronger position in dealing with speculative capital flows, dealing margins were widened to $2\frac{1}{4}$ per cent. The implication for sterling with a new parity of $2.60 was an obligation on the U.K. monetary authorities to support the rate of exchange within the limits of $2.54 and $2.66.

What could be observed in these arrangements was the first realignment of *all* exchange rates since the Bretton Woods agreement in 1944.

45. The Group of Ten communiqué.

The opinion was widely held that the situation had been retrieved only at the eleventh hour and then only temporarily. In their communiqué, the finance ministers therefore agreed that discussions should be promptly undertaken, particularly within the context of I.M.F., to consider more permanent arrangements for the reform of the international monetary system. It was agreed to direct attention to the appropriate monetary means of stabilising exchange rates and ensuring convertibility: to the proper role of gold, of reserve currencies and of special drawing rights; to the permissible margin of fluctuation on either side of agreed parities and to other means of establishing flexibility; to measures appropriate to dealing with the movement of short-term capital.

It therefore transpired that the weakness of the Bretton Woods agreement led ultimately to a world monetary crisis which was temporarily resolved only by long and patient multilateral negotiation.

46. Breakdown of the Smithsonian agreement. The agreement was observed for only a few months. During 1972 one country after another broke away to apply a number of variations on "*floating rates*".

In 1978 the international monetary system comprises two blocs centred upon the German mark and the U.S. dollar which are floating against each other. A third group of currencies including sterling, the French franc and the Italian lira have floated against both.

The arrangement centred upon the mark is known as "*the snake in the tunnel*". The participating currencies limit the range of their movements against each other within a much narrower band than that permitted by the Smithsonian agreement. They then float in unison against the other currencies. Such a degree of co-operation is seen by some as a stepping stone to full European monetary union. The countries which have participated are Benelux, West Germany, Norway, Sweden and Denmark.

Adherence to this narrow band of exchange rates poses problems to the extent that rates of inflation differ markedly from one country to another. Inflation has been much less severe in Germany than in France and the U.K. for example, a factor which has not permitted either country to participate.

47. A "dirty" float. Governments have attempted to limit the severity of exchange rate movements through central bank intervention in the market, i.e. exchange rates have not floated freely or cleanly.

Intervention is periodic rather than continuous and has taken three forms. Central monetary reserves, in the case of the U.K. the Exchange Equalisation Account, are used to make sales or purchases at spot (present) rates. In this way the rate is artificially influenced. Secondly, the authorities may operate in a similar way in the forward market to influence the future spot value. This may serve to deter speculation against the currency. Thirdly, changes in domestic interest rates may influence short-term capital movements. This last measure is particularly important in the U.K. which has been particularly prone to such movements.

48. Future stability of exchange rates? It is widely agreed that a more orderly and stable system than the present one would be highly desirable and a number of technically possible solutions have been proposed. As yet there is no indication that any of them will be adopted and in 1978 the international monetary system faces an uncertain future.

THE WORLD BANK GROUP

49. Objectives. It has been noted that the ulterior purpose of the I.M.F. is the promotion of international trade as a means of rising world living standards. Similarly, the World Bank Group which is concerned with increasing the flow of investment in the developing countries may be said to have the same objectives. The more rapidly the economies of the developing countries expand the fuller the part they can play in international trade.

50. International Bank for Reconstruction and Development (I.B.R.D.). Basically this is an international investment bank financed by the developed nations and which makes loans to Governments for approved projects for periods up to thirty-five years at the substantial interest rate of $5\frac{1}{2}$ per cent.

A criticism of I.B.R.D. has been that the debt service burden at this rate of interest has grown so rapidly that during the 1960s it was absorbing 10 per cent of the export income of the developing countries, thus jeopardising their economic programmes.

51. International Development Association (I.D.A.). This organisation is also financed by the Governments of the developed countries. It was set up because of the inability of some developing countries either to qualify projects for I.B.R.D. support or to meet the high interest charges. The loan terms are liberal with easily staged repayments and no interest other than a $\frac{3}{4}$–1 per cent service charge.

52. International Finance Corporation (I.F.C.). Unlike I.B.R.D. and I.D.A., the I.F.C. which was set up in 1956 does not make loans to Governments. Along with private investors it participates in private industrial enterprises.

PROGRESS TEST 12

1. Explain how a rate of exchange is reached. **(1)**
2. What do you understand by a variable exchange rate system? **(2)**
3. Explain how an exchange rate may be actively stabilised. **(3(b))**

4. What do you understand by "exchange control"? **(4)**

5. Where exchange rates are stabilised, what will be the effects of a payments disequilibrium? **(5(*b*))**

6. Explain the price-specie flow mechanism. **(6)**

7. What were the main features of the gold standard? **(7)**

8. How was equilibrium supposedly restored on a full gold standard? **(8)**

9. What were the main disadvantages of the gold standard? **(9(*b*))**

10. Criticise the concept of the price-specie flow mechanism. **(10)**

11. What is the significance of changes in income to the balance of payments? **(11)**

12. Explain one of the variations to the full gold standard. **(12)**

13. Why was the gold standard abandoned? **(13)**

14. What are the purposes of an exchange-control system? **(16)**

15. What are the disadvantages of exchange control? **(18)**

16. Define an "adjustable peg". **(21)**

17. What are the shortcomings of the theory of purchasing power parity? **(22)**

18. Upon what factors does a successful devaluation depend? **(24–27)**

19. Compare the main arguments for and against fluctuating exchange rates. **(28, 29)**

20. Appraise the case for an adjustable-peg system. **(30)**

21. List the objectives of I.M.F. **(31)**

22. What are "drawing rights"? **(33)**

23. What policy does the I.M.F. pursue in respect of exchange control? **(35)**

24. Assess the success of the I.M.F.'s operations. **(36–38)**

25. Explain the nature of the world liquidity problem. **(40)**

26. What are "Special Drawing Rights"? **(41)**

27. What was the Smithsonian Agreement? **(44)**

28. Outline the present exchange rate system. **(46)**

29. What do you understand by a "dirty float"? **(47)**

30. List the institutions which fall within the World Bank Group. **(49–52)**

31. What are the objectives of the World Bank Group? **(49)**

PART FOUR
GOVERNMENT AND INDUSTRY

CHAPTER XIII

Industrial Structure

PROBLEMS OF DEFINITION

1. Introduction. This part of the book concerns itself with the intervention of government in industrial life. It might intervene at the size level (Monopolies and Mergers), on location decisions (Regional Problems) or to change ownership (Nationalisation) and its justification will be couched in terms of improving the industrial structure of the country. Unfortunately politicians seldom define the "better industrial structure" which they are seeking; rarely do they offer criteria by which their efforts can be judged. They may make noises about "improving efficiency" but again the meaning of this concept is left in abeyance. This chapter tries to repair these omissions by offering an economic and organisational framework in which government intervention policies can be evaluated.

2. What is a firm? This appears to be a trite question until it is realised that the local corner newsagent, the main street dry cleaner and Unilevers are all called firms in common language, yet their size, their methods of organisation and their economic impact are so widely disparate that a unique definition seems impracticable.

Economic theory defines a firm as a mechanism for transferring inputs into outputs and it assumes a single decision making process undertaken by an entrepreneur. The economist then assumes the firm's sole aim is to maximise profit and he studies the price/output policies of the firm under various types of competition. The theoretical economist is not concerned with the internal organisational workings of a firm important though they are for decision making.

Applied economists accept the first part of the definition (inputs into outputs) but they must also study the ownership control problem because of its impact on policy making (*see* 4–9), they question the aims of the company (*see* 10–14) and its pursuit of efficiency (*see* 15–18). Problems of size variation (*see* 19–20) are also of importance.

The widening of the economists' interests in the firm should be of use to governments as they chase the dream of the perfect industrial structure.

3. What is an industry? An industry is equally difficult to define, e.g. is chocolate making a self-contained industry or part of the confectionary industry or even the food industry? This definitional problem might appear to be pure semantics but in monopoly studies firms are said to dominate a market or industry. Obviously in this case some degree of definitional accuracy is required.

Statistically, the government has designated twenty-five Industrial Orders under the British Standard Industrial Classification (B.S.I.C.), e.g. V is Metal Manufacture, VIII is Vehicles and X is Textiles. The Orders are then sub-divided into small industries and eventually into products.

For example:

Order	—	Electrical goods industry
Industry	—	Domestic and electrical appliances
Product	—	Electrical cookers, refrigerators

OWNERSHIP, CONTROL AND POWER

4. Introduction. Four potential power elements can be delineated in a firm, shareholders, directors, management and workers. The traditional simple idea was that the shareholders (the owners) elected directors (the controllers), who appointed managers to run the day-to-day business; the workers were merely a human resource input. In a small firm the ownership and control factor would be amalgamated in the owner's hands.

However today the inter-relationship of the four is infinitely more complex in any firm above a small to medium size. The changes have arisen because society's perception of the status or role of each partner has altered and society in general has developed a more participatory philosophy of life.

5. Shareholders. The traditional shareholder was an individual with a big or small stake in one firm who really believed that he could influence the company via the annual general meeting when the directors were elected. Today the major shareholders are the institutions, e.g. pension funds, insurance companies, who hold 40–45 per cent of all British private equity. How and to what purpose they exercise this considerable power is a matter of some controversy.

On paper they should be able to pressurise firms to act in an efficient manner because this will benefit their investment but the institutions have a paranoic fear of publically arguing with management because of the effect on share prices, therefore any pressure for good or bad is exerted behind the scenes. Some union leaders would like a voice in the distribution of institutional funds allegedly to increase levels of industrial investment but they refuse to discuss by what criteria the investment would be made.

6. Directors. In practice directors are no longer beholden to the shareholders' meeting because, through the use of proxy votes and the institutional votes, directors have become self-perpetuating, changes usually only occurring through board room arguments and divisions.

Today the main debate revolves around the role of the non-executive directors. Many years ago most boards would have non-executive members but from the 1950s fashion changed, it was felt that these type of directors were for decorative purposes and many companies switched to full-time executive directors. Now doubt is creeping in, particularly with so many poor industrial performances and company scandals. Current opinion again favours non-executive directors but to have a watch-dog role, this belief extends to a suggestion that Britain should copy German and some U.S.A. companies in having an executive board and a supervisory board, the latter representing shareholder, worker and financial interests.

7. Management. Their role has not changed but there has been a marked reappraisal of the power of that role. Many organisational students, Galbraith in particular, believe that management forms cliques and by controlling information flows to directors and workers they can effectively direct the running of the company to safeguard their own interests. Interestingly, East-European commentators have noted the phenomena in socialist industries. Galbraith has named this new power base the techno-structure. Its influence will depend on the level of management under discussion and the executive power of the directors.

8. Workers. They now have far more legal rights, i.e. security of employment and trades union activity but the main new interest is worker involvement in policy making. Many ideas are canvassed, worker directors, worker co-operatives, consultative committees to name but a few. However, evaluation of the various methods are outside the scope of this book but any discussion about mergers, nationalisation and restructuring must recognise that a worker's labour gives him some rights in the policy making processes of their firm.

9. Conclusion. The control problem of the modern firm becomes even more complicated because some critics feel they ought to be accountable to the public at large, either through some form of government representation or by allowing consumers a voice in company affairs. (*See* 13.)

Clearly the last quarter of the twentieth century will see a significant change in the real concept of a firm but it is very easy for opponents of the traditional firm to become obsessed with ownership and control problems and totally ignore the purposes and efficiency problems which are at the heart of industrial success.

AIMS OF A FIRM

10. Profit maximisation. Standard economic theory of the firm assumes that its sole aim is to maximise profits and all decision taking is geared to that end. Laymen also suggest that a business is trying to make as much money as possible. These views are over simplified and ignore the intricate workings of the modern company. The concept of profit maximisation, apart from the problem of measuring profit (*see* 16), is difficult to interpret in a meaningful practical way. (*See also* I, 20–6.)

11. Problems of profit maximisation.

(*a*) The premise is based on a marginal analysis whereas firms tend to use average precepts, e.g. a firm has far more knowledge of average rather than marginal costs, thus the company has no precise guide to decisions which will maximise profits.

(*b*) A company might not know if it was maximising profits because it has always to make a choice between different policy options. Suppose it chooses policy A, then, with hindsight, it realises policy B or C might have produced better profit figures, yet history cannot be reversed. As information costs are not negligible the firm never acts on anything approaching perfect knowledge thus it may never know whether it is achieving maximum profits.

(c) The time scale of profit making is an important consideration. It is possible to make large-scale, short-period profits but in so doing damage the long-term health of the company. Similarly firms often accept short-run losses to build up business.

(d) The assumption of profit maximisation ignores the fact that a business organisation is made up of individuals often coalescing into groups motivated by a whole range of objectives, psychological, social as well as economic (*see* 12(*d*)), and the objectives of these groups are not necessarily profit orientated.

12. Alternative aims. There is an ever increasing research literature on business aims other than profit maximisation. Below are brief sketches of the major schools of opinion with their protagonists' names in brackets.

(*a*) *Managerial discretion* (*Williamson*). Management will always seek profit to satisfy the shareholders but they also have their own needs, e.g. status from empire building or non-taxable perks, all of which are costs charged out of profits. Williamson suggests this idea is more applicable to large organisation management who may be remote from day-to-day money-making decisions.

(*b*) *Sales revenue maximisation* (*Baumol*). Sales maximisation is good for the morale of workers, customers and financiers so the company tries to maximise sales within the constraint of adequate profits.

(*c*) *Managerial growth* (*Maris*). The company is a bureaucratic structure whose performance will be judged on growth and security. Management feels its prestige will arise out of company growth; being a big company manager creates its own status.

(*d*) *Behavioural theory* (*Cyert and March*). A company is a human organisation with a wide range of goals, expectations and choices overladen with uncertainties. Therefore any decision will be a compromise between a coalition of interests; that such decisions should produce profit maximisation seems unlikely.

(*e*) *X-theory inefficiency* (*Leibenstein*). A firm is split between the utility functions of its various human components and unless there is a policing system, e.g. intense competition or profit sharing, inefficiencies will creep into the company as its members seek their own objectives. For example a company in a monopolistic position may settle for a quiet life without too many pressures.

In general the common thread of the new thinking is that if a firm seeks satisfactory levels of profit to stay in business then its various levels or organisation pursue their own objectives.

13. Social role. The discussion so far on aims has assumed the firm to be self-contained but in fact it operates in the community, therefore should its aims contain obligations to the people at large. Types of question involved here are: What costs should a company incur to avoid pollution? Should it employ certain numbers of handicapped people? Should it create jobs for the young unemployed? What are its attitudes to women and Catholic midgets? The more zealous advocates of the social role envisage the company as a social service, whereas vigorous opponents argue that managements are trained to make profit and there are no known criteria for linking business and social decisions. There are no easy answers to the argument but most bigger companies have become sensitive to the social implications of their business policies. (*See* E. J. Morgan. "Social Responsibility and Private Enterprise" in the U.K. *National Westminster Bank Review*, May 1977.)

14. Private and public ownership. The tangled arguments on company aims have assumed private ownership but the modern firm may be sustained by government money or it may be nationalised. Nearly two generations of nationalisation in practice have failed to unravel the aims of a nationalised organisation (XVIII, 23–8) so the chances of solving the aims problem of a half government owned company seem remote.

The basic dilemma is the role of profit (*see* **15**) and its relations to social need. Some people try to find a middle road by asking companies to act in the national interest but this is surely a subjective nebulous idea unless a country is at total war. Ultimately a country's industrial organisations must make efficient use (*see below*) of the nation's scarce resources.

XIII. INDUSTRIAL STRUCTURE 211

COMPANY EFFICIENCY

15. Profits. In Western societies and increasingly in Marxist controlled countries profit (surplus for Marxists) is used as an efficiency test but **16–21** will show this relationship can have pitfalls and efficiency is itself a difficult concept to measure in practical terms.

Profits have four functions.

(*a*) They are a source of funds for investment. (In Britain approximately 75 per cent of investment comes from undistributed profits.)

(*b*) They act as an incentive to undertake business risks. Individuals are willing to run the risk of supplying goods and services because they hope to make a profit.

(*c*) Profits are an allocative device as past profits or the chance of future ones attract resources into a business.

(*d*) They serve as a test of efficiency in the sense that companies making large profit are thought to be efficient. This can be a narrow view of efficiency and the point is taken up in **17**.

Profits have a vital role to play and no economy can organise itself without the pursuit of profits. Critics of profits confuse the making of them, which is a necessity, with the distribution and ownership of them which is a socio-political question.

16. Problems of defining profits. No effort was made to define profits in **15** and apart from accountants and enlightened economists few people realise what an elusive concept it is. Conventionally, profit is defined as the difference between total revenue and total costs. This is accurate but ignores huge difficulties of defining revenues and costs and in particular such terms as asset and stock valuation and depreciation.

Currently there is heated debate on how to allow for the impact of inflation on asset valuation because different accounting methods can produce totally different profit figures. In 1975 companies were showing profit on paper, yet in practice, in terms of liquidity, were near bankruptcy. In 1977 a leading motor manufacturer using one accounting method showed profit of £59 million, another method produced profits of £7 million.

Profits will always be used as a guide to economic performance but blind faith should never be put in a single set of profit figures.

17. Profits and efficiency. Given the warnings of **16**, profits are used as efficiency criteria. As an absolute figure, e.g. last year

Company X made £100,000 profits, they are valueless but must be expressed as a percentage, usually of capital or possibly turnover. (Retailers may consider profit in relation to selling space.)

If a company has a return on capital of x per cent, how is this to be judged good or bad? Possible criteria are:

(a) Does x per cent attract new investors?

(b) Is it sufficient for internal resource growth?

(c) How does it compare with similarly situated companies?

(d) How does it compare with previous performance? This can be a dubious argument because there is a hidden implication that x should always be increasing, which is an impossible business situation.

When all these questions have been answered one final question must be asked. In what circumstances were the profits made? Did they arise out of a monopolistic situation? Were they the result of government subsidy or protection? If the answers are "yes" then how efficient was the company? Given the ambivalences surrounding the use of profits to test business efficiency there is always a search for alternative criteria.

18. Alternative efficiency tests. Because the financial measurement of efficiency is so fraught with accounting difficulties there has always been a desire to find more precise measurements based on the relationship between factor inputs and output. Even here there are measurement problems. For example, the input labour will vary tremendously as to effort, skill and attitudes and it is arguable how accurately wages measure these variations. Also nobody can evaluate the exact interdependence of capital, labour and management in producing a given output.

The most common form of this method is "technical efficiency" when a firm tries to operate at the lowest possible average cost, thereby producing a given output with the least possible input or alternatively maximising the output from a fixed input.

The company's efficiency might also be judged by their innovating record measured through their ability to produce new goods or better production methods. Better is, of course, a subjective word because the new idea might for example lay off many people thus causing social hardship. Obviously efficiency is impossible to measure precisely, but that is no excuse for attacking the pursuit of efficiency because all societies are faced with the reality of scarce resources and they must devise systems of using the resources effectively. That is the true meaning of efficiency, it does not represent an economic attack on human dignity as some critics suggest.

19. Business size and efficiency. Private companies have grown enormously over the last fifty years (*see* XV) and the justification for the growth has usually been to achieve efficiency through scale economies. Since 1950 governments have vastly increased their involvement with industry, and again have often justified their actions with the desire to obtain scale economies. This argument stretches through most of the remaining chapters of the book, is it therefore a valid argument?

Scale economies simply mean that as a firm expands output its costs do not rise in the same proportion, therefore costs per unit fall. The saving arises because bigger companies have cost advantages (scale economies) in finance, labour, management, technology and resource purchase. Traditionally, Henry Ford was the industrialist who first stumbled on the idea with the mass production of his Model-T.

Diagrammatically the situation is shown as:

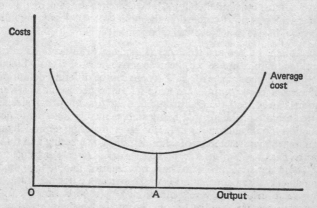

FIG. 5 *Average total cost curve.* Traditionally, the curve is considered to be saucer-shaped.

The crucial question for industrialists and policy makers is where does the point *OA* (minimum average cost) occur because

afterwards costs rise through scale diseconomies (market satur-
ation, rising labour costs, management difficulties)?

Industries have argued the cost curve is very elongated, almost
L-shaped (*see* Fig. 6) therefore it makes sense for companies to

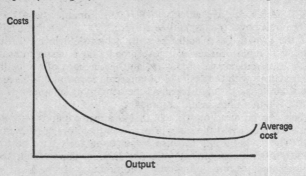

FIG. 6 *An L-shaped average total cost curve.* The curve continues to decline over a very substantial output.

grow almost indefinitely but recent research is showing disturbing
facts which seriously question the policy of recklessly pursuing
the goal of size to achieve scale economies.

20. Doubts on size and efficiency. Efficiency arguments based on
scale economies are very difficult to prove because it is so difficult
to measure economies of scale. There can be different definitions
of average costs, outputs are seldom homogeneous and cost variations can be realistically attributed to factors other than size. So
great are the problems that many studies merely investigate production inputs and outputs. This is an engineering approach and
ignores the vital elements of administration, marketing and transport. (*See* C. A. Smith, *Readings on Theory of Firm*, Penguin.)

These statistical problems have not deterred people from making a generalised correlation between size and efficiency but even
this relationship is severely questioned by reports ranging from
ten-year academic studies to congressional investigations of conglomerates (*see* XV, 15). Time and again the results show no link
between profitability and size of business. The obstacle facing the
big company is the traditional diseconomy of management.
Management expertise seems to disintegrate as companies grow.
Indeed most large companies acknowledge the problem and react

XIII. INDUSTRIAL STRUCTURE   215

through decentralisation of decision taking, as they want their managers to be closer to grass roots output and money making and not become involved with bureaucratic empire building (*see* 12(*a*)).

Sociologists have shown that humans react more favourably to the small firm ambience and this has obvious implications for problems of size and efficiency.

22. Summary. Efficiency is the moonbeam chased by successive governments but few of them show awareness of the problems of definition which surely must be solved before coherent policies can be formulated and used.

Illustrated below are different performance concepts in the period 1967–76:

Company growth (total return as percentage of shareholders' original investment) 1967–76

1. Associated Dairies
2. Ladbrokes
3. Manchester Liners
4. Dixons Photographic
5. Racal
6. Jefferson Smurfit
7. Costain
8. Coral Leisure
9. Cavenham
10. B.S.R.

Largest increases in pre-tax profits 1967–76

1. J. Laing
2. Mothercare
3. Jefferson Smurfit
4. Hanson Trust
5. Croda International
6. Ladbrokes
7. Racal Electrics
8. R. Costain
9. Dixons Photographic
10. B.S.R.

Largest sales growth 1967–76

1. Croda International
2. Cavenham
3. Hanson Trust
4. Tri centrol
5. Associated Dairies
6. Coral Leisure
7. Racal
8. B.S.R.
9. Mothercare
10. Ready Mixed Concrete Ltd.

Source: *Management Today*, June 1977, p. 75

PRESENT INDUSTRIAL STRUCTURE

22. In general. Britain's mixed economy can be described as a wide variety of markets. A market is those parts of the economy where output is sold so that production costs are met by the supply of goods and services. The non-market sector is where output is not sold but allocated (e.g. health and educational services), and is paid for out of taxation. In the late 1970s Britain's non-market sector accounts for approximately 40 per cent of our Gross Domestic Product.

The spectrum of markets covers the whole textbook range:

(a) The near perfect market, e.g. currency and commodity markets.

(b) Imperfect markets where several companies compete actively against each other, e.g. supermarkets, confectionery, breweries, cosmetics.

(c) Markets dominated by a few large companies, e.g. petrol, fertilisers, ice cream (i.e. oligopolistic markets).

(d) Single suppliers, e.g. National Coal Board and the Post Office.

23. Galbraith thesis. J. K. Galbraith the American economist has long argued that the above market classification does not represent a realistic picture of Western economies. He suggests two categories:

(a) *Market economy.* Many small firms exist in a variety of industries but their work is unplanned and they seldom have long production runs. They have little power (except perhaps in small geographical areas) over prices, their consumers or the government.

(b) *Planned economy.* Most industries are dominated by big companies with huge, expensive technology. Because of the big financial involvement the firms must try to dictate to the consumer over prices, quantities and qualities of output. To help their domination they are closely involved with the government at many levels of management.

Critics of Galbraith say he ignores the interdependence of big and small firms for sub-contract work and that he over-emphasises the power of big companies to manipulate demand. Business history reveals some terrible demand miscalculations and also shows a surprising fluidity in the rise and fall of big companies.

It would also be bizarre news to British companies that governments work in their favour, nevertheless Galbraith does well to highlight the changing pattern of industrial structure and to show how it differs from the traditional economic textbook. These new perspectives are especially valuable in dealing with monopoly and merger problems.

24. Private industry and government. As the remaining chapters show industry and government are now entangled so remorselessly that it is pointless to argue for an economy with a total private industrial sector.

Four examples of the involvement are given below.

(*a*) The impact of government policies on industry, e.g. transport policy on civil engineers and car producers.

(*b*) The government as buyer and seller, e.g. defence contracts, nationalised industries.

(*c*) The impact of big firm policies on the economy, e.g. petrol, chemicals and drugs.

(*d*) Government use of subsidies and taxes for social purposes.

Governments are going to involve themselves with industry but what criteria have they for their interventionist policies?

GUIDELINES FOR GOVERNMENT POLICY ON INDUSTRIAL STRUCTURE

25. Basic situation. Despite Galbraith (*see* **23**) all firms operate in fairly uncontrolled markets and if government is dissatisfied with private industry, the analysis must be within three elements of the market, viz. market structure, conduct and performance.

R. T. Nelson summarised the areas of investigation in the following diagram (R. T. Nelson, "Industrial Economics". *Economics*, Summer 1974) (*see* Fig. 7).

The dotted arrows between the market boxes indicate the common belief on the causal relations but research evidence suggests the relationship is not so obvious, e.g. changes in market performance could alter structures, performance now could vary conduct in the future. Despite these reservations the basic premise is that governments will be trying to influence activities within the boxes because they believe the current market situation is

(*a*) not producing economic effectiveness;

(*b*) not reflecting the community's social values and desires.

Economics via welfare theory offers guidelines to the government, but non-market believers put their trust in civil servants

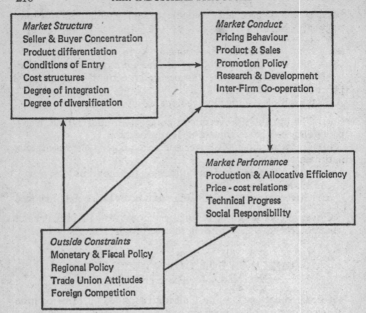

FIG. 7 *An analysis of the functioning of a market.* The diagram
suggests causal relationships within the market.

pursuing the national interest as the basis for governments altering the industrial structure.

26. Welfare theory. This paragraph is a very simple interpretation
of a most complex piece of theory which centres on a concept
called the Pareto Optimum. This optimum is achieved when it is
impossible to devise a policy which makes one person "better off"
without making someone else "worse off". Better and worse
imply higher and lower levels of satisfaction. Should the Pareto
Optimum be realised then an optimum allocation of resources
will be achieved.

As an example consider the following. (Assume a two-product
model economy.)

	Price	Marginal Cost (MC)		Price	MC
Cars	£2,000	£1,500	Washing Machine	£200	£300

Price > MC

Price < MC

i.e. the utility to the consumer (measured by price) exceeds the value of the productive resources utilised.

i.e. the utility to the consumer is less than the value of productive resources utilised.

In this situation it would benefit the consumers to switch resources from washing machine manufacturing to car producing.

For example, switch £1,500 of resources

Benefits — consumer gains an extra £2,000 of cars

Losses — consumer loses $\dfrac{£(1,500 \times 200)}{300}$

$= £1,000$ of machines

∴ Benefits are greater than losses.

This movement of resources will continue until price = MC

For example,

	Price	MC		Price	MC
Cars	£1,500	£1,500	Washing Machines	£300	£300

Now a £1,500 switch produces a gain of £1,500 value of cars but a loss of £1,500 of machines, so no consumer gain would materialise.

The main lesson is that at the optimum position the value of each good to society must equal the costs incurred by society in producing the good. This position is the price = marginal cost equilibrium position of perfect competition and is an argument for allocating resources by encouraging a perfect market situation to exist.

27. Criticisms of welfare analysis. The major pragmatic criticisms of welfare theory concepts are:

(a) The theory tends to concentrate on private costs and benefits whilst ignoring social costs and benefits which are called externalities, e.g. a firm working in a market situation may create pollution which affects the community outside the immediate market environment, thus it is argued market price does not reflect a true social valuation.

(b) Given the presence of almost immovable monopolistic elements, e.g. large companies, unions with a closed shop policy, in the modern market situation no government is in a position to pursue policies based on the existence of a perfect market.

28. Consequence of criticism. Because of the above doubts the modern policy maker has tended to wander along two avenues of thought.

(a) *Market improvement ideas.* This means attaching the social and economic defects of the market system through the use for example of subsidies, taxation, anti-monopoly policies. Such policies still leave choice decisions in the grip of the consumer and producer.

(b) *Market replacement ideas.* Examples here are the education and health services and nationalisation as originally conceived in its socialist pristineness. Here choice is much more in the hands of the bureaucrats.

The latter idea has grown remarkably in the last twenty years and has become quite fashionable because its supporters believe something called social justice will thus be achieved. (*See* **I, 41.**)

29. Criticism of market replacement ideas. These beliefs, now the conventional wisdom, are in fact under severe intellectual attack. Three major protagonists are A. Downs, *An Economic Theory of Democracy*, Harper, New York 1957; W. A. Niskanen, *Bureaucracy and Representative Government*, Aldine Atherton, 1971; S. Brittan, "Government and the Market Economy", *Hobart Papers*, Institute of Economic Affairs, 1971.

The basic attack centres on the belief that bureaucrats and planners are men without sordid human motivation, who have divine insights into the needs of other men and can allocate resources to satisfy these needs apparently without any allocative criteria. The critics suggest bureaucratic organisations are human maximisers (like producers and consumers) and they seek to maximise their budgets because herein lies the path to bureaucratic satisfactions, e.g. good salaries, promotion, job security and prestige. Politicians also act in the same way to maximise votes. Thus a bureaucracy perhaps allied to a production interest can convince a government that a certain policy is a vote winner, but to believe or prove that the policy makes economic sense in terms of resource allocation is another matter altogether.

Indeed it is a mystery to economists why the anti-market forces place such faith in the bureaucratic decision maker, for the latter needs the combined talents of a Benedictine monk and Einstein to justify the faith placed in him.

30. Conclusion. This chapter has shown the difficulties of searching for a perfect industrial structure, the rest of the chapters study governments making this search. In evaluating government actions and the advice given to governments, it will benefit readers to refer back to this chapter to establish whether decisions are being taken for identifiable economic and social ends or merely for short-term political gain.

PROGRESS TEST 13

1. Describe the difficulties in defining a firm. **(2)**
2. What is the British Standard Industrial Classification? **(3)**
3. Explain a techno-structure. **(7)**
4. Discuss the problems of using profit maximisation as the single goal of a firm. **(11)**
5. What is meant by the behavioural theory of the firm? **(12)**
6. Outline the functions of profit. **(15)**
7. Explain what is meant by scale economies. **(19)**
8. Suggest two criticisms of Galbraith's view of the modern economy. **(23)**
9. What is the Pareto Optimum? **(26)**
10. Explain a "market replacement" policy. **(28)**

CHAPTER XIV

General Government Policy Towards Industry

PHILOSOPHY OF RELATIONSHIP

1. Area of study. In Chapter I an examination was made of the macroeconomic foundation for government economic policy after 1945. Only then was it recognised that the Government should bear the responsibility for the management of the economy at a high level of economic activity through the control of the aggregate level of demand.

Despite this new aim of economic policy, governments retained their interests in the microeconomic aspects of our lives particularly with regard to the shape, size and performance of industry. This interest can be traced back in a small way for many centuries but it began to grow through the late nineteenth century.

The inter-war years 1919–39 saw more active efforts to reshape the structure of industry but the real turning point has come since 1945 when government intervention has become more politically acceptable, consequently as the last chapter showed the government–industry relationship has deepened considerably (*see* XIII, 24).

This chapter studies the basic thinking which has underpinned the growth of the relationship.

2. Laissez-faire attitudes. The vast majority of nineteenth-century thinkers believed that national economic and social benefits would be maximised through the summation of the efforts of each individual consumer and producer working unrestrictedly towards their own aims within the parameters of the economic laws of Supply and Demand. Economic theorists of the time believed that the laws would work most effectively within a perfectly competitive framework which (*see* E. Seddon, *Economics of Public Finance* (3rd Ed.) Macdonald & Evans Handbook, V) would produce the most efficient allocation of resources and the maximisation of consumer satisfaction.

These beliefs encouraged governments to refrain from intervening in economic life unless they were trying to prevent groups of individuals co-operating to restrain trade. However, although the nineteenth century saw a great growth in economic prosperity there were periods of economic depression and many people lived in conditions of considerable human squalor, so doubts were raised about the validity of the *laissez-faire* principles as a method of improving man's material well-being.

3. Decline in laissez-faire attitudes. The twentieth century has seen an almost total absence of people who believe in a complete laissez-faire economy. Three historical developments have moulded this change.

(*a*) *Change in the role of government*. It is clear that the aims of different individuals and organisations are not necessarily complementary, they are more likely to conflict. Thus the government must create an environment in which the individual can pursue his own interest but only at the limited expense of others. Originally this doctrine was applied via the law to general human conduct but the last hundred years has seen it applied to the clash of economic interests, e.g. high prices benefit the producer, low prices the consumer; a single individual can conflict with himself as worker and consumer.

(*b*) *Growth of industrial organisations*. Advances in technology with the required huge financial commitment plus the growth of markets based on rising living standards and massed communications has produced large scale business organisations straddling international boundaries (*see* XVII). Allied with the phenomena, labour has become organised on a large scale at least at the national level, therefore economic policies based on a perfect competition analysis will have difficulty in relating to the existing world.

Currently economic theory is endeavouring to analyse the new business world of giants rather than small individuals, but until the intellectual exercise is complete the policy makers lack the neat economic certainties of their great-grandparents.

(*c*) *Growth of socialist thought*. Through the nineteenth century many men, the most significant one being Marx, argued that there were no naturalistic laws of economics and that man's problems arose out of the private ownership of resources which caused men to compete rather than co-operate with each other. Consequently the allocation of resources could be undertaken in a just fashion by rational decisions owing nothing to the laws of supply and demand; the achievement of such a society would also bring human harmony. The emotional appeal of such reasoning was obvious and its adherents argue that the state should be the neutral holders of the nation's resources, allocating them in the most beneficial fashion. This philosophy was the necessary under-pinning to justify the increasing interventionist role of government. Given these major historical circumstances it seems inevitable that today we should be living in an infinitely complex economic society in which the role of the government has apparently become predominant.

4. Role of Government in industry today. Since 1945 Governments have faced a changing industrial scene without the comforting security of a precise microeconomic analysis which would guide their industrial policies.

A pragmatic approach has been followed although successive governments have believed that industrial inadequacies, however defined, are at the root of the macro problems of inflation, external financial deficits and low economic growth. They seem to reject the idea that sensible macro policies might create an economic environment in which industry can flourish.

This method has produced many policy contradictions because no clear evidence exists to conclusively answer such problems as the correlation of company size and efficiency (*see* XIII, **19**), the causal relationships of investment, technology and growth and the relative costs of unemployment and over-manning. Government uncertainties on the nature and purpose of their industrial role has created confusion and indecision in the business community.

Today government involvement with industry grows through regulation, exhortation and financial aid and yet nobody in political circles can offer a comprehensive rationale to explain the various policies.

5. Basic problem of Government intervention. Government has always created a legal framework in which industry must exist and although there is some resentment at the extension of the legal aspects, particularly in labour employment, the real problem and controversy arise when governments become financially involved with private industry.

The government usually justifies its monetary help on the basis of national interest whilst critics of the aid argue it is wasteful to subsidise inefficient companies which cannot work using normal financial channels.

National interest can be interpreted from three view points.

(a) Political, e.g. defence.

(b) Economics, e.g. technology, balance of payments.

(c) Social, e.g. unemployment, environment.

Unfortunately, these aims can conflict, e.g. technology creates unemployment, nuclear fuels may cause a health hazard, therefore government help to a firm for one reason can create other problems and there is also the danger that ailing companies regard government as an all the year round Father Christmas.

A further serious worry is the control the government is able to exercise once it has dispensed the tax payers' money to industry because many companies which have received financial assistance, prosper for a while but then their managerial and financial inadequacies seem to reoccur.

6. Future developments. All Western countries have witnessed the growing entanglement of government and industry but countries where the relationship has been less intense (Germany and America) have healthier economies than countries which have allowed the relationship to develop (Great Britain and Italy).

In the late 1970s there has been an intellectual reaction to the government's role in industry and a desire to re-examine the benefits of depending more heavily on the market mechanisms (*see* XIII, 29). The new thinkers do not advocate a return to a total *laissez-faire* position (*see* 2) but they believe that an economic system does need a signalling system if resources are to be allocated effectively. The anti-market system supporters have never overcome the lack of allocation criteria in their analysis. The market argument suggests the price mechanism should be allowed to operate freely with the government only intervening when there is a clearly defined social cost arising from the market operation. Such views have crept into the workings of the nationalised industries (*see* XVIII) and the preliminary activities of the National Enterprise Board (**11**(*b*)) suggest it believes in economic reason rather than social day-dreaming.

It is too early to judge whether the new radicalism will replace the current interventionist conventional wisdom but it is significant that the advanced Marxist countries are experimenting in liberating their industries through market mechanisms, to solve the fundamental resource allocation problem.

AN OUTLINE OF BRITISH GOVERNMENT
INTERVENTIONISM

7. Controls. The government exercises control over the industrial sector by the use of rationing, licensing quotas and price fixing; it hopes to allocate resources through bureaucratic decision to achieve some defined need.

After 1945, the consequences of the War created severe shortages and the Labour administration had to rely on the old wartime controls but by the end of the decade the controls seemed to exist for doctrinaire reasons and both consumers and producers felt trapped and without incentive.

The incoming Conservative government of 1951 embarked on a policy of dismantling the controls. They were helped by an expansion of world trade and a severe fall in commodity prices which allowed British industry to prosper.

Yet by the late 1950s there was growing evidence that Britain was slipping behind her European rivals in the prosperity race. Strangely the British government looked at France which had been experimenting with economic planning (rather than Germany which was still very market orientated) and decided that Britain ought to indulge in economic planning.

Curiously it was a Conservative government which introduced this new facet of interventionism.

8. Planning. Economic planning might take two forms:

(*a*) *Imperative planning.* This involves a government control of output decisions of the private sector. Indeed it is questionable whether a private sector could exist in this situation.

(*b*) *Indicative planning.* This is planning by consent and was the basis of the French experience (**7**). Government and industry co-operate in deciding how best to utilise resources to attain agreed goals which are usually expressed in percentage increases in output. It is also hoped the planning produces mutual respect and understanding between both partners (three partners if industry is sub-divided between management and labour).

9. British planning. Planning in Britain was pioneered by the Conservative government in the early 1960s and was taken up by the Wilson administration from 1964.

(*a*) *Conservative contribution.* In 1962 the National Economic Development Council was formed and is still in being. It consists of two parts:

(*i*) Top Council. Representatives of both sides of industry and the government. The Chairman is the Prime Minister or the Chancellor.

(*ii*) The Office. A body of economic and industrial experts led by a Director General to carry out day to day research and suggest economic strategies for consideration by the Council.

N.E.D.C.'s terms of reference were to examine the economic performance of the nation and to identify the obstacles to achieving faster rates of economic growth. In 1963 N.E.D.C. produced a plan based on the reports from a cross section of seventeen industries. The plan assessed the sectoral implications of a 4 per cent rate of growth up to 1965 and stressed the need for greater training facilities and improvements in labour mobility. However, these ideas were never formulated into a coherent plan and N.E.D.C. has scarcely been more than a talking shop and an intelligent pressure group.

(*b*) *Labour contribution.* Theoretically it would seem that a Labour government would favour planning as a major economic tool but in practice this has not been the case. George Brown in 1965 produced a plan which was no more than a series of economic aspirations and consequently it had no effect. The government also formed N.E.D.C. working parties for the major industries to highlight the strengths and weaknesses of the industries. These were christened little Neddies. The working parties have assumed a greater role under the Callaghan government's Industrial Strategy (12). This policy also has some leanings towards a planning exercise (13(*c*)) but only as part of a general industrial policy.

In general, for several reasons (*see below*), economic planning has had little pragmatic acceptance in Britain.

10. Problems of planning.

(*a*) There is insufficient theoretical or statistical evidence to suggest how the economic variables, macro or micro, interact to produce economic success or failure. It is very difficult to disaggregate the economy in order to see how the total economy works.

(*b*) Only France has had a coinciding of prosperity and planning and it is too simplistic to accept this is a certain causal relationship. The Socialist countries using imperative planning (8(*a*)) have had no great economic success relative to the West.

(*c*) Indicative planning (8(*b*)) depends on very full and free co-operation between government and industry but in Britain the confidence for such co-operation never appears to exist.

11. Institutions for intervention. Within the last decade Labour politicians have favoured specially created bodies to deliberately help industry to restructure itself to obtain a better productive performance. As with planning it is not an original idea but is derived from Italian experience.

(a) *1967 Industrial Re-organisation Corporation (I.R.C.)*. It consisted of a board and an executive and its main function was to promote the re-organisation of industry particularly to improve the quality of management by closing the gaps between well and badly managed firms. It had £150 million of government money to take share interests in companies but it was expected to sell its stake when the necessary improvements had been made. I.R.C. was required to work commercially and not merely to prop up ailing companies.

In the four years of its existence it was involved in ninety projects, its interest centring on the motor car, electronic, ball-bearing, fishing and scientific industries.

Critics often attacked I.R.C. for the arrogant attitudes of its executives who had a passion for re-vamping British industry according to their own pet notions but on balance as with any investment body it had successes and failures.

I.R.C. was killed by the Conservative government of 1970 who were committed (at least for two years) against specific political intervention in industry.

(b) *1976 National Enterprise Board (N.E.B.)*. It arose out of the 1975 Industry Act and is similar in concept to I.R.C. although it appears to be operating on a bigger scale. N.E.B. functions are:

(i) To establish, maintain or develop industrial undertakings.

(ii) To promote the reorganisation of industries.

(iii) To take over and manage public owned securities.

(iv) To extend public ownership into profitable manufacturing areas.

(v) To promote industrial democracy.

It has £1,000 million to use to buy into or to lend to companies and it must act commercially. (In its first year of operation it made a return of 11.8 per cent on its shareholdings.)

N.E.B.'s range of investments is quite staggering despite most of its time and money being spent between British Leyland and Rolls Royce (Aero-division). Besides these two giants it is involved in computers, machine tools, office equipment, tanning, spark erosion machines, miniature televisions, clock making, medical supplies, rubber and plastics. It is also hovering over the electrical generating industry. In practice, N.E.B. has four areas of operations, acting as a holding company (XV, **14**) restructuring industry, selling Britain overseas and helping small companies. (*See The Economist*, 7th May, 1977.)

N.E.B. like I.R.C. is a state agency bridging the gap between public and private sectors. The critics and supporters of such bodies debate on the use of public money in the private sector and whether market capital could do the same job of making British industry more efficient without the use of taxpayers' money.

12. Industrial strategy. Labour governments since 1974 have felt that an overall policy towards industry is required rather than a series of piecemeal steps. The strategy has evolved out of the 1975 Industrial Act which produced N.E.B. (**11**(*b*)), Planning and Information Agreements (**13**(*c, d*)) and a White Paper (1975 Cmnd. 6315).

This further urge to improve industry was triggered by several articles from Oxford economists Eltis and Bacon (e.g. *National Westminster Bank Review*, Autumn 1975: *The Sunday Times* 14th November, 1976). Their basic thesis was that Britain had shifted too many resources out of marketable goods (manufactured goods and services) into non-marketable goods (health, education, leisure, administration) thus creating several economic dangers:

(*a*) The non-marketable goods are non-exportable.

(*b*) Allocation decisions move from economics into political pressure groups.

(*c*) The financing of their production particularly in a declining economy is likely to be inflationary.

(*d*) The non-marketable goods do not produce future wealth except in a vague social way.

The basis of the strategy has been to reverse the flow of resources back into manufacturing industry and to really identify the future successful sectors and firms and to give them every aid.

13. Components of the industrial strategy.

(*a*) *National Enterprise Board* (**11**(*b*)). This is clearly the major government instrument but its value and success may depend on information flowing from the other aspects of the strategy discussed below.

(b) *Sector working parties.* Working parties have been established for thirty-nine varied sectors of British industry to study the structure and performance of their sectors. The reports investigate such factors as:

(i) Statistics on size/growth rates, foreign trade and demand forecasts.

(ii) The impact of government present and future policies on the sector.

(iii) Ideas for performance improvement, e.g. technology optimum size, import substitution.

Each working party has to establish the growth points in its own sector and to clarify the inter-sector relationships. The autumn of 1977 is too early to judge the success of the working parties but their initial reports and analysis have been realistic but as always idea implementation is the difficult task.

(c) *Planning agreements.* The 1975 Industry Act asked the country's 200 largest companies to enter into voluntary planning agreements with the Government. The companies will give information on such matters as investment and pricing policies, employment and productivity, exports and imports product development. The government feels such information will make its own industrial policy decisions more rational and it will improve the relations between government and industry. By mid 1977 few companies had bothered with the agreements. Exceptions were Leyland, Chrysler, Babcock & Wilcox, Clarke Chapman, G.E.C. and Reyrolle Parsons.

In general this aspect of the strategy has been a failure, even the nationalised industries have fought shy of the agreements.

(d) *Information agreements.* The government have always argued that workers should have more involvement with industrial decision taking. The Secretary of State for Trade and Industry can ask a firm for information on employment, output, sales, productivity investment and acquisitions. This information can then be discussed with the trades unions.

Information agreements have never developed because of the fears about the revealing of commercial secrets. Whether this new style of industrial involvement will actually bring the much heralded improvement in British industrial efficiency is open to doubt because there is always the problem of whether central government can actually effect the factors which contribute to industrial efficiency.

14. Conclusions. It is indicated in XIII, **19–20** that efficiency is a difficult concept to measure. A recent investigation by Pratten (C. F. Pratten, "Efficiency of British Industry," *Lloyds Bank Review*, January 1977), argues that our poor record is not statistically attributable to poor investment levels or a lack of competitive markets. He suggests two problems:

(*a*) *Payment systems.* Relative to our competitors our pay structures are less linked to skill, merit and quality of work. Two decades of incomes policies have not helped this phenomena.

(*b*) *Attitudes.* Pratten detects different attitudes to the work situation in this country, e.g.:

    (*i*) Do we actually believe in making profits?

    (*ii*) Do the British actually enjoy the us/them conflict in industry?

    (*iii*) Have the British different work-leisure preferences from other nationalities?

If Pratten's analysis is correct, it could be argued that persistent government interventionist policies have not been conducive to establishing a more rational economic climate in industry, thus it is difficult to see how attitudes will change.

PROGRESS TEST 14

1. Describe the basis of a *laissez-faire* economic policy. (2)

2. How has the growth of large industrial organisations led to the decline of such policies? (3(*b*))

3. Outline the basic problem of government intervention in industry. (5)

4. Why has there been a reaction against the government's interventionist role in the 1970s? (6)

5. When were controls last a vital part of our economic policy? (7)

6. What is indicative planning? (8(*b*))

7. Explain the organisation of N.E.D.C. (9(*a*))

8. Why was the I.R.C. abolished in 1970? (11)

9. What are the main functions of N.E.B.? (11(*b*))

10. Outline the main points of Mr Callaghan's industrial strategy. (12)

CHAPTER XV

Size and Monopolies

THE LARGE SCALE

1. Introduction. Within the last seventy years in all Western countries, big companies have taken an ever increasing share of industrial output. In Britain for example the largest hundred companies in 1909 took 16 per cent of manufacturing output, by 1971 the figure was 41 per cent. Between 1935 and 1972 the number of registered companies fell from 140,000 to 60,000 mostly through the demise of small companies.

This development creates concern, for there appears to be an over concentration of economic power in few hands although it is not clear who actually wields the power.

This chapter investigates the reasons for the growth of industrial size and then examines its competitive impact. Subsequent chapters look at the problems associated with mergers (*see* XVI) and the growth of industrial giants across international boundaries (*see* XVII).

REASONS FOR GROWTH IN INDUSTRIAL SIZE

2. Mass markets. The size and geographical spread of markets has increased considerably in the last hundred years. Reasons for this are:

(*a*) Population growth giving potentially more customers.

(*b*) Improved transport facilities which speeds up distribution.

(*c*) World-wide radio and television narrow cultural and social differences which eases the marketing of standardised products.

3. International competition. Because of the last point a nation's industries are competing at an international level and there is a belief that only big companies can compete at this level. This view has influenced the government's thinking on mergers. (*See* XVI, 7, 24.)

4. Economies of scale. Economies of scale were explained in XIII, **19**. Despite the difficulties of measuring them and the growing suspicion that the optimal scale of production is lower than exists in big companies, the lure of the synergy principle (2+2 = 5) in terms of production costs has ensured that companies will grow.

5. Diversification. No company, because of demand fluctuation, can afford to be a single product firm therefore companies have always wanted to diversify into new product markets. The easiest way of diversifying is to buy up a company in the new market and this policy is bound to produce larger companies.

6. Product development. The industrial world is increasingly based on science and technology and as products develop and improve (often in hope rather than fulfilment) a big and costly research injection is required. The development can be so costly only a big firm can undertake it.

7. Capital intensive industries. Many industries by their nature need huge capital equipment, e.g. fuel and energy, rail and air transport, car and aircraft manufacturing, so these industries will inevitably be dominated by big companies.

8. Managerial politics. It is suggested in XIII, **12**(c) that managerial status can be measured by organisational size. This point can be linked to the psychology of managers who tend to be power seekers, consequently the managerial ethic will respond favourably to the pursuit of company growth.

9. Size begets size. The previous reasons will cause companies to become bigger. If they then wish to expand and merge, the merger is between much larger units than was the case twenty-five years ago and so growth becomes an accelerating process.

SMALL COMPANIES

10. Survival. Despite the foregoing reasons the small company (usually defined as employing 200 or fewer people) still dominates by number all Western economies, although interestingly its decline has been more marked in Great Britain than anywhere else.

Small companies will always exist where any of the following social and economic conditions persist.

(a) Small markets, e.g. plumbing.

(b) Non-standardised product where quality and detail are important selling considerations.

(c) In areas where there is a small labour pool.

(d) Small companies because of their intimacy and informality enjoy better labour relations.

(e) Manager/owners of small companies enjoy the power of sole control so they ignore economic arguments for expansion because growth would require expanding the management base and they fear a loss of identity.

GROWTH METHODS

11. Introduction. Most big business organisations have grown by acquisition and various types of organisation have developed for controlling these empires. The major classifications are given below.

12. Integration.

(a) *Vertical.* To turn raw materials into finished products requires a chain of productive processes with different companies providing one process or link in the chain. Vertical integration occurs when a firm reaches forward or back in the chain to take over a customer or a supplier. They do this to guarantee supplies or to have more control over outlets. This method is now practised on a widespread scale; well known examples occur in the beer, oil, building, clothing and shoe industries.

(b) *Horizontal.* In this method companies at the same level in the productive chain come together basically to cut down competition and reduce distribution costs. Again, it is a common form of organisation with obvious examples over the years in the motor, hotel, entertainment, brewing, biscuit and confectionery industries.

13. Inter-locking directorates. Several companies appear to exist independently but in fact their board of directors overlap considerably in membership so the company policies will have a coherent thrust. This organisational type is difficult to identify, the best known example exists in the South African diamond industry.

14. Holding company. This is a method of holding together a business empire. A company is set up merely to be a significant shareholder in a collection of other firms and the controlling interest of the holding company is the real power behind all the other firms. It is a common device (look at the stock exchange quotations to see the word "holdings" after a company's name). Unilever is so organised and the massive British Shoe Corporation is in a business empire controlled by Sears Holdings. The National Enterprise Board (XIV, 11(*b*)) is acting as a government holding company to organise those companies with a large involvement of government money.

15. Conglomerate. It is an American word to describe a business empire based on financial and managerial expertise rather than production and marketing needs. The empire will consist of a range of companies operating in a random non-competing and non-complementary series of industries. The controlling company will have (or think they have) financial and managerial skills which they inject into ailing or under-valued companies hoping to revitalise the firms; for whose gain is questionable.

Conglomerate economic performance is now under a cloud of suspicion in America and although the species is rare in Britain one of the few examples, Slater Walker, did not inspire confidence.

Conglomerates raise anxieties because:

(*a*) A big financial unit buying into a new market could narrow the chances of other possible entrants.

(*b*) The centre of the conglomerate may use cross subsidisation policies (**43**) or in the multinational sense doubtful transfer pricing policies.

(*c*) They may lack financial soundness. Congressional investigators found that growth was often based on the issue of endless new shares and true financial returns were locked in a tangle of balance sheets.

(*d*) If the conglomerates were successful they represented a source of considerable economic power, the analysis of which was outside conventional economic theory.

FEARS OF INDUSTRIAL SIZE

16. Introduction. As **2–9** suggested the growth of company size seems inevitable and it is also inevitable in society that any power centre which grows quickly will arouse fear and suspicion. This section outlines these fears concentrating finally on fear of mono-

poly for this way is capable of economic evaluation, whereas the
other misgivings have a socio-political basis.

17. Social and economic power. As companies grow their power
to influence the community through investment, pricing and employment policies correspondingly grows but paradoxically the
men who make the policy decisions become obscure, lost in the
web of their bureaucratic empires and responsible to nobody.
Critics argue that communities are beholden to invisible men who
have greater power than elected governments. (*See also* XIII,
29.) This argument seems exaggerated and difficult to prove but
society must guard itself against potential power threats although
in the advanced world, governments are still considerably more
powerful than companies.

18. Social purpose of industry. This argument was mentioned in
XIII, 13. The worry is whether the potential economic advantages of size are outweighed by social costs. For example, does
work on large scale production units debilitate the human per-
sonality, does the vastness of large scale business empires reduce
human dignity? These questions are of course not confined to
business, they must be asked of any large scale organisation,
schools, local government or hospitals. Alternatively, it can be
argued only big companies can afford to employ handicapped
people, sponsor sport and fund educational institutions; so big
companies make a more positive contribution to life in general
than do small companies.

The social purpose of industry is a vital and fascinating question but can not be answered in an economic context.

MONOPOLIES

19. What is a monopoly? The word monopoly has provoked fear
almost throughout the history of mankind but it is most difficult
to define the word for practical economic and legislative purposes. Theoretically a perfect monopolist would be a producer
facing a totally inelastic demand curve being able to change any
price he wishes, but this is too unrealistic and better definitions
are required.

20. A single producer. A monopolist has been defined as the
single producer of a good in a market. However, this definition
has two weaknesses.

(a) *Branding*. A branded good is made by one firm but brands compete, e.g. Only G. & J. Greenall make "Vladivar" vodka, but they are not a monopoly because they sell their product in a highly competitive market.

(b) *Overlapping markets*. Only British Rail provide a train market but that market is a part of the bigger transport market which is fiercely competitive.

21. A lack of substitutes. A firm producing a good for which there is no close substitute is in a monopolistic position. In practice this market situation seldom exists unless the producer has control over a basic raw material, exclusive patent rights or legal protection. The G.P.O. is an excellent example because its services are heavily guarded by the law.

22. Market concentration. Given the definitional problems many economists and legislators have tried to define monopoly power through concentration ratios, i.e. what share of output, sales or assets in an industry is in the hands of a given number of companies (five companies are often used in this exercise). It is best to use output or sales share figures because share of assets will vary with the capital intensive nature of the industry (*see* Table XXIII).

The use of concentration ratios appears to give a degree of precision to monopoly definition but there are many difficulties.

(a) How are the boundaries of the market defined, e.g. are boiled sweets in the same or different markets to bars of chocolate and mints? To what extent does an industry differ from a market?

(b) How are multi-brand firms to be treated? Distillers have about 80 per cent of the whisky market but they produce a variety of whisky brands all with their own brand-loyal customers. If Distillers allow the separate whisky producers a large degree of marketing freedom, is it a competitive or monopolistic market?

(c) There can be significant variations in concentration ratios between area, national, regional and international markets, e.g. two firms could dominate the Scottish market but their impact would be slight on the British market and even less in Europe. Another aspect of this problem is how to allow for import shares in the home market.

(d) There is evidence that concentration ratios increase with the age of an industry and also with lack of growth in a market. Therefore competition is seemingly a natural element associated with new, dynamic and growing industries.

The value of concentration ratios is a matter of dispute. "It has not been established that there is a unique correlation between the degree of concentration and either the degree of discretion available to the firm, the types of business practices pursued or the character of the economic effects." (J. F. Pickering, *Industrial Structure and Market Conduct*. Martin Robertson, p. 21.)

TABLE XXIII.   CONCENTRATION RATIOS IN BRITAIN ABOVE
50 PER CENT 1971

Order	Industry	Number of products analysed	Sales concentration 5 largest companies
III	Food, drink, tobacco	12	57
V	Chemicals	14	64
VI	Metal manufacturers	3	61
IX	Electrical engineering	8	63
XI	Vehicles	4	73
XVI	Bricks, glass, pottery, cement	5	53

(*Source: 1971 Census Production.*)

23. Market domination. A simplified view of concentration is to try to assess one company's share of a market, given the problems of defining market (**22**(*a*)), and then to arbitrarily select a figure of domination. British policy used to use 33⅓ per cent now it uses 25 per cent (**52**(*a*)).

24. Size. A common fault is to equate company size and monopoly, Marxists are very guilty of this sloppy thinking. Big companies usually operate in highly competitive markets whereas smaller companies may dominate their own smaller market; the classic monopolist is the village shop in the remote village for their pricing power is very strong.

25. Summary. A precise definition of a monopoly is not feasible, so anti-monopoly legislators will construct an arbitrary definition. They must then balance the arguments for and against monopolies.

ARGUMENTS AGAINST MONOPOLIES

26. Higher prices. A monopolistic market price may be greater than the competitive market price because the lack of substitutes (**21**) gives the producer a more inelastic demand. Economic theory also indicates that a monopolist's price is greater than marginal cost (*see* Fig. 8) which also has implications for resource allocation (XIII, **26**).

27. Inefficient resource allocation. Economic theory argues that the most efficient resource allocation occurs under conditions of perfect competition, where price = marginal cost and all factors are paid the value of their marginal product (XIII, **26**). It is argued in **26** that monopoly prices are above marginal cost and the inelastic demand in the product market increases trade union power over wages in the labour market. (J. D. S. Appleton, *Labour Economics*. Macdonald & Evans, p. 13.)

Applied economists, e.g. Liebenstein "Allocative Efficiency v. X-efficiency". *American Economic Review*, vol. 56, 1966) also argue that lack of competitive pressure reduces the incentive on companies to use their resources in the most efficient manner.

28. Restriction of choice. The consumer is forced to buy from the monopolist and he has no adequate redress if his purchase is unsatisfactory. The ultimate power of the buyer is to take his custom elsewhere without undue cost.

29. Lack of innovation. If a company has little competition there is no incentive to improve its product, its efficiency or indeed any aspect of its business behaviour. Should these attitudes grow and prevail in an economy stagnation must be the final result. All nations which have enjoyed industrial success at any moment of history have done so on the bedrock of innovation.

30. Political domination. In a small country or a particular region of a bigger country one company can monopolise the area's economic life, e.g. American Sugar Corporation in pre-Castro Cuba. A major part of the resources flow into the company eventually allowing it to dominate the economic, social and political life of the area.

ARGUMENTS IN FAVOUR OF MONOPOLY

31. Benefits from economies of scale. If the benefits accrue in accord with theory (XIII, **19**) then costs should be lower and consumers will gain via lower prices.

Many cases exist, e.g. cars and television sets, where volume production has lowered prices but we lack knowledge of any correlation between optimum production levels and market shares, i.e. at what level of output do economies come into play?

32. Costs of innovation. The American economist, Schumpeter has argued that the accelerating dominance of science and technology in industry was bound to increase the costs of innovation to a level that only market dominating firms could afford research and development.

This argument has been used by governments to justify nationalisation in certain cases (steel and aircraft) and also the formation of big units in private industry (computers and cars) (*see* I, **25**).

33. Stabilising economic force. Any economy is subject to short-term economic fluctuations and companies in highly competitive situations operating possibly with low profit margins are prone to go bankrupt with consequent waste of resources. The company in a monopolistic position is less prone to violent demand fluctuations and can offer greater security to the work force and shareholders.

34. Costs of competition. Because of traditional economic theory, competition has been elevated to the position of an absolute good but in fact competition can incur considerable costs:

(*a*) *Cut-price wars.* In the short period consumers gain from price wars but ultimately they lead to quality reductions, low profits and investment and the driving out of companies, all situations which ultimately work against the consumer.

(*b*) *Marketing costs.* A fiercely competitive market is bound to increase marketing costs as firms fight for their share of the market. At worst marketing costs may become the largest single cost element for some products, e.g. with certain drugs and cosmetics marketing accounts for 30–45 per cent of total costs.

35. Summary. The problem of dealing sensibly with monopolies is underlined by the contradictory nature of the traditional arguments for and against. One school of opinion suggests the need to concentrate on the behaviour of monopolists, do they in fact operate restrictive practices which would seriously affect consumer freedom?

EXAMPLES OF RESTRICTIVE PRACTICES

36. Resale price maintenance. Manufacturers force retailers, through threats of withdrawing supplies, to charge a standard price for a commodity thus effectively restricting price competition in the retail trade. This practice was banned in Great Britain in 1964 except for the sale of books (**61**).

37. Full line forcing. A manufacturer insists that the retailer takes all his product lines and not just those which the retailer feels are good sellers.

38. Exclusive dealings. A group of manufacturers or a single monopolist ensure their products are only handled by specific outlets, thus a consumer's choice is restricted. The petrol and beer industries use this practice although in these cases most customers have easy access to a range of outlets. The main fear of exclusive dealings is they restrict freedom of entry to a market and this is an essential condition of competition (**53**(*b*)).

39. Import restrictions. A market dominator in country A agrees not to export to country B if a firm in the latter country offers a reciprocal agreement. In the past Swedish and British match manufacturers have used the system.

40. Restrictive tendering. In certain industries, e.g. civil engineering, the customer orders his product by asking suppliers to submit a tender for the work. It is not unknown for the market leaders to privately agree who will do the work and then fix the tender to ensure their desires are met. More sophisticated methods can be devised and the customer finds difficulty in proving that his true choice is being restricted.

41. Price fixing. The dominating firms in the market agree to charge the same price perhaps only lowering them to drive out newcomers. Open price-fixing is usually illegal but it is easy to have informal price agreements (**60**(*b*)).

42. Aggregated rebates. Rebates are given to a customer who remains loyal to the producer. This practice may seem innocuous but the period of expected loyalty may stretch over a number of years, thus newcomers would have to offer almost non-profitable terms to gain a foothold in the market. This method is fairly common in the shipping industry.

43. Cross-subsidisation. A company with products in many markets may use the profits from a monopolised market to subsidise its goods in another market, to drive out competition and create a second monopoly. It may also use profits from an established product to subsidise negative costs flows from products in the early stages of their life cycle.

44. Arguments for restrictive practices. Conventionally restrictive practices are condemned for restricting customer choice and protecting the inefficient producer but companies can defend these practices on the following grounds:

(a) Price cutting can create long-term costs in the effects on profits and investment (**34**(a)).

(b) The practices stabilise the business environment and create confidence which leads to more investment.

(c) Pooling of technical agreements cuts down on costs of research and information.

PROBLEMS OF FRAMING MONOPOLY LEGISLATION

45. What is competition? Anti-monopoly legislation is trying to increase the competitive nature of markets but competition is itself a vague concept. Economic theory concentrates on price competition but in the growing number of oligopolistic markets (markets containing a few big companies actively competing with each other) excessive price competition is frowned on because if one company cuts prices significantly, the others will have to follow, no extra sales will accrue thus revenue and profit will fall. Oligopolists prefer administered prices which is a polite way of saying unofficial price fixing.

These companies compete via their commodity, its use and design and through promotional schemes. Even in the retail trade where price competition is obviously present it is uncertain if customer loyalty is just a function of price or whether other variables, e.g. shop amenities, are important.

46. Multi-product firms. Today many companies supply a variety of products to a vast complex of markets and any one firm may be faced with the total textbook range of competitive situations. Satisfactory analysis requires knowledge of the companies policy in each market, e.g. How are overhead costs allocated in the market prices? Is there cross-subsidisation of prices (43)? If the products come from individual units within a big company, what freedom of policy decisions exists in the units?

47. Home and international competition. Many companies operate in home and world markets. They may argue that a secure monopolistic domestic market gives them the confidence to attack the export trade. A similar argument implies that only big companies can effectively compete internationally (3). Governments will be torn between protecting the home consumer from monopoly and encouraging exports.

48. Distinction between economies of scale and market domination. Most companies claim that big market shares enable them to reap the economies of scale but seldom is this claim quantified. Investigators of this argument must ask the following type of question:

(a) Are the economies in one plant or through the whole company?

(b) Are the economies technical, financial or administrative?

(c) What market share is necessary to achieve these economies?

(d) Are the economies producing lower costs and prices?

49. Guide lines for companies. In controlling monopolies, governments have to choose between a pragmatic approach, which is non-judicial, and a legalistic approach. The first method treats every monopolistic situation on its merits. This seems equitable but companies claim they are unsure which commercial policies will prove acceptable. They may be tempted to restrict competition if government policy seems indecisive.

A legal situation clarifies the situation for a company but an inflexible legal attitude to market domination might not be in the public interest for, as 31–4 indicated, benefits can arise from monopolistic situations.

50. Use of economic criteria. The economic textbook approach to monopolies would be to judge them on the basis of the allocation and efficient use of resources. These criteria obviously should not be ignored but their use does pose problems.

The resource allocation analysis contrasts perfect competition and monopoly but in practice, the competitive situation is difficult to define (45). Efficient use of resources is similarly difficult to evaluate (XIII, 15–20). Governments may also turn a blind eye to the economic deficiencies of a specific monopoly for political (e.g. defence needs) or social (e.g. employment) reasons.

BRITISH ANTI-MONOPOLY LEGISLATION

51. Alternative methods of attack.

(a) *Regulation of structures*. The government is concerned with the size of companies supplying a market. It will try to prevent any firm or group of firms obtaining more than a specific share of the market. This method requires information on concentration ratios (22) and is the backbone of American monopoly control.

(b) *Regulation of behaviour*. A monopolist offends by using restrictive practices (36–43) and governments will try to attack these practices. This approach has formed part of the British legislation (56–60).

(c) *Regulation of performance*. Theory argues that the monopolist will operate inefficiently therefore his performance must be monitored. The obvious criteria are price/cost relationships, profit levels, innovation record and ability to meet demand, unfortunately it is difficult to define acceptable levels of performance, e.g. what is a satisfactory level of innovation. Supposing profit levels are higher in a monopolistic as opposed to a competitive market; is this a result of market domination or greater efficiency? The British Monopolies Commission (52) has concentrated on studying performance in monopolistic situations.

THE 1948 MONOPOLIES & RESTRICTIVE PRACTICES (INJURY & CONTROL) ACT

52. Monopolies commission. A commission was established to investigate monopolised markets which were referred to it by the government. The criteria for investigation were:

(a) A third of output is produced by a single firm or more than two companies working together (now 25 per cent of output).

(b) Firms in the industry are deliberately trying to restrict competition.

The Commission tries to establish the presence of restrictive practices and then to evaluate whether this behaviour is in the public interest. It also studies the economic performance of the companies under review.

A report with recommendations is submitted to the Department of Trade and Parliament but only the government can take action (usually it quietly suggests to the firm that different behaviour would be appreciated); in this respect the Commission is powerless.

53. Established principles. Although essentially pragmatic the Commission's work has evolved definite strands of thought.

(a) The most damaging result of restricting competition is a reduction in incentives to innovate.

(b) Freedom of entry is the essential condition of competition. This view supports the exhaustive research done by the American economist, Bain.

(c) Very high profits and return on capital are probable indication of a lack of competition, although a Monopolies Commission report on the pet food industry said the average capital return of 46.7 per cent (national manufacturing average 16.2 per cent) achieved by Pedigree Ltd. was the result of efficiency rather than market domination and high prices.

(d) More intensive competition is likely to be oligopolistic (45), therefore company size and market shares may be an irrelevant measure of monopoly. In the detergent market two companies, Unilever and Procter Gamble, dominate to the extent of 45 per cent market share each, yet the market is extremely competitive.

54. Achievements. During its long existence the Commission has investigated many industries, e.g. electric light bulbs, dental goods, detergents, glass making, photographic films, brewing, cellulosic fibres, matches, car accessories, breakfast cereals, frozen foods, tobacco, petrol, infant milk foods and pet foods.

The Commission can scarcely claim to have made significant changes in the competitive structures of British industry and it has often been criticised (55), nevertheless its reports have been very informative and they revealed the horrific depth of restrictive practices. The early findings were so bleak they prompted the government to formulate the tougher legislation of the 1956 Act (56).

55. Criticisms of Monopolies Commission.

(a) The body lacks power. Very few recommendations have been enforced by the government and the force of bad publicity has been a seven day wonder, so Imperial Tobacco still control Gallagher and film distribution is still dominated by Rank and A.B.C.

(b) When the Commission's suggestions are followed quaint results can follow. Kodak cut their prices and nearly drove their main competitor out of business; the detergent companies produced with little advertising a new low priced product whose sales were very low.

(c) The Commission was too slow. Up to 1965 this was a valid criticism some reports taking up to four years to be completed. Since then the staff has been increased and the time taken has been cut down to about two years.

(d) Is the impact of the Commission worth the cost? The cost of the reports may be considerable if the Commission's research costs are added to the time and effort needed by companies to prepare their submission. Unilever complained that they spent many thousands of pounds to show the efficiency of their Birds Eye division; a proof accepted by the Commission thus causing Unilever to wonder about the point of the operation.

Even if the Commission attacks a company's behaviour and performance little is achieved in improving the competitive nature of a market and only a great optimist would suggest the Commission has had a significant influence on British competitive structures.

The validity of this criticism is confirmed by the need to introduce the 1956 Legislation.

THE 1956 RESTRICTIVE TRADE PRACTICES ACT

56. Introduction. The Act was the outcome of the 1955 Collective Discrimination Report which revealed that restrictive practices were rife in at least eighty industries and the practices were against the public interest for they frustrated the innovators and created very rigid markets. A tougher body than the Monopolies Commission was required.

57. Main principles. The Act created two new institutions.

(a) *Registrar of restrictive practices.* The office registered any agreements between two or more companies which placed restrictions on the price of goods supplied, the conditions of sale, the quantity of goods produced and the category of person supplied.

The Registrar codified the agreements and if companies wished to maintain their agreements they justified them to the Court of Restrictive Practices (63(a)).

(b) *The Court of Restrictive Practices.* This is a proper legally organised court although the judge has lay advisers and the defendants are assumed guilty, i.e. they have to show their practices are in the public interest. This term is so vague, the Act laid down gateways or arguments which must be used in the defence submission.

58. Gateways.

(a) The restriction protects the public from danger in the sale or installation of the good.

(b) The removal of the restriction would deny the public specific and substantial benefits.

(c) The restriction helps the participants to secure fair terms for the supply of goods from firms who are dominant suppliers.

(d) The restriction protects people against restrictions imposed by persons who are not party to the agreement.

(e) The removal of the restriction would seriously affect employment in an area dominated by the parties.

(f) The removal of the restriction would probably cause substantial reduction in the export earnings of the parties to the agreement.

(g) The restriction is necessary for the maintenance of another restrictive agreement which the Court has ruled to be in the public interest.

Defendants have to quantify their evidence and it has proved difficult to get agreements through the courts (60(c)). If firms are not willing to submit their case to the courts they must abandon the agreement or else be fined.

59. Use of the gateways.
Relatively few cases have come before the courts but the Court's decisions have not always satisfied economists, e.g. the Cement Makers Federation were allowed to have common delivered prices to reduce business risk and the Black Bolt and Nut Association were allowed price fixing to save their customers shopping around, whilst the scrap iron industry successfully claimed their minimum price agreement kept prices

down. On the other hand several price fixing agreements were thrown out. (For a list of interesting cases *see* J. F. Pickering, *Industrial Structure and Market Conduct*. Martin Robertson, pp. 287–91.)

60. Results of the Act. In the first two years of the Act over 2,000 practices were registered so it had a definite flushing out effect. In general three main points can be made:

(*a*) The Registrar's reports indicate a confidence that most markets are now operated without formal agreements.

(*b*) The above point hides two vital facts, viz.

(*i*) Formal agreements have been replaced by informal agreement or co-operation agreed in conversation between interested business parties.

(*ii*) Price leadership has developed where firms in an industry raise their prices accidentally at the same time. The Government's Price Commission almost sanctifies this process by allowing firms to put in simultaneous price rises.

(*c*) Judges' decisions do not appear to be commercially consistent so firms are still uncertain about the acceptability of their behaviour. However, the Court is obviously free from the pressure of political influence which has affected the Monopolies Commission.

On balance the Court has been useful particularly in opening up access to markets.

SUBSEQUENT LEGISLATION

61. 1964 Abolition of Resale Price Maintenance (R.P.M.). R.P.M. was a basic price fixing device (36) and was declared illegal in 1964. Any company wishing to continue with the practice had to apply to the Restrictive Practices Court using a number of gateways established for R.P.M., e.g. the number of retail outlets would be reduced and after sales service would be diminished. The Act was a total success and R.P.M. is now a rarity in the British economy.

62. 1968 Restrictive Practices Act. This was a tidying up piece of legislation with three points worth noting.

(*a*) Informal agreements must be registered although proof of their existence is difficult to obtain.

(*b*) A restriction is permitted if it does not prevent competition.

(*c*) A temporary exemption for agreements is allowable if they assist import substitutes or product standardisation.

63. 1973 Fair Trading Act. The Act covered the wide field of consumer protection but some points were relevant to this section.

(*a*) The Registrar's role was taken over by the Director General of Fair Trading, e.g. in August 1977 he threatened the Ready Mixed Concrete Industry with court action for fixing prices.

(*b*) The Director is responsible for identifying monopolies operating against the public interest. He can refer them to the Monopolies Commission (as can the Secretary of State for Prices if the Prices Commission from their price investigations suspect an abuse of monopoly power).

(*c*) Monopoly is defined as one supplier having a 25 per cent market share. If two companies, via an agreement, have this size of share then it is investigated by the Restrictive Practices Court not the Monopolies Commission.

(*d*) The provisions of the 1956 Act were extended to the supply of services.

(*e*) The Monopolies Commission were given guide lines for their studies although the criteria were wonderfully vague, e.g. "the desirability of maintaining and promoting a balanced distribution of industry and employment in the U.K."

E.E.C. LEGISLATION

64. Basic ideas. The ultimate ideal is for all member states to harmonise their company and trade legislation but this situation is far distant and the E.E.C. has concerned itself with inter-state flows of trade.

Article 85 of the Treaty of Rome bans agreements between inter-state companies to fix prices, share markets or to limit production, investment and technical development. Companies can justify their agreements if they improve distribution, production or technical progress. I.C.I. were once fined for persisting with a banned price agreement.

Article 86 prohibits the exercising of market power to keep prices up, production down or to keep new firms out of the market.

THE PROMOTION OF COMPETITION

65. The problem. Anti-trust legislation is really concerned with the discrepancies between maximum profit and social net benefit arising from a lack of genuine competition. The discrepancy shows itself through excessive prices and poor product development.

To produce competitive markets Britain has tried the pragmatic approach (Monopolies Commission, **52**) and a legalistic approach (Restrictive Practices Court, **57**) yet there is still unease about the dynamic qualities of British industry.

Monopoly policies have underlying them the pursuit of perfect competition but such an action itself incurs costs; e.g. too many small firms could endanger genuine scale economies, therefore a vital need is a clear cut concept of effective competition.

66. Possible solutions. Government monopoly policy should ensure that all markets have sufficient firms to offer genuine choice to suppliers and there should be realistic freedom of entry to a market. Ideas on prices are more complicated because even in perfect competition there is only one price so pursuit of price competition could be a red herring. The best course of action is to monitor price-cost-profit relationships.

To help achieve these ends three actions are suggested.

(*a*) More foreign trade should be encouraged as long as it is fair competition. There are risks to the balance of payments and employment but in the last twenty years foreign firms have been a significant stimulus to British industry.

(*b*) Company law should insist on greater disclosure of performance information by companies. The balance sheet is a useless guide and informed opinion has only scanty evidence to judge a firm's performance.

(*c*) Governments should adopt tougher anti-merger measures. Market domination usually comes from acquisition rather than a company's internal growth yet government merger policy has been very indecisive (*see* XVI). Oligopolistic markets (**45**) are now so common, that a harsh merger policy may be too late but governments should quickly explore the possibilities of such action.

Fears of decreasing market competition in Britain have grown since the 1960s with the rapid increase in the number of mergers occurring in British industry.

PROGRESS TEST 15

1. Give three reasons for the growth of large scale industrial organisations. (2–9)

2. Distinguish between vertical and horizontal integration (12)

3. What is a conglomerate? (15)

4. Explain the phrase "market concentration". (22)

5. Examine the costs of competition. (34)

6. What is cross-subsidisation? (43)

7. Distinguish between scale economies and market domination. (48)

8. Explain structure regulation in monopoly legislation. (51)

9. Outline the main principles followed by the Monopolies Commission. (53)

10. Suggest three methods of increasing competition. (66)

The Problems and Control of Mergers

GROWTH OF MERGERS

1. What is a merger? A merger is the coming together of two or more companies so the over-all policies of the new organisation are determined by a single board of directors. Many words besides merger are used to describe this process, e.g. take-over, acquisition, amalgamation, absorption and fusion. The various words try to distinguish between the method of merging, e.g. were the parties agreeable, were the parties of equal size? In this chapter "merger" will be used for all situations.

2. History of mergers. At specific periods of time since the nineteenth century there has been a rapid acceleration in the numbers of mergers. The variations in merger rates depend on economic disturbances, e.g. technology, economic growth and cheap capital.

(*a*) The first noticeable growth was in the late nineteenth century, e.g. wallpapers and distilling, where there was a period of rapid technological change and declining profits.

(*b*) The 1920s saw the emergence of the big five in banking, four railway companies, I.C.I. and the fast growth of Unilever. The prime stimulant was depressed trade with the need to reduce competition and rationalise manufacturing processes.

(*c*) The next merger boom occurred in the late 1960s and early 1970s (*see* Table XXIV) the main reasons being changing technology, prosperity (cheap and plentiful finance) and fear of foreign competition.

There was also government encouragement (**24, 25**).

REASONS FOR MERGERS

3. Marketing reasons.

(*a*) *Domination.* A company wishes to expand its market share and feels it has not the growth potential within its own resources

BRITISH GOVERNMENT POLICY TOWARDS MERGERS

18. Government reaction to mergers. Through the 1950s and the early 1960s the Government took no action against mergers as such. Indeed in many industries, e.g. aircraft and textiles, governments actively encouraged mergers which produced bigger industrial units.

From 1964 the merger boom accelerated (*see* Table XXIV) with a new facet emerging. This was a growing proportion of mergers involving two big companies, e.g. G.E.C. and English Electric; Boots and Timothy Whites. Fears of market domination rapidly grew and the fears deepened when the acquiring company was foreign, e.g. Chrysler and Rootes; Nestlé and Crosse & Blackwell (*see* Table XXV: increasing concentration of net assets).

The feeling of the time was expressed by Mr Crosland, Minister at the Department of Trade and Industry.

"Mergers raise profound political and social as well as economic issues. A very large firm has a pervasive influence on people's lives. We can lay down certain principles—they are good if they lead to better management or greater economies of scale, bad if they lead to inertia, a dangerous lack of competition or any abuse of market power. The difficulty comes in applying these general concepts to particular situations." (Speech to Manchester Chamber of Commerce, 2nd February, 1969.)

TABLE XXV.   NUMBER OF FIRMS REQUIRED TO ACCOUNT FOR 50 PER CENT OF NET ASSETS IN DIFFERENT INDUSTRIES

Industry	End 1957	End 1967
Drink	12	4
Textiles	8	3
Food	7	4
Vehicles	5	2
Clothing and footwear	3	1
Paper and printing	6	3
Wholesale distribution	21	14

Source: A Survey of Mergers 1958–68. H.M.S.O. (1970) Appendix 10

19. Principles behind intervention. Governments will contemplate intervening if:

(a) There may be a divergence of social and private interests, e.g. will the merger produce factory closures and unemployment?

(b) The merger is not in line with the government's view of the "correct industrial structure".

ACTION AGAINST MERGERS

20. 1965 Monopolies & Mergers. The main features were:

(a) The Department of Trade to investigate any merger which creates or increases a monopoly in the supply of any good or service in the U.K. The value of any assets to be taken over must exceed £5 million. (This will cover any significant merger.)

(b) The Department of Trade to investigate the merger of any independent newspapers whose combined circulation is over 500,000. (This is designed to ensure a variety of opinion in the mass media.)

(c) The Department of Trade will investigate any merger involving a foreign company gaining a major shareholding in a British company.

(d) The Department of Trade can refer any merger to the Monopolies Commission for further investigation. The latter to report within six months. (*See* **22–3** and Table XXVI.)

(e) Parliament has the power to unscramble a merger which has taken place. (Note that the administration is now in the hands of the Office of Fair Trading.)

21. The nature of the investigation. The Department of Trade seeks information about the companies involved in the merger, the motivation behind the merger, demand factors, market structure, the efficiencies expected to accrue from the merger and any likely effects on the balance of payments (*see Mergers, A Guide to Board of Trade Practices.* H.M.S.O. 1969).

22. Results. Since the Act over 900 proposed or actual mergers have been investigated but only about 3 per cent have been referred to the Monopolies Commission and an even smaller figure have been deemed to be against the public interest. Consequently there are no real criteria of what constitutes the "Commission's views", however, mere threats of reference by the government have caused many mergers to collapse, e.g. Redland–Marley; Read–Bowater.

Such evidence confirms Newbould's view that many mergers are unplanned and the realisation that the Monopolies Commission will require quantifiable justifications daunts the merger partners. Sometimes companies have escaped a reference by giving the government assurances about the new companies' behaviour, e.g. not to use price discrimination or to restrict supply. There are obvious misgivings about such vague promises; for how long will civil servants monitor the behaviour, what action follows any breaking of the assurances?

TABLE XXVI.   MONITORING OF MERGERS

Year	Mergers examined	References to Commission
1965	50	1
1966	60	6
1967	90	1
1968	130	2
1969	110	2
1970	90	4
1971	110	2
1972	120	4
1973	85	10

Sources: Department of Trade Journals

23. Some findings of the Monopolies Commission.

(a) Merger of Ross Group and Associated Fisheries. Disallowed because it would lead to market domination in the Humber ports without strengthening the industry.

(b) Merger of Boots and Glaxo. Disallowed because it is more beneficial to have a variety of research interests.

(c) Merger of British Match Corporation and Wilkinson Sword. Allowed because it would inject new management into British Match and give Wilkinson more overseas contacts.

(d) Merger of Barclays, Lloyds and Martins. Merger between the two big banks disallowed because it would diminish competition. Martins could join either of the big banks (Barclays and Martins joined).

(e) Merger of British Motor Corporation and Pressed Steel. Allowed because of product integration and export potential.

GOVERNMENT IN FAVOUR OF MERGERS

24. Basis of action. This chapter has concentrated on the control of mergers but government has also encouraged mergers. Chapter XIV showed that politicians wish to produce an efficient industrial structure and big companies because of their technological know-how and their ability to compete effectively against overseas firms form an essential part of the structure, thus Governments have been tempted to encourage the formation of big units. This attitude has been prevalent in shipbuilding (before nationalisation), machine tools, motor cars, textiles and computers.

25. Action. The Labour party has dominated government since 1964 and despite ideological fears of big business they have actively encouraged mergers through their interventionist bodies I.R.C. (*see* XIV, 11(*a*))and N.E.B. (*see* XIV, 11(*b*)). It can be argued that nationalising the steel, shipbuilding and aircraft industries is simply large scale merging policy.

Significantly I.R.C. inspired mergers escaped reference to the Monopolies Commission and the government appeared to have contradictory policies on mergers but this pragmatic approach was justified by the complexity of evaluating a merger proposal.

26. Summary. Establishing a sensible policy towards mergers is a complicated operation because big companies, in either an economic or social view, are not inherently good or bad. However, governments may argue they do not have the machinery to continuously vet business behaviour and the safest policy is a tough attitude to mergers, e.g. in America any merger which creates a market share above 4 per cent is barred. Such a policy would incur costs but at least it would be a comparatively simple policy. Its effect on government interventionist policies (*see* XIV, 11–13) would be interesting.

PROGRESS TEST 16

1. Define a "merger". (1)
2. Give two marketing reasons for the growth of mergers. (3)
3. Why might fear be a reason for mergers? (8)

4. Outline the social worries associated with mergers.   (13)

5. Examine Newbould's findings on mergers.   (14)

6. Suggest possible benefits of mergers.   (16)

7. What principles lie behind government merger intervention?   (19)

8. Describe the main results of the 1965 merger legislation.   (22)

9. Why might governments be in favour of mergers?   (24)

10. Explain why a logical merger policy is difficult to formulate.   (26)

CHAPTER XVII

Multinational Corporations

NATURE OF MULTINATIONALS

1. Introduction. So far the discussion of industrial size has been confined to inside National boundaries but many commentators believe the key big company/government problem to centre on the growth and activities of multinational enterprises. Simply, they are companies which have production plants in many countries but the control and decision-taking units of the company are in one country. This chapter will analyse the nature of these commercial mammoths and investigate the reasons for the large scale worries which they seem to generate.

2. Definition. Any definition must be arbitrary but the following seems adequate "A combination of companies of different nationality connected by means of shareholdings, managerial control or contract and constituting a single economic entity." (R. E. Tindall, *Multinational Enterprises*. Oceania Publications. New York 1975, p. 1.) Pickering, less legally, suggests a multinational will have annual sales of at least £100 million, 25 per cent of which will be earned by overseas plants. The multinational will have production facilities in six or more countries. (J. Pickering, *Industrial Concentration*. Martin Robertson 1974, p. 175.)

The country which contains the head office of the multinational is known as the parent country, the other countries containing production or distribution plants are called host countries.

3. Who are the multinationals? The multinationals are in fact household names and below are a very small selection of them listed by parent country:

    (*a*) *U.S.A.* General Motors, Du Pont, Esso, I.B.M., Gillette, I.T.T., Ford.

    (*b*) *U.K.* British Leyland, B.P., Dunlop, I.C.I.

    (*c*) *Europe.* Volkswagen, Phillips, Ciba-Geigy, Nestlé, Siemens, Volvo-Saab.

Sometimes a multinational might have significant decision taking units in more than one country, e.g. Unilever.

4. Significance of multinationals. Four quotations illustrate the power of multinationals.

"To a remarkable extent the ownership and control of both production and distribution, outside of the Communist countries has passed into the hands of gigantic corporate organisations." (C. S. Burchill, *The Multinational Corporation Queens Quarterly*. Spring 1970, p. 3.)

"Given an expanding world economy and the rise of the multinational corporation, national boundaries may follow the history of state boundaries in the U.S.A. which failed to confine the American corporation and prevent the growth of a national economy. It represents a move beyond international trade into internationalisation of production." (G. Paguet, *Multinational Firm and The Nation State*. Collier Macmillan 1972, p. 1.)

"The really significant resources are now technology and management. These assets enjoy the quality of mobility as well as scarcity. Manufacturing operations formerly found in a few nations are now widely dispersing throughout the world." (R. A. Mathews in Paguet, *see above*, p. 154.)

"On the basis of output amongst the top 100 countries and enterprises with a volume exceeding £2m, 54 are enterprises and 46 are countries." (A. Sampson, *The Sovereign State*. Hodder & Stoughton 1973, p. 270.)

In fact in terms of gross national product if General Motors were a state it would rank fourteenth in the world.

These are sweeping statements but seeking specificity it can be noted that in Great Britain in 1973, 13 per cent of output and 20 per cent of exports were produced by multinationals. In certain fields, e.g. breakfast cereals, razor blades and petrol, the figure rose to 40 per cent.

The problem of multinational power is treated as an essentially modern problem but articles warning of the impact of Singer, Heinz and other American corporations in Britain were written at the beginning of this century. Whilst an American businessman wrote in 1902, "When the duty exceeds the cost of separate managers and plants then it will be an economy to erect works in the country that our customers can more cheaply be supplied from." (R. E. Tindall, p. 9.) Compare this with a modern thought, "It is just not possible for a mere exporter to become a major long term factor in a market in the second half of the twentieth century." (President of Pfizer & Co. Ltd.)

5. Growth of American multinationals. The concept of companies seeking and developing factories in other countries grew in the second half of the nineteenth century, e.g. Bayer Chemicals, a German firm opened in New York in 1876, Russia in 1882 and France in 1908, whilst Singer of America moved into Scotland in 1867. Movement has always been two ways between America and Europe but until recently the American concerns have dominated the scene. The reasons for this are:

(*a*) The general faster growth of the American economy produced a big demand for labour saving consumer durables, which had a high income elasticity. This demand was a tremendous stimulation to innovation.

(*b*) The over-all growth of mass consumer demand automatically initiated the search for new mass production techniques.

(*c*) The obsession of American industry with finding good managers; they were not content with a belief often found in Europe that management still is an inherited gift which can be passed down in families. For the Americans, management is a science rather than an art and they have devoted vast resources to obtaining efficient management techniques.

(*d*) The American anti-monopoly laws have always been severe, thus companies have been tempted to go overseas rather than form alliances at home.

Therefore economic history has given the American company the natural ingredients for growth namely, big markets, technology and good management. Nationally they grew big and by the Second World War the firms were facing tremendous oligopolistic competition. Post-1945 home competitive pressures were intensive, whilst in Europe living standards were expanding rapidly but labour costs were lower than in the U.S.A., these factors made an American invasion of Europe inevitable.

Interestingly since the mid 1960s the same circumstances of tough competition, rising living standards and lower labour costs are pushing the European and American multinationals in to the Third World.

6. Growth of European multinationals. The European multi-nationals have as long a history as their American counterparts but the scope and scale of their growth has been much more limited and significant development did not occur until the 1950s.

As with the American experience, European multinational growth has come with rising incomes, increasing management techniques and the impact of research and development, al-though the product mix seems different with the European multi-nationals producing more working class and luxury goods. How-ever, certain differences can be detected in the European picture.

The ownership of European companies is strongly influenced by families, banks or governments rather than private share-holders and dynamic profit-orientated management, thus the Europeans have lacked the aggressive stimuli to vigorously ex-pand. Also European businessmen, perhaps because of their trading history, have placed more weight on the value of exports. On average Europe exports 26 per cent of her G.N.P., the Americans only 7 per cent, so the concept of attacking foreign markets from production plants in the market is alien to the European experience.

The conservatism of the Europeans is revealed in that their first steps to becoming multinationals are often taken in coun-tries close to their geographical boundaries and possibly because they wish to follow common linguistic and cultural patterns.

Evidence also suggests the Europeans are bigger diversifiers, some Americans are almost single industry companies, e.g. I.B.M., Kelloggs. This situation may arise from the size potential of home markets.

Rather oddly the recent European multinational boom has been helped by America which was interested in attracting foreign capital for balance of payments reasons. In 1966 an office was opened in Paris to provide information about America for European businessmen. Some of the attractions offered were:

(*a*) Access to the largest market in the world.

(*b*) The ease of raising capital on the Euro-dollar market.

(*c*) A more rigorous implementation of the Buy America Act made it difficult for the simple exporter to sell direct to America.

(*d*) The benefits of exposure to American competitive business methods.

But the size of initial investment in America, at least £80–100 million, often tempted the Europeans to attack the American market by buying into smallish local firms and utilising their capital and managerial assets.

7. Summary. The multinationals' have become a huge influence on the international business scene and consequently are the social and political landscape of nearly every country in the world (even communist countries are encouraging their activities).

Pessimists predict that by the late 1980s, a significant share of world output will be in the hands of a few multinationals. The potential of the multinationals to create either economic good or social and economic cost is awe inspiring. The next section investigates this power for good and bad.

THE ADVANTAGES AND DISADVANTAGES OF MULTINATIONALS

8. Introduction. "It is run by foreigners. It rigs its intra company transfer prices. It imports foreign labour practices. It doesn't import foreign labour practices. It underpays. It overpays. It competes unfairly with local firms. It is in cahoots with local firms. The technology it brings to the Third World is old fashioned; no it is too modern. Nobody can control it. It wrecks balances of payments. It plays governments off against each other. Won't it please come and invest. Let it bloody well go home." (*The Economist*, 24th January, 1976, p. 68.) In this context "it" refers to multinationals and the passage sardonically reflects the amazing conflict of feelings about multinationals.

This section tries to rationally investigate the good and bad points relating to these international giants. The normal procedure of separating the advantages and disadvantages will not be used. Instead the investigation will centre on the main areas of controversy.

9. Balance of payments. The multinationals move large quantities of goods and capital around the world to suit their own strategies and these movements can influence countries, balance of payments and exchange rates.

(*a*) *Capital.* If a multinational invests in an overseas subsidiary, superficially there is capital outflow from the parent country and an inflow to the host country. Over the years the flows will be reversed as the debt is repaid and profits return to the head office. However, the impact of the flows will depend on:

(*i*) Where was the capital raised? In these days of international capital markets, there is no guarantee that the capital will be raised in the parent or indeed the host country.

(*ii*) The movements of profits will depend on the shareholding structure of the parent company and on its method of control over its subsidiaries.

Some multinational critics argue that the capital flows will seriously affect exchange rates but it is more likely that the capital moves in response to changes in exchange rates, i.e. it does not cause the fluctuations.

(*b*) *Goods*. Multinationals will try to rationalise production on an international level, therefore they will be moving components and semi-finished goods in and out of countries. A sudden change in production policy, e.g. if Fords switch all body-making from Great Britain to Germany, could alter a country's flow of imports and exports. Also a multinational may decide to bring in components from another subsidiary rather than buy locally thus influencing import totals.

In general the balance of payments effects may be greater for a developing rather than a developed nation because the latter will be both a host and a parent country thus the movements of capital and goods are likely to cancel out.

10. Technology. Technology has always been a stimulus for multinationals (*see* **5**(*b*)) so they are going to be innovators bringing new ideas and methods into host countries. Unfortunately, many host countries will be developing nations and their technological needs are a continuous source of debate. One school of thought believes that to copy the newest Western technology will bring fast economic growth whereas the other school argues that a copying technique ignores the total differences of economic and social structures, e.g. is it sensible to use labour saving technology when the nation's cheapest resource is labour?

Another view of technology is that it has replaced share ownership as the source of power in a company. If the parent company controls the technology its formal share relationship with the subsidiaries is a red herring. The role of the multinationals with respect to technology is neutral, the real question is society's perspective on technology.

11. Manpower.

(a) *Management level.* Many host countries believe that the multinationals prefer their management to be parent country nationals thus stifling the development of local talent. The contrary view is that modern international management methods act as an incentive to local companies. There is no firm evidence to significantly support either view.

(b) *Worker level.* This is a major controversial area revolving around multinational impact on local labour market wage levels and the structure of industrial relations. There is more myth than evidence to feed the debate but it should be noted that the multinational tradition is to seek efficiency (implying high pay-levels) and the honouring of local laws. Unfortunately in Great Britain our system of industrial relations is built on tradition rather than the law, thus in the interests of economic efficiency a multinational might view the tradition with a jaundiced eye. (In May 1977 the workers of I.B.M. in Britain overwhelmingly voted against being unionised by compulsion.) The relationship of unions and the multinationals is discussed in 20–22.

12. Efficiency. As implied in 10 the multinationals when building in a new country seek efficiency otherwise the operation is pointless. The host country is nervous whether the invasion will kill or stimulate local companies and the host government will probably become increasingly involved in the industrial structure. As always it is dangerous to generalise about the multinational effects.

13. Markets. Three major problems occur within local market structures.

(a) *Market shares.* If the multinational has a commanding share of a local market what should be the host's reactions? The response may depend on the strength of antitrust legislation or the ability to merge local companies into a viable competitive force. An oligopolistic market structure seems inevitable with the coming of the multinationals to a country. The real local sufferers may be the medium-sized companies, for the genuinely small company can usually find a place in the market.

(b) *Pricing decisions.* Multinationals will operate in many markets using international production techniques but what will determine the price-cost ratio in any given market. Cross-subsidisation may be used so that prices and profits in a strong established market are used to subsidise a price war against local companies in another market. If a multinational is operating in so many markets with a spread of production units, is there any chance of using the marginal techniques of pricing which theoretically lead to the optimum use of recources.

(c) *Buying locally.* A multinational will want to integrate its production techniques probably on an international scale and this will have balance of payment implications (*see* 8(*b*)) the buying policy of the multinationals can affect the general economic well being of local companies, e.g. in a Third World country would the multinational buy locally at high cost to stimulate the local economic structure?

14. Tax avoidance. It is claimed that multinationals can avoid paying their correct company taxes by showing false profits through the manipulation of transfer pricing. The latter is the name given to the prices charged to each other by the different parts of the multinational empire as they exchange components and semi-finished goods. The charge is based on the assumption that some plants of the empire will be in countries which have low rates of company taxation. The multinational accountants then ensure by rigging the transfer prices that high profits are made in the low tax countries and low profits in high tax countries. Proof of this practice would require an investigation far outside the scope of this book.

MULTINATIONALS AND GOVERNMENTS

15. Basic problem. It has been shown in 8–14 how individual aspects of an economy can be affected by multinational activity but governments, and in particular Third World governments, have to assess the comprehensive economic and social effects of the multinational presence.

The host government/company relationship is perhaps the most controversial area of the whole multinational debate. The main worries can be divided into three.

16. Global strategy. The multinationals plan their output capacity and sales targets in terms of the world economy rather than a national one, thus a decision to transfer or expand resources is taken irrespective of local effects. Even more importantly the decision is not in the hands of the host government.

The realities of the situation may be different as resource transfer is often an economic nonsense (because of tied up capital) and governments do have the power to control capital movements across their boundaries.

17. Attitudes of parent countries. There are fears that parent country governments may persuade their multinationals to deal more favourably with politically acceptable countries or even worse to use the multinationals as a front for intelligence activities. There is some evidence of I.T.T. involvement in Chilean politics but it would be ludicrous to tar all multinationals with this brush.

18. General attitudes to host countries. The attitude of multinationals to the economic, social and cultural aspirations of host countries is often questioned. Most of the industrial giants argue that to politically antagonise host governments would amount to business suicide. However, it is not known how many pursue the positive policies of British American Tobacco which always uses local management and ploughs back profits into the local community.

19. Conclusions. The irony of the relationship is that as governments become more abusive and regulatory towards the multinationals the latter will find the host's economic climate less inviting and thus the host government may well lose the capital and technological infusion it so desperately requires. Some system of controls based on a mutual appreciation of each other's needs seems very necessary.

MULTINATIONALS AND TRADE UNIONS

20. Basic worries of unions. Trade unions are always apprehensive of big national companies; when a company becomes international it becomes a positive bogeyman which can be blamed for all mankind's evils.

More rational unionists fear the multinational power in the three areas of employment transfer (American unions claim that in the period 1966–9, 400,000 jobs were moved from U.S.A. to Europe), wage levels and national patterns of industrial relations.

21. Union reaction. Forward thinking trade unionists envisage international agreements (with the multinationals) to obtain:

(*a*) Simultaneous negotiations on major issues at all subsidiaries.

(*b*) To aid (*a*), integrated bargaining to establish common demands.

(*c*) The building up of international information systems to assist trade union bargainers.

(*d*) To organise action in plants to help workers who are in dispute elsewhere in the multinational.

So far the only successful agreements have come in the chemical and glass making industries and the only significant multinational union is the International Chemical Federation.

22. Difficulties of international union agreement. The achievement of effective international union co-operation faces many hurdles. Below is a list of the main obstacles.

(*a*) *Variations in philosophy.* Unions in different countries have a varying philosophical appreciation of their roles. In America, trade unions have a free market, profit orientated view of the world; a European Communist union has the opposite ideology, the British socialist unions have a confused perspective of their environment, and in Japan their unions are usually company based.

(*b*) *Variations in industrial law.* The function of the law in industrial relations varies tremendously between countries both in principle and detail. The German framework centres on industrial law, whereas in Britain we believe in custom and practice. Thus any international agreement would have to make legal sense in all countries, e.g. sympathy strikes are legal in some countries but not in others.

(*c*) *Variations in wage determination.* Wage determination is a prime part of collective bargaining and the methodology can vary significantly in a single country let alone across nations. Imagine the problems of internationalising wage agreements between countries which have or do not have income policies. Linking with (*b*), it is essential to know if a wage contract is legally binding?

(*d*) *Union organisational abilities.* Apart from the American unions it is most doubtful if any other unions have the management skill and financial resources to organise themselves across national boundaries. Indeed most admit to the problems of meaningfully organising their home activities.

However, despite these frightening hazards unions will clearly, at the political level, join with their governments and any international body to try to control the dangers, real or otherwise of the multinational.

CONTROL OF THE MULTINATIONALS

23. Introduction. From the previous sections, a potential conflict of interest emerges between managements that operate in a world context and governments which work on the national scene. Increasingly the multinational is regarded, without too much concrete evidence, as a sinister new form of imperialism.

The objections of states can be summarised as loss of national pride, the historical fear of absentee ownership and the growth of unknown decision takers who operate outside the democratic control mechanism. The most pessimistic multinational watchers prophesy that by the end of the twentieth century the nation will be an obsolescent concept. Perhaps it will, but there seems no reason to seriously blame the multinationals for this amazing political and constitutional change.

Nevertheless, given the unknown quality of the multinational, (What really is its *raison d'être*?) the mystery will produce fear and governments will try to erase the devilry by controlling the demon. This section investigates the parameters of control policy.

24. History of controls. In the 1960s and early 1970s governments and international bodies published a host of tracts about multinational control most of the suggestions being fairly gentle and untroublesome, e.g. local equity participation, the quicker promotion of local personnel, the use of local suppliers and the harmonisation of company investment policies with government economic requirements.

These attitudes reflected a belief that both multinationals and nation states had a part to play in world economic and social progress. Then in the mid 1970s the price of world economic growth began to falter and the nation states searched for scapegoats and after the Arabs they chose the multinationals.

Attitudes hardened and hostility grew particularly in the Third World, the United Nations and trade unions movements. There was talk of stringent controls such as states becoming compulsorily the major shareholder or the drawing up of international guide lines to regulate multinational behaviour. Some poorer countries incredibly argued that the West should give them the multinationals. The Western nations despite their own fears of the multinationals drew back from the wilder proposals but began a desperate search for their own control system.

25. Basic thoughts for control. Western countries have never rationalised their views on the costs and benefits of industrial size within their own boundaries, so their thoughts on international control are tentative.

(*a*) *Shared ownership*. The host country to have an equity share in the subsidiary to influence the companies' decision taking. This argument simplifies the vastly complex question of ownership and control, the cloudy relationship of shareholder and manager. Share participation could lead to apparent rather than effective control.

(*b*) *Local managers to be locals*. Some companies already follow this policy (**18**) but to establish it as a principle is questionable for management's task is to better his company not to work for some ill defined concept of national interest. Presumably economic efficiency and hence prosperity depends on the best managers being at the top, irrespective of colour, race or creed.

(*c*) *Anti-trust legislation*. Countries may design an active policy to prevent foreigners buying into national companies. (As France did under the presidency of General de Gaulle.) This policy presupposes the government has a very clear picture of its required industrial structure, which seems an unlikely phenomenon judged by Britain's performance over the last two decades. None of the above control points seem very useful because of the difficulties outlined below.

26. Difficulties. Any control system must overcome two extreme difficulties.

(*a*) *Power of a single country*. A single country can only act against the subsidiary of a multinational and over-reaction may drive out much needed foreign capital. There seems a need for concerted action, which leads to the second difficulty.

(*b*) *International agreement*. If the activities of the multinationals are to be restricted, countries must act together and formalise international agreements on company, merger and industrial relations law. Such agreements appear impossible because so many countries would be involved all with highly local ised traditions. Even the E.E.C. cannot seem to evolve a satisfactory Community policy on mergers (*see* XV, **64**).

A further difficulty is that many developed countries are both parent and host to multinationals so their attitudes are bound to be ambivalent. The most likely development is that each country will bargain with a variety of multinationals to develop a *modus operandi* for the successful running of their economies.

CONCLUSIONS ON MULTINATIONALS

27. Summary. The dilemma of the nation state is that it cannot live easily with or without the multinationals. Each state must prime its own relationships with each multinational for there is no single concept of a multinational or a state.

Perhaps the whole problem can be summarised by quoting Hymer, "The coming age of multinational corporations should represent a great step forward in the efficiency with which the world uses its economic resources but it will create grave social and political problems and will be very uneven in exploiting and distributing the benefits of modern science and technology." (S. Hymer in *Multinational Firm and the Nation State*, G. Paguet. Collier Macmillan 1972, p. 63.)

PROGRESS TEST 17

1. Give a definition of multinational companies.   (2)
2. Name four multinationals.   (3)
3. Explain the growth of American multinationals.   (5)
4. How has America tried to attract European multinationals?   (6)
5. What is the effect of multinationals on the balance of payments?   (9)
6. Describe the impact of multinationals on manpower.   (11)
7. Outline the problems arising from multinational pricing decisions.   (13(*b*))
8. What is the likely attitude of multinationals to the host countries?   (18)
9. Why do unions worry about multinationals?   (20)
10. Outline the history of attempts to control multinationals.   (24)

CHAPTER XVIII

Nationalised Industries

BACKGROUND OF THE NATIONALISED INDUSTRIES

1. Definition. In November 1976 the National Economic Development Office published a wide ranging investigation of the British nationalised industries. (H.M.S.O.) They offered this definition of such industries. A public corporation whose:

(*a*) Assets are in public ownership and vested in a public corporation.

(*b*) Boards are appointed by a Secretary of State.

(*c*) Board members are not civil servants.

(*d*) The corporation is primarily engaged in industrial or other trading activities.

It is a tight definition concentrating on the production and sale of goods and services thus the major source of revenue is the customer. It excludes such bodies as regional water authorities, port authorities, the Bank of England and the National Enterprise Board. The problem of the status of British Leyland, Rolls Royce Aero-Engines and other companies dominated by government money is avoided. This chapter will concentrate on the traditional nationalised industries as designated in Table XXVII.

2. Impact of nationalised industries. The nationalised industries play a significant role in the British economy. Together they account for more than a tenth of the Gross Domestic Product and nearly one fifth of total fixed investment. The four biggest employers (besides the government itself) are nationalised industries. They occupy a dominant position in the supply of steel, transport, energy and communications. About a third of all plant and equipment bought by British industry is consumed by the nationalised sector whilst they are the sole domestic customer for several areas of British industry.

The nature of the beast is summed up by W. G. Shepherd, "The problems of the nationalised industries are complex and

TABLE XXVII.   NATIONALISED INDUSTRIES AND THE
U.K. ECONOMY 1975

	Value added £m.	% G.D.P.	Employment '000s	% U.K.	Fixed investment £m.	% U.K.
British Airways	279	0.3	53	0.2	82	0.4
British Gas	745	0.8	102	0.4	349	1.7
British Rail	1,118	1.2	254	1.0	205	1.0
British Steel	745	0.8	220	0.9	410	2.0
Electricity[1]	1,397	1.5	167	0.7	595	2.9
Coal Board	1,397	1.5	312	1.2	185	0.9
Post Office	2,608	2.8	421	1.8	923	4.5
National Bus Company	186	0.2	70	0.3	21	0.1
National Freight Corporation	186	0.2	45	0.2	—	—
Total	8,662	9.3	1,644	6.7	2,770	13.5
Other National industries	372	0.4	47	0.2	164	0.8
Other public corporations	1,304	1.4	261	1.1	943	4.6
TOTAL	10,337	11.1	1,952	8.0	3,877	19.0

[1]Electricity only England and Wales.

(*Source:* The Economist, *27th November, 1976, p.* 15 (*figures may not add because of rounding.*))

changing. With their many operations and outputs the industries are enormously diverse and they are closely involved in the adjustment problems of the entire economy with important social effects frequently linked to their actions. No single economic criterion for organising and operating the nationalised industries has been found appropriate." (*Economic Performance under Public Ownership.* Yale University Press, 1965.) In a nutshell the British nationalised industries are very large business organisations with a vital economic influence yet they have to perform a social role and there are no clear guide lines for establishing criteria to evaluate the success of their combined economic and social achievements.

3. Myths. Serious debate on the complex industrial problem is severely handicapped by political prejudices which have created myths about the nationalised industries. Below are some examples:

(a) *All nationalised industries lose money*. As Table XXX shows this is not true. British Rail probably has lost most money but internationally it is difficult to make profit out of running a major railway network whether they are publicly or privately owned. Simple profit levels are never a satisfactory test of efficiency.

(b) *Nationalised industries are a U.K. phenomenon*. All Western nations have nationalised industries, usually in the public utilities, and government involvement in this field can be traced back to the late nineteenth century. Furthermore many countries have developed nationalised interests in other industries and even in individual companies, e.g. in Sweden the alcohol industry, in France, Renault. Each country has evolved a nationalised sector best suited to its own traditions and modes of business organisation.

(c) *Nationalised industries are pure monopolies*. The competitive position of the industries varies significantly. The Post Office is near enough to a pure monopoly, whilst British Rail is in fierce competition with private road transport, private and public air transport. (In 1975 British Rail accounted for only 8 per cent of passenger travel; the 1964 figure was 12 per cent.) The energy industries compete amongst themselves and with the private oil industry.

(d) *Total nationalisation leads to economic salvation*. Myths (a)–(c) are in the minds of right wing political people, the salvation myth belongs to the left. There is no scrap of economic or business theory or indeed, pragmatic evidence to support this piece of nineteenth century dogma. Cruelly the industrial performance of the socialist countries where nationalisation is total is admitted by themselves to be well below Western standards.

ARGUMENTS FOR NATIONALISATION

4. To prevent abuse of monopoly power. Competition through the presence of several firms would be very wasteful of resources in certain industries, e.g. gas, electricity, rail, postal communications and water because the capital intensiveness of the industries would make plant duplication extremely costly. Without nationalisation single private firm domination would be inevitable and the community would be exposed to the potential abuses of monopoly power (*see* XV). Government control of monopolies never seems entirely satisfactory therefore nationalisation puts the monopoly power into public rather than private hands.

5. Economies of scale. There is a fear that in certain industries firms might be too small to maximise scale economies. This would be serious if the industry was capital intensive and competing in world markets. Failure to achieve the economies gives low profits which further reduces investment incentives. Either the vicious circle continues until near bankruptcy or the City encourages private mergers which might lead to the fear of monopoly argument given above. Both situations are unattractive and so the government steps in with nationalisation plans. This argument was behind the 1967 steel nationalisation and the 1977 shipbuilding take-over.

6. Control of the economy. This is really a political argument which suggests that if the government is to successfully run the economy, the traditional monetary and fiscal policies are inadequate and the government must control the major industries whose decisions on investment, prices and employment policies can have far reaching effects on the economy.

7. Social benefits. Some industries have an element of social benefit in their output but the social cost is so high that private profit could not cover the cost, thus without nationalisation the social benefits could not be obtained. Examples occur in post and transport where services are provided at below cost of production to remote areas. There have also been suggestions that low income families should receive financial assistance towards their fuel bills.

The social argument is sometimes advanced to safeguard jobs, e.g. in 1977 there were calls to nationalise Plesseys, the big telecommunications manufacturing firm, but this is a dangerous argument because no industry can provide jobs indefinitely if there is no product demand.

8. Government as main customer. Some industries, e.g. aircraft, shipbuilding, generating equipment are heavily dependent on the government for orders. They are also often technologically advanced industries so their demise would scarcely be in the national interest. It is argued that if these industries were state owned it would be easier for the government to have an overall buying and production plan to avoid the uncertainties which presently plague the industries.

9. Redistribution of resources. This is another political argument based on old-fashioned doctrine. It is assumed that nationalisation means a transfer of control over the means of production to the workers who would also gain from a distribution of the profits. So far nationalisation has meant a transfer of power to the state and as will be seen in **29–52** a change of ownership has not eased some extremely complex problems of control, investment and pricing policies.

10. Summary. The case for nationalisation rests on three broad strands:

(a) Certain industries depend on size of operation and private control might entail serious monopolistic dangers in terms of price and output policy.

(b) Industries may have certain social obligations which a totally profit orientated structure could not meet.

(c) A change in ownership of industry produces an economic and social Utopia.

The first point can be economically researched and debated, whilst the final point is an act of faith. However, the middle argument is the tricky one because it entails seeking a balance between economic and social ends, a situation which is at the heart of modern life.

ARGUMENTS AGAINST NATIONALISATION

11. Creation of monopoly. In Britain nationalisation so far always involves a single supplier of a good or service although the possibility of substitutes exist (**3(c)**) so the government is creating a monopoly with all its inherent dangers. This argument rejects the thesis of **4** that a government monopoly is more amenable to control. It is felt that the government has far more weapons to guard its monopoly power (e.g. the use of taxes and subsidies to protect coal against oil) and that ultimately there is no higher authority to protect the consumer against government monopoly power. Believers in this argument contend that monopoly, irrespective of ownership, is potentially dangerous to consumer satisfaction and resource allocation. The case of the monopoly power of British Rail is often cited when they hardly ever provide a

buffet service on their Sunday trains, leaving the consumer without a practicable alternative.

12. No profit motive. The aims of the nationalised industries are
seldom clearly defined in profit terms (*see* **23–28**), so the management lack any incentive to improve their efficiency by the usual
control standards of private enterprise. Later sections will try to
clarify what are the aims of the industries and the aspirations of
their managements. To simply correlate profit and efficiency is
naïve (*see* XIII) and traditional economic theory of the firm
exaggerates the role of profit in private industry decision taking,
yet a concept of working for a high rate of return seems more
reasonable than the whimsicalities of R. Pryke who wrote, "The
aim of those in charge of the nationalised industries is to meet
the needs of the consumer at the lowest possible price, to act as
a model employer and in general to help maximise the welfare of
the nation." (*Public Enterprise in Practice*. MacGibbon and Kee
1977, p. 460.)

13. Diseconomies of scale. The nationalised industries are very
big and face the danger of suffering from diseconomies of scale.
Over-bureaucratisation is the chief fear and there are many signs
of the industries suffering from too much centralisation, poor
communications, red tape and the other well-known evils of
organisational size. The management seem aware of the problems
and all the industries have endured many restructuring operations but the benefits are not so obvious.

Another diseconomy can arise from market contraction with
subsequent rises in costs per unit. In private industry diversification is the answer but the nationalised industries live in a market
straight-jacket and diversification is frowned upon (*see* **35(c)**).

14. Political interference. Constitutionally the politician is supposed to keep at arm's length from day-to-day management of
the industries (*see* **29–33**) but the whole history is marred by a
persistent over ruling of sound business decisions for nebulous
political gain. The political culprits have an exotic philosophical
range from Heath to Benn (*see* **27**).

The record of intervention undermines the control of the
economy argument (**6**) which is based on a quaint belief in the
economic rationality of politicians. The nationalised industries
have been used by both parties as a lifeboat to rescue the sinking

economy but unfortunately this role is beyond any single group of industries whoever owns them.

15. Fears for democracy. This is a pure political argument based on the premise that democracy rests on a multi-dimension sharing of productive resources ownership and the greater the share enjoyed by the state, the less power there is for the people. At the extreme of a total Socialist state this could be true but the nationalisation structure in Britain, even with the addition of aerospace and shipbuilding, seems a long way removed from this danger.

16. Summary. The arguments against nationalisation depend on two major thrusts:

(*a*) State monopoly given the quality of political thinking and integrity may be even more dangerous than private monopoly which can at least be controlled by the law.

(*b*) The nationalised industries lack adequate concrete economic and social aims to guide their managers' decision-taking, so the danger of resource wastage must be high.

17. Conclusions on 4–16. The supporters and opponents of nationalisation forget a vital point, viz. nationalisation cannot be inherently good or bad. This is a logical absurdity. Essentially it is a method of business organisation which ought to be evaluated by business criteria. (This does not preclude social costs and benefits.) It is not, and this absolutely devalues debate, the heralding of the Red Dawn.

The nationalisation of public utilities is easy to justify on economic grounds but the nationalisation of the whole retail trade would be a piece of economic fantasy. Real difficulties of debate occur when the nationalisation of steel, cars or drugs are proposed. In these complex arguments, economists must avoid twisting their economic facts and theories to suit their political prejudices.

Finally it must be remembered that nationalisation is only one method of government involvement with industry. The next twenty years may see more subtle and satisfying ways of realising a successful working relationship between government and industry, total *laissez-faire* and total nationalisation are obsolete and irrelevant ways of fashioning a desirable industrial structure.

METHODS OF ORGANISATION

18. Department of state. This was an early idea in which the enterprise was organised through a specific minister and his department, e.g. the Post Office used to be run by a minister with the title Post Master General.

19. Local authorities. Most local authorities through their committee system and officials provide a range of non-social services, e.g. buses and markets.

20. Public boards. The traditional British method of running a state industry is to create a board (equivalent to a board of directors) responsible to a Government minister and hence to Parliament. The board is responsible for the day-to-day running of the industry but remains accountable to the representatives of the people (*see* 29–35).

21. Government holding company. The last twenty years has seen an ever increasing injection of government money into private companies, so that many companies are effectively controlled by the government. In the past the government has been a dormant shareholder but in the mid seventies it has sought a more creative role. The Labour administration of 1974 copying the Italians have used the National Enterprise Board as a holding company to cement together their growing business empire. Presumably the companies involved are pressurised to follow some general government objectives, e.g. British Leyland–N.E.B. discussions on the future of a new Mini. However as stated in 1 this type of situation is still not regarded as pure nationalisation.

PROBLEMS OF NATIONALISED INDUSTRIES

22. Outline of problems. The ideal way to run a nationalised industry would be to recruit high calibre management talent and leave them to run the industry. Lip service is paid to the ideal but there have been many deviations for a variety of reasons.

(*a*) Governments have used the industries as tools of macro-economic policy (*see* III, 20) and long-term investment and pricing decisions by management have been sacrificed for often spurious short-term economic political gain (*see* 52).

(*b*) The industries have been used to prop up failing areas of British technology, e.g. British Airways have bought aircraft they did not want and the Electricity Generating Board have been ordered to build unwanted power stations. (Ince 1971, Drax B 1977.)

(c) They have to provide a social service to some consumers (telegram service) and some employees (maintaining inefficient pits).

These examples reflect the broad span of problems facing the nationalised industries, i.e. what are their aims, what is their relationship to their political masters and how should they conduct their financial and commercial affairs?

PROBLEM OF DEFINING AIMS

23. Introduction. Whatever political motivation produces a nationalised industry it must be given some basic aims unless rational management decision taking becomes an impossibility. There have been four periods in the evolution of the aims of the nationalised industries although the last period will be seen to be regressive.

24. Period I 1948–61. This was the great maternity period, when numbers of nationalised industries were born and various statutory obligations were laid down. Broadly there was a desire to meet the demand for the products and to change prices which allowed the industries to break even over a period of time. In fact the aims were staggeringly vague as a guide to practicing management, e.g. the N.C.B. was expected to provide coal at prices and qualities best calculated to further the public interest; the electricity industry had to provide electricity to those who wanted it and to cheapen supplies as far as was practicable.

There was no clarification of the public interest, no efficiency criteria were established thus management was left in the dark and performance was disappointing.

25. Period II 1961–67. In 1961 the government, trying to rectify the lack of purpose, published *The Financial and Economic Obligations of the Nationalised Industries* (Cmnd. 1337). Industries were required to balance their books over a five year period after providing for interest and depreciation, at historic cost, provision was also made for the building up of reserves. Finally financial targets were to be set for the first time, with each industry having a target rate of return on capital based on its capabilities and needs, e.g. Electricity Boards 12.4 per cent; British European Airways 6 per cent; Post Office 8 per cent.

The Government also promised the Boards greater freedom to fix prices and promised to give a written explanation of any intervention on prices. Subsequently Select Committee Reports reprimanded governments for ignoring this policy of non-intervention.

26. Period III 1967–71. In 1967 the Labour government published *Nationalised Industries—A Review of Economic and Financial Objectives* (Cmnd. 3437). The basic concern was with the tremendous increase in nationalised industry investment which was consuming an ever growing share of scarce capital resources.

The major concept was the use of discounted cash flow techniques to evaluate proposed investment plans in order to keep them in line with national resource utilisation. It was suggested that no project should be undertaken if the likely rate of return was below 8 per cent which was deemed to be a comparable rate with the private sector. The government also required a pricing policy that would ensure the customer paid the true cost of the service, although if wider social benefits were involved the government promised to make a subsidy towards the cost of the benefit.

On balance this White Paper was slightly odd for a Labour government, for its philosophy was definitely profit orientated with social obligations taking a back seat.

27. Period IV 1971 onwards. The Conservative government of Mr Heath came to power in 1970 on a platform of applying almost nineteenth century principles of *laissez-faire* to the industrial structure. They wanted to hive off many of the periphery activities of the nationalised industries and to make the remainder highly profit orientated. Government intervention would be out.

By late 1972 as inflation was beginning to accelerate the nationalised industries were ordered to peg their prices the consequence of which were staggering losses in 1974 (*see* Table XXX). Target rates of return, and discounted cash flow techniques vanished. (There is still no method of allowing for social obligations in accounting terms.) The Labour government of 1974 rekindled the fire of profit orientation for the nationalised sector by allowing huge price rises to enable the previous years' losses to be eradicated. Mr Kaufman for the government made the interesting comment, "Socialists forget that every £1 million of profit made by the G.P.O. is £1 million of Public Expenditure for housing and the real social services." (*Trade and Industry*, 25th March 1977.) Nevertheless, Government interference was still to be seen when Mr Benn in 1977 ordered the Gas Industry to raise its prices because it was competing too efficiently with the other fuel industries. Almost immediately the Prices Commission accused the Gas Council of making abnormal profit. Undeterred Mr Benn then ordered the Electricity Generating Board to build a power station for which there was no demand.

Still the government was worried about the nationalised role and they commissioned an investigation by N.E.D.O. (*see* 1). Unfortunately, the main debate on the report centred on the idea of creating a new management structure, an idea howled down by all interested parties and intelligent onlookers.

28. Summary. By the autumn of 1977 roughly 20–30 years after the birth of the nationalised industries the community still had not evolved a clear purpose for them. Opponents believed they ought to charge very low prices and miraculously make enormous profits, supporters viewed them as a huge social service free of normal financial constraints. An academic arrived at the delightful position where the nationalised industries could ignore market forces and consumer preferences would be transmitted through the ballot box (M. Lipton. What is Nationalisation For? *Lloyds Bank Review*, July 1976).

This continuing confusion on aims plagues much of the thinking about subsequent problems.

THE PROBLEM OF PUBLIC ACCOUNTABILITY

29. Introduction. Whereas the board of directors of a private company is responsible to its shareholders, the board of a nationalised industry is ultimately responsible to the electorate via Parliament. This is a nebulous concept and the Acts of Parliament establishing the industries deliberately offered no rigid solution in the belief that experience would evolve a satisfactory method of accountability. Below is a broad outline of the system that has evolved.

30. The Minister. The Minister responsible for the industry has been the main instrument of control. Certain statutory obligations are placed on him. He appoints board members, fixes their salaries and approves major policy decisions, e.g. investment programmes. He can also direct the boards to conduct the business in the public interest.

As a general rule the boards and their management take day-to-day decisions and the Minister has a big say in over-all policy. Unfortunately at times of political and economic crisis, the borderline between the two decision areas disappears (*see* 22 and 27).

Parliamentary back-benchers also complain about their inability to even marginally influence the policies of the nationalised industries. At question times, questions seem to investigate the Minister rather than the industry.

31. Select committees. Since 1951 all-party select committees have acted as Parliamentary watch-dogs over the industries. They have the power to send for people, paper and records and from 1956 they have investigated the boards' reports and accounts. Their aim is to inform Parliament about the aims and activities of the industries.

The select committees have performed well for their reports are rational and free from political bias, whilst they have won the confidence of the boards. However, their reports tend by nature to be retrospective and it is difficult to specify progress which can be attributed to the committees.

32. Consultative councils. Each industry has a consultative council (composed of lay people) with a statutory obligation to act as general advisers to their boards particularly from the consumers' views, e.g. they often have the right to veto price increases. The councils are organised on a regional basis but they exist in a limbo as the vast mass of the people are unaware of their existence except possibly for the Post Office Consumers' Council.

33. Problems of the system. The N.E.D.O. report (1) identified four problem areas in the accountability relationships:

(*a*) A mutual lack of trust and understanding between the boards and the government (politicians and civil servants).

(*b*) A total confusion about the respective roles of all the bodies involved.

(*c*) There is no framework for evolving long-term policy objectives and no continuity of support when decisions are reached. For example, plans for investment and manpower have a time scale well in excess of Parliamentary life and political expediency.

(*d*) No system exists for measuring performance and assessing managerial competence.

However, it is too simple and unrealistic to draw up single guide-lines for commercial and social policy decisions or to clearly designate the ministerial and corporate spheres of influence. Given the vast economic power and social influence of the nationalised industries, governments are going to interfere.

34. N.E.D.O. suggestion. The need is to establish between government and the industries a relationship based on trust, continuity and accountability. To achieve this aim N.E.D.O. wanted to create a Policy Committee between the Minister and the boards. It would consist of the board chairman and some members, senior civil servants, trades unions, consumers and independents (Presumably a person who consumes nothing?). The committee would establish corporate objectives and the strategies needed to achieve them. Performance criteria would be created. Ministers could not intervene except in extreme circumstances when they could over ride a decision.

The chances of the plan coming into operation are slight, as two major criticisms are levelled at it:

(*a*) It represents the creation of another bureaucratic body which reduces the status of the board and further befogs the accountability relationship.

(*b*) There is still an obvious loophole for government intervention.

35. Conclusions. As with the aims issue, no real forward progress has been made towards a coherent accountability system. N.E.D.O. did stress points which ought to figure in the continuing discussions:

(*a*) The nationalised industries are now becoming considerably wider than the public utilities therefore blanket success tests may be inappropriate.

(*b*) Agreed efficiency monitoring systems must be developed unless political subjectivity becomes the only basis of debate.

(*c*) Politicians must realise they are dealing with huge technological industries which can not be used to solve short-term political problems. The Government and the boards are operating in different time dimensions.

COMPETITION

36. Relations with private industry. The nationalised industries and their private counterparts live in the same commercial world, at least two-thirds of nationalised output is bought by the private commercial sector and the nationalised concerns, because of their big investment programmes (*see* Tables XXVII and XXVIII), are huge buyers of plant and equipment. Below are some of the problems posed by the relationship.

(*a*) *Pricing policies.* Should nationalised industries sell cheaply to subsidise the cost structure of private industry? If they do, how are their own losses to be financed and does such non-market force pricing lead to poor resource utilisation (*see* 38–48).

(*b*) *Buying policies.* Should nationalised industries invest in schemes, unjustified by their own demand forecasts, to guarantee jobs in the private sector? If they do what is the effect on their own cost and price framework?

(*c*) *Diversification policies.* What are the boundaries of the commercial interests of the nationalised industries, e.g. do British Rail need to own hotels, or should British Airways provide package holidays? Conservatives have tended to define the boundaries very narrowly but this goes against all industrial experience because as demand patterns change companies must diversify, e.g. the major tobacco companies are into food and cosmetics. As electricity demand appears to be almost stagnant, should the boards diversify or are the activities and resources of the nationalised industries to be historically determined forever? As *The Economist* said, "Without development we might still have a nationalised stage coach company with all the problems of the coachmen's union." (*The Economist*, 27th November, 1976, p. 17.) The counter argument is that nationalised industry competition is theoretically unfair because they can never go bankrupt because of government finance; but what is the effect of management incentive of no development, does stagnation produce good management?

37. Competition between nationalised industries. Several nationalised industries are in severe competition with each other, e.g. rail/air, gas/electricity/coal, but it is difficult to establish what is the most beneficial nature of that competition. If competition does stimulate efficiency then the public must gain but does the consumer gain from the possible wastes of competition, e.g.

different gas and electricity meter readers and show rooms, or the advertising campaigns of the different industries.

The answers are not obvious and it is perhaps a problem of competition practice rather than a particular aspect of national-isation.

PRICING POLICIES

38. Role of prices in nationalised industries. Four possible roles for prices may be determined by looking at the history of pricing policies.

(a) Fixed to maximise profits. In this case, theory of the firms principles would be applied (*see* **40**).

(b) Fixed to provide a basic service at a price that all sections of the community can afford with the implication that a financial loss may be made.

(c) Fixed to satisfy the government's economic strategy, e.g. prices kept down as a bargaining ploy to seek an incomes policy.

(d) Fixed to strike a balance between (a) and (b). The indus-tries are obliged to make profit but they have to meet certain de-finable social obligations. Thus the industry seeks a satisfactory profit given a social constraint. This fits the satisfying principle from the modern theories of the firm (*see* XIII, **12**).

Should policy (b), (c) or even (d) be used, the industry will need a subsidy which has economic consequences of its own (*see* **44**). Alternatively if policy (a) was rigorously applied it would prompt the question—why nationalise the industry in the first place? Clearly pricing policy can not be realistically divined from prob-lems of the purposes of nationalised industries.

39. History of nationalised prices. The layman believes that nationalised industry prices have always been very high relative to the private sector but reality is more complicated.

Between 1960–75 the nationalised prices to the consumer rose on average by 8.4 per cent per annum, whilst the total retail price index rose by 7.2 per cent per annum. Over the same period a price index of nationalised industry outputs, purchased by manu-facturing industry, increased less rapidly than those of total basic materials and fuel purchased by the manufacturing sector.

Although the average price rise is higher than the retail index, the average masks periods when prices were kept artificially low for political reasons, big losses were incurred then prices were allowed to rocket over a short time period, much to the consumer's horror. This process occurred in the early 1960s and 1970s. Such abrupt price changes turn the industries' demand forecasts into a lottery, e.g. in the 1960s low electricity prices increased demand and production potential was built up, then prices were raised to an economic level, demand fell and the industry had an excess of production capacity.

A long-term study of the pricing policy reveals no rationale other than political expediency with all the economic nonsense that such a Marx Brothers' policy is bound to produce.

40. Price theory and the nationalised industries. For all practical purposes nationalised industries are monopoly suppliers of goods and services and using basic economic theory their price/output policies ought to give them supernormal profits. They sell an

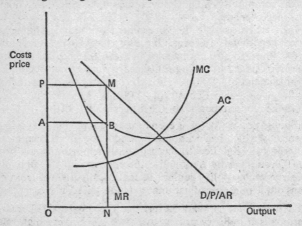

FIG. 8   *Price and output policy in monopoly.* The monopolist has the power to restrict the output to *ON*, in order to achieve a price *OP* substantially above the lowest point on the average cost curve. Competition would have forced a larger output, minimum average cost and a lower price.

output of *ON* for a price of *OP* which gives then a supernormal profit of *APMB*. However, one reason for nationalising an industry is to avoid this situation (*see* 4) therefore what should be the pricing policy of a nationalised industry?

Economic theory suggests that if we wish to maximise welfare and resource allocation then a policy of equating price and marginal cost should be pursued.

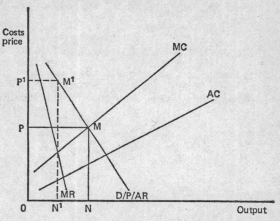

FIG. 9 *Price and output in a competitive market.* Competition obliges the supplier to produce an output consistent with marginal cost (the extra cost of one more unit of output), equalling the price it achieves. Thus *ON* sells at *OP* which equals marginal cost of *NM*.

In this situation an output of *ON* is sold at a price of *OP*. The price is lower and output greater than in the profit maximising situation where price would be *OP¹* and output *ON¹*.) The White Paper of 1967 seemed to endorse this policy, "The consumer should pay the true costs of the goods and services he consumes in every case where they can be suitably identified." (Cmnd. 3437, para. 18). The government suggested the use of long-run marginal costs which would include a provision for the replacement of fixed capital. There were three suggestions for deviating from the general rule.

(*a*) If there was spare capacity in an industry, the price should be lowered to short-run marginal costs to attract more custom.

(*b*) If there was excess short-run demand then price should be raised as a rationing device.

(*c*) If it is difficult to allocate costs to specific services then two-part tariffs (*see* **47**) should be used with prices proportionate to marginal cost.

However, the principle of equating price and marginal cost has been attacked on many grounds and these difficulties are discussed below.

DIFFICULTIES OF MARGINAL COST PRICING

41. Falling average cost curves. Nationalised industries are usually capital intensive thus in the long run because of scale economies they should enjoy falling average costs. This situation also

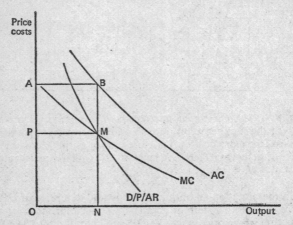

FIG. 10 *Price and output policy with falling marginal cost.* When due to scale economies marginal costs rather than rising, continue to fall, the competitive rule of equating *MC* with *P/AR* would result in a loss of *PABM.*

ensures a falling marginal cost curve which creates a problem for the *MC* = price relationship. Clearly at a price of *OP* the industry is making a loss of *PABM* which would have to be financed out of tax revenues, a situation creating two worries.

(*a*) There is a redistribution of income from the tax payer to the consumer based on no obvious criteria of equity, need or resource allocation (*see* **44**).

(b) Price policy might become a facet of taxation policy which is a piece of economic irrationality.

42. Measuring marginal costs. Marginal cost is an elusive concept in any industry but in capital intensive industries the problem is very complex. The time period chosen is of great significance because the cost of meeting an increase of demand of one unit in period t is not necessarily the same as meeting the identical demand increase in period $(t+1)$. Consider the problems facing the electricity generating boards. Assuming no change in the total number of customers, the demand varies by time of day, day of week, week of year and through the vagaries of climate. Varying output to meet these changes produces a myriad of marginal costs. Consider further the decision whether to build a new power station costing millions of pounds but which in the long run is a marginal cost!

Theoretically the industry will have a multitude of marginal costs which might be reflected in a complex tariff system. But the information costs of calculating and metering the system make it only worthwhile for very large customers. Also if the producer is facing an inelastic demand, subtle price differences will have little effect on consumption decisions.

43. Marginal social costs. The management of nationalised industries usually accepts that they have to meet certain social obligations but nobody (despite many gallant mathematical exercises) knows how to allow for these costs within the framework of marginal costing. How are the social costs and benefits of the telegram service to be evaluated? What is the social value of putting electricity cables underground rather than on overhead pylons?

The industries often argue that their social elements should be clearly designated and then the government should pay for them by direct subsidy.

44. Subsidising prices. It is shown in **41** and **43** that governments may have to subsidise various nationalised industry activities but this policy itself has dangers.

(a) Large subsidies can quickly increase the volume of public expenditure, a step which depending on the financing of the expenditure, can be inflationary (*see* VI, 14, 17).

(b) If subsidies are just cheap finance for the maintenance of inefficiently operated services then they represent a misallocation of the nation's resources. The continuous availability of subsidies can also undermine the rigour of management decision taking as the stimulant of financial control is removed.

(c) As already stated (41(a)) subsidies paid for out of tax revenue ensure that the taxpayer is subsidising the consumer and yet the rationale of this subsidy is not clear on either social or economic grounds. Some Labour Party members have suggested, rather wildly, that rail commuting is a middle-class pleasure and to subsidise it creates a regressive distribution of income. If a country branch line is subsidised then presumably the reason for subsidy is living in a pleasant area which seems a debatable excuse for handing out government money.

45. Side effects of marginal cost pricing. If the price of the output is related to the true cost of providing the output then various odd social and economic side effects could develop, e.g.

(a) Coal mine efficiencies and hence costs vary enormously for a variety of technical and geographical reasons so if prices were related to marginal costs consumers would be charged a big range of prices depending solely on the regional source of their fuel. Consumers would bitterly resent this luck element in their coal bills and if demand was elastic the sales of the inefficient pits would collapse and the remaining pits might not be able to meet the nation's demand for coal.

(b) British Rail provides three basic passenger services—long distance Inter-City, commuters and short-distance branch lines. If the true costs of the second and third categories were reflected in prices then:

(i) Commuters might be forced on to city roads with terrifying consequences for congestion costs.

(ii) Branch line passengers might desert the rail service which would seriously affect Inter-City because the branch lines are a feeder service.

ALTERNATIVE PRICING POLICIES

46. Average cost pricing. Average costs are easier to calculate and by ensuring prices were linked to them, deficits would be less likely to occur. Despite these attractions the problem of allocating costs remains because the fixed cost sector of total costs is very large and to allocate a percentage to any specific output cost seems arbitrary. Fixed costs are now so important that the industries can become involved in a vicious circle; as price rises, sales drop (depending on demand elasticities) and unit costs rise thus tending to push prices up again.

In some industries average costs might be difficult to define in an economically meaningful way, e.g. 45(*b*) showed three elements of British Rail passenger service. Would rail average costs be for all services combined or for the individual sector? If the former case was true, the branch lines would be hugely subsidised by Inter-City. What are the social and economic values of this type of cross-subsidisation?

47. Two-part tariffs. This is a popular system used by the gas, post and electricity organisations. The price is made up of:

(*a*) A fixed charge to make a significant contribution to the fixed costs, i.e. an average cost approach.

(*b*) A running charge which attempts to cover the cost of producing extra units of output, i.e. a marginal cost approach.

48. Summary. The pricing policies of the nationalised industries are infinitely complex, interwoven as they are with the vagueness of the industries' aims and the heavy handed interference of politicians but until the purpose of the nationalised industries has been established pricing policy will not be a rational economic phenomenon.

INVESTMENT POLICIES

49. Importance of nationalised investment. The following tables give some impression of the sheer magnitude of the nationalised industries investment programmes. These high levels which are inevitable given the nature of the industries, produce several problems, which will be investigated in the next paragraphs.

50. Investment levels. Because the industries are capital intensive, the level of investment will always be high but this statement disguises the fact that the actual size will tend to fluctuate wildly as big replacement and expansion programmes are undertaken, e.g. the electrification of the London–Glasgow rail link and the development of North Sea gas. The level of investment will largely depend on long-term demand forecasts and scientific estimates of future technological developments, both of which are areas of calculation which can be easily but disastrously wrong. For example the electrification of the Glasgow–London rail link, from

TABLE XXVIII.   INVESTMENT LEVELS GREAT BRITAIN (£m.)

	Total investment	Public Corporation investment
1966	8,079	1,738
1968	9,182	1,844
1970	9,453	1,679
1972	9,862	1,506
1974	10,124	1,738
1976	9,562	1,889

(*Source: Economic Trends, June 1977.*)

TABLE XXIX.   NATIONAL LOANS FUND NET LENDING (£m.)

	1967/8	1969/70	1971/2	1973/4	1975/6
Post Office	200	240	296.7	313.4	30.1
Coal	76	−11.1	44.2	18.6	97.4
Electricity	379.9	320.3	194	−115.9	81.4
Gas	262.2	158.1	187.9	−38	−76.9
Steel	175	31.2	144.5	−3	130.9
Aviation	17.4	−20.3	43.4	−36.1	35.7
Transport	88.2	16.2	44.5	34.7	122.2

(*Source: Annual Abstract of Statistics 1976.*)

planning to completion, took about fifteen years, so its success depended on guesses at long-term rail demand. Short-term demand forecasting is hazardous but time scales of over five years rely more on faith than statistics.

The time scale can also undermine the technological size of investment plans as designers have to work out possible future production techniques; the electrical generating bodies have persistently suffered from this problem through the breaking down of new equipment and because of the raging scientific and political debate on the role of nuclear fuel.

Fear of government actions has also tended to push the industries into short-term piece meal decisions rather than allow them the luxury of long-term strategies, e.g. Caves suggested that the Post Office had ignored the role of telecommunications (R. E. Caves, *Britain's Economic Prospects*, Allen & Unwin 1968, p. 18.) indeed by the summer of 1977 the Chester Committee suggested that the Post Office's mail and telecommunications operations should be split.

51. Raising the capital. The nationalised industries between them raise well over £1,000 million per annum not all of which can be self-financed. The scale of the borrowing raises several problems.

Each of the industries has a statutory limit to its borrowing powers and each needs Ministerial approval to raise and spend the money but they can borrow working capital without prior approval. Up to 1956 (with the exception of the N.C.B.) they borrowed on long dated fixed interest stock. The rates were low and unrelated to risk so there was a danger of unfinancially controlled investment which would be wasteful of the nation's resources.

In 1958 the industries started to borrow from the Treasury and in 1968 they commenced borrowing from the National Loans Fund (*see* Table XXIX) at more commercial rates of interest. All the managements would like the power to significantly extend their borrowing from the national and international private capital markets. Such a course of action would give them more commercial rigour and free them from the irrationalities of government decision taking. However, although private borrowing has increased the Treasury has misgivings about the policy for three reasons:

(*a*) *Social objectives.* The social obligations of the industries makes it difficult to forecast risk factors and rates of return, thus the private lender lacks the normal commercial mechanism for judging investment opportunity.

(*b*) *Market impact.* The amounts of money involved are so large it would distort the market for conventional private users.

(*c*) *Effects on economy* (**52(*a*)**). The investment programmes have been used as a tool of demand management and the Treasury are reluctant to relax control over the programme. They also fear the balance of payments consequences of too much overseas fund raising.

52. Economic policies and investment levels. Throughout this chapter it has been clear that the nationalised industries have been bedevilled by government interference often based on short-term considerations. Investment policy making has been no exception to the above assertion for all British governments have used nationalised industries' investment plans as a weapon of counter cyclical finance (*see* V, **20**). Plans have been cut or invented, pushed back or brought forward without reference to the needs of the industry concerned (Mr. Heath and Mr. Benn have ordered power stations to be built for the expediency of creating jobs in politically sensitive areas).

This policy has so many pitfalls that governments' continuing adherence to it seems amazing. Some of the difficulties are:

(*a*) *Time lags.* What is the lag after the decision to increase or reduce a programme before the economic effects materialise?

(*b*) *Relation of private and nationalised investment.* What is the effect of sudden changes in public corporation investment on private firms who are the main customers and suppliers?

(*c*) *Inflexibility of investment.* Investment is essentially a long run phenomenon, its results determining industrial patterns in five to ten years time. Does anybody know the results of persistent short-run changes on these patterns?

Finally it must be noted that if governments indulge in arbitrary price fixing policies for the nationalised industries it can create fantasy in the investment process (**39**).

NATIONALISED INDUSTRIES—SUCCESS OR FAILURE

53. Guidelines. To judge the success of any organisation it is necessary to see if its objectives have been achieved. Unfortunately, as has been seen through the whole chapter, the objectives of the nationalised industries have been both many and muddʾed. The ideas below indicate some areas into which government policy has pushed the nationalised boards.

(*a*) A pricing policy to promote the best use of resources and to obtain a commercial rate of return on investment.

(*b*) To promote social welfare by policies of low prices and high wages.

(*c*) To have the industries as engine rooms for research and innovation.

(*d*) To use the industries as a tool for wider economic objectives, e.g. anti-inflationary and regional policies.

Clearly they have been expected to be all things to all men and any critic or supporter can find an objective which has or has not been achieved.

54. Criteria of success. From the vagueness of aims two general principles can be identified.

(*a*) The industries are users of scarce resources therefore they should obtain the efficient utilisation of their resources by effective output, pricing and investment policies which implies the seeking of profit returns commensurate with private industry.

(*b*) If the above was the only criteria, there would be no point in nationalising the industries as they could be organised in the conventional private way. The industries are taken over because they may have to provide non-profitable services for social reasons or to offer external economies, e.g. British Rail running non-paying rail links for the Scottish tourist industry.

Therefore any evaluation must be based on some attempt to balance (*a*) and (*b*) as extremes of either principle would destroy the other.

55. Evaluation. At the simplest level in profit terms (*see* Table XXX) the industries have had good and bad years but so have all private firms. It is also debatable whether profit is a reliable guide anyway.

TABLE XXX.   NATIONALISED INDUSTRIES, PROFITS AND LOSSES, 1966–76 (£m)

	1966	1968	1970	1972	1974	1975	1976
Coal	0.2	35	9	−118	−112	35	46
Electricity	85	55	65	−23	−176	−265	9
Gas	11	−13	14	15	−42	−44	25
Rail	−135	−147	10	−26	−158	−61	na
Steel	—	−21	10	−45	56	89	−246
G.P.O.							
Mail	1	4	−25	−13	−62	−109	148
Telecom.	39	35	61	58	−61	−195	155

(*Source: Economics 1, 27th November, 1976 p. 16.*)

Supporters of the nationalised industries particularly Pryke have made a strong case for the efficiency of the industries using measurements of innovation and labour productivity based on the fruitful pursuit of scale economies, good labour relations and realistic wage bargaining systems. Unfortunately many private firms could establish similar cases. Pryke also ignores diseconomies of scale which could produce the poor service to consumers which has been well chronicled, e.g. disappearing gas board maintenance men and similarly elusive British Rail buffet cars.

The basic gulf between critics and supporters really rests on the ownership criteria. Are governments and civil servants possessed of divine economic and social judgements or are they more reckless spendthrifts?

In reality the ownership question is another example of the long list of Marxist fallacies because the key to success is management efficiency not ownership. Equally evident is the fact that the economic criteria must take priority over the social criteria although the latter must not be ignored. Consequently the nationalised industries ought to pursue a policy of achieving satisfactory profits (using commercial criteria) based on the constraint of clearly designated social obligations.

On this criteria the public corporations in Great Britain based as they are on public utilities have performed well when politicians have kept to the side lines. It is noticeable in the non-utility area, i.e. steel, serious problems, largely due to political ineptitude, have developed.

Obviously nationalisation is not a matter of political theology, of achieving heaven or hell, it is a subject requiring economic evaluation.

PROGRESS TEST 18

1. Describe the significance of the nationalised industries on the British economy. **(2)**

2. Give two arguments in favour of nationalisation. **(4–9)**

3. Give two arguments against nationalisation. **(11–15)**

4. What is meant by the accountability of nationalised industries? **(29)**

5. Explain the effect of nationalised industries pricing policy on private industry. **(36(a))**

6. Outline the role of prices for nationalised industries. **(38)**

7. Define marginal social costs. **(43)**

8. Explain a two-part tariff. **(47)**

9. Why is the Treasury suspicious of private capital raising by nationalised industries? **(51)**

10. Suggest criteria for measuring the success of nationalised industries. **(54)**

CHAPTER XIX

Government and the Regional Economic Problem

NATURE OF THE PROBLEM

1. Introduction. Throughout history differing regions within countries have had varying levels of prosperity as the free play of economic forces has produced the rise and fall of industries. In one period a region might have full employment and relatively high income levels, within a generation or two the region has begun to economically decay and its peoples' living standards have fallen below the national average. Alternatively a region can initially be very poor then perhaps the discovery of a valuable resource can bring prosperity to the area.

Prior to the twentieth century, governments would view these changes as natural and unalterable, they would only interfere if they thought the situation might produce political upheaval. Even then the intervention would not try to reverse economic forces but merely give help to those suffering from change. England has a long history of this assistance through the Poor Laws.

However, since the 1930s when the unemployment figures were so appalling (*see* Table XXXIII) and for the reasons outlined in 3–7 British governments have given a high priority to the economic and social problems of the regions.

This chapter sketches in the policies and discusses their successes and failures. Regional problems are not confined to Britain and the views of the European Economic Community on their regional troubles are analysed at the end of the chapter.

2. Characteristics of poorer regions. The poorer regions will exhibit some or all of the following features.

(*a*) The region relies for its employment on a few traditional industries, the demand for whose products is in decline (probably permanently). These areas are suffering from structural unemployment.

(b) The region's industries may also have a relative cost disadvantage because of their distance from major markets.

(c) Because of the above factors, unemployment will be much higher than the national average.

(d) Levels of income will be relatively low although the effects may be modified by the transfer of money through government welfare schemes.

(e) Because of (c) the levels of demand in the region will be low thus adversely affecting the service industries whose demand is bound to be localised.

(f) Educational attainment will be lower as evidence suggests that in the poorer regions fewer children stay at school after the statutory leaving age. This circumstance will affect the skill levels of the local labour market.

(g) Many poorer areas suffer from a net migration of population. Superficially this ought to help the unemployment figures but unfortunately younger people tend to leave thus reducing the dynamism of the locality. It also leaves a high proportion of older people who are difficult to retrain if they are structurally unemployed.

(h) The "infrastructure" of the regions is poor, i.e. the quality of housing, schools, hospitals, communications and amenities are below a desirable standard.

(i) All these factors are likely to induce in the regions low productivity (*N.I.E.R. Review*, November 1968) and low returns on investment (*Guardian*, 18th November 1969, p. 23) which makes it even more difficult to ease their economic difficulties.

Should a high proportion of these factors prevail in a region the quality of economic and social life of its people will be below an acceptable level prevailing in the rest of the country.

REASONS FOR GOVERNMENT CONCERN WITH THE PROBLEM

3. Waste of resources. Labour is a productive resource which is wasted if it is under-utilised. This argument is open to debate for it can be argued that ever accelerating technology is undermining the conventional attitudes and structures of employment. (J. D. S. Appleton, *Labour Economics*. Macdonald & Evans (*see* XI,30).)

4. Social problems. The poorer regions are likely to have a higher proportion of the long-term unemployed. These people and their families, despite the Welfare State, suffer great social, economic and psychological hardship and they become entangled in a poverty trap from which it is very difficult to escape.

5. Conflicting economic policies. A government's economic policy particularly in its demand management is trying to influence the economic conditions of the whole country. Therefore the need of separate policies for different regions can run counter to the basic macroeconomic policy objectives, e.g. a country with a high rate of inflation may cut demand, tighten credit and introduce an incomes policy. All measures which will worsen conditions in the poorer regions, whereas policies to help the regions are likely to increase demand. "A more even distribution of economic prosperity would counteract the inflationary effects of regional concentrations of excess demand, thus facilitating the management of the economy." (E. Roll, *Public Administration.* Spring 1966.)

6. Congestion costs. If people move out of the declining areas to more prosperous regions they will create a growing pressure on the demand for houses, transport and social services in their new environment, thus raising the costs of living and creating intolerable social pressures. Theoretically, the congestion costs could reach a level which would tempt people and firms out of the congested areas back to the declining regions. Fears of overcrowding in major conurbations was a dominant factor in the New Town Policy (15) pursued by governments over the last thirty years.

7. Summary. Regional backwardness presents so many economic and social problems that governments have felt bound to intervene with the free play of market forces. During the 1970s a new strand of thought developed which argued that the problems were created by over-centralised decision taking and consequently more political power ought to be devolved to the regions. This argument lies behind the call for self-determination or devolution which takes the regional problem into a far larger dimension. The rest of the chapter looks at the conventional problems but the new issue is briefly mentioned in 34.

THE BASIS OF GOVERNMENT REACTION

8. Introduction. Basic economic theory offers little help to governments which are trying to ease the problems of regional imbalance. Traditional welfare theory deals with individuals, whereas regional policy is working in arbitrarily defined geographical areas with a variety of economic and social structures.

Theoretical concepts also presuppose maximising objectives, e.g. a consumer maximises satisfaction, a firm maximises profit, but what is being maximised in regional policy? Is it the welfare of the people living there now or the welfare of some future population? Is the government trying to maximise the income *per capita* of the region? If so does it devise policies to raise income for a constant population or should it try to move the poorer sections of the population out of the region? Governments, being pragmatists, seem to have the simple measurable objective of trying to reduce the level of unemployment and the more subjective aim of improving living standards within the less prosperous regions.

In general terms governments have had two broad policy options, each with attendant difficulties, either move industry into the region or move the people out.

9. Moving workers out of an area. The government through various financial aid schemes tries to subsidise workers who are prepared to find work outside the poorer regions. However, the economic and social costs are very high, e.g. the cost of new housing, leaving family and friends and disruption of children's education. The size of these costs plus the difficulties outlined below have disencouraged governments from making really committed efforts to encourage labour mobility. Mobility costs are really the costs of human investment and finance needs to be raised to cover the cost. For capital investment an economy has capital markets but lending on human investment is risky for conventional financial institutions because there is no collateral. To bridge this gap Hartley (K. Hartley, *Problems of Economic Policy*. Allen & Unwin 1977, p. 183) suggests the establishment of a state manpower bank to finance training and mobility.

10. Difficulties of mobility policy.

(a) The people with the incentive to move are probably the skilled workers and to denude an area of its skilled manpower further damages its industrial credibility.

(b) If sufficient numbers move to seriously reduce unemployment levels, then there will be a further drop in demand levels in the region and it will suffer from a reverse multiplier effect which could keep up the level of unemployment.

(c) The policy if successful could create congestion costs else-where (6).

(d) A significant migration of people would lead to a serious under utilisation of the social services already provided in the regions.

11. Bringing industry into regions. The fundamental government policy has been to persuade or bribe firms to open new plants in the less prosperous areas by the use of capital cost reducing or labour cost reducing policies, e.g. investment grants or the Regional Employment Premium (17(b)). As with the labour mobility policy, questions can be raised about the wisdom of such inducements to companies.

12. Difficulties of moving industry.

(a) Are firms persuaded to locate in areas in which they are not maximising their efficiency according to location theory (21). If so, is there a misallocation of resources?

(b) Is there a temptation for companies to move to a poorer region to obtain all the incentive money and then pull out? Critics of Courtaulds suggested the company did this with its plant in Skelmersdale.

(c) By offering companies substantial assistance to defray capital costs does the government encourage the establishment of capital intensive companies with a consequent low demand for labour.

(d) There is evidence to suggest that the regional inducements are most profitable to (i) firms in warehousing and distribution which need little labour; (ii) companies with simple assembly line units which use largely female labour. Neither of these types will effectively help to reduce male unemployment.

(e) Does anybody know the economic effects on the competi-tive cost structure of companies which establish plants in areas to which they would not have gone by free choice? Lord Stokes, when Managing Director of British Leyland, argued that the location of a lorry plant in Scotland in the late 1960s added an extra £58 to the cost of a lorry. How do you evaluate the impact of this additional cost in world markets against the provision of jobs in Scotland?

BRITISH REGIONAL LEGISLATION

13. Introduction. R. Turner ("Government Policy on Location". *Economics*, Summer 1966) suggested that British regional legislation has had three common characteristics:

(*a*) It defines geographical areas in which companies and local authorities qualify for government assistance.

(*b*) It defines the range of industries qualifying for aid.

(*c*) It sets out the available financial benefits.

In principle most of the legislative Acts are similar varying only in detail, e.g. altering the regional boundaries, defining new areas or changing the type of incentive aid. This section outlines the major legislation but only discusses significant conceptual changes.

14. Pre-1945.

(*a*) *1934 Special Areas Act.* Four particularly depressed areas, West Cumberland, the North-East Coast, South Wales and Central Scotland were designated special areas and industry therein was made eligible for Government assistance. However, the Act had no real effect as the financial aid was slight and most industries were so depressed they had no incentive to develop anywhere.

(*b*) *1937–40 Barlow Commission.* This body was asked to study the twin problems of backward areas and congested conurbations. They recommended the establishment of a central body to:

(*i*) Re-develop the congested urban areas.

(*ii*) To disperse industry from those areas.

(*iii*) To promote a reasonable balance of industrial development throughout Great Britain.

The outbreak of war sank these recommendations and no post-war government was prepared to formulate such a strong centralised policy although some of Barlow's thinking was found in the 1945 legislation.

15. 1945–59.

(*a*) *1945 The Distribution of Industry Act.* This Act slightly enlarged the 1934 Special Areas, e.g. the inclusion of parts of North Wales and South Lancashire. It rechristened them "development areas" and gave the Board of Trade powers to build new factories for leasing on trading estates. There was also aid towards the capital cost of moving.

(*b*) *1946 New Towns Act. 1947 Town & Country Planning Act.*
These two Acts are not technically involved with regional economic problems but they represented a new idea which argued that
the location of people and industry together with physical planning are all elements in the search for that elusive concept, the
improvement of the quality of life. The 1947 Act introduced a
vital new weapon, Industrial Development Certificates (I.D.C.s).
They are needed to support applications for planning permission
for industrial development above a certain size, outside the development areas. In these non-development areas planning permission without an I.D.C. is invalid, although the actual granting
of a planning application lies in the hands of the Local Authority.
The Department of Industry is now responsible for issuing
I.D.C.s. The I.D.C. represents a negative control to help the
regions; negative in the sense that a company refused an I.D.C.
for building in the South-East may still not decide to build in a
development area.

16. 1960–66.

(*a*) *1960 Local Employment Act.* Previous legislation was re-
pealed and the old areas were replaced by "development districts" which were localities with unemployment rates of $4\frac{1}{2}$ per
cent and above (or a district where that figure might be achieved
in the near future). The new districts were smaller than the areas
thus fewer people were in localities receiving aid. Capital was
provided for new buildings and local authorities were given considerable powers and finance to improve their infrastructure
(2(*h*)).

(*b*) *1963 Local Employment Act.* Aid was extended to places
within commuting distance of the development districts and to
overspill development of any city within a district, even if the
overspill community was outside the district. The quantity of
capital aid for buildings was increased and for the first time
grants were given for the installation of machinery. The Government also promised to use its purchasing requirements to help
firms in the development districts.

(*c*) *1964 Regional Planning.* The advent of a Labour government brought a renewed interest in the concept of planning.
George Brown believed the country's geographical economic in-
equalities had to be solved on a regional level. By magic the
country acquired eight regions (Scotland, Northern, North-
West, Yorkshire and Humberside, East Midlands, West Mid-

lands, Wales and South-West) and each region was given the present of a

(*i*) Regional Planning Board. This was a committee of top civil servants from all government departments in the region and its task was to co-ordinate government activity in the regions. The boards were also responsible for producing plans to promote growth in their region.

(*ii*) Regional Economic Planning Council. The Councils consisted of twenty-five part-time members, men and women of distinction in their locality. Their functions were to assist with the drawing up and implementation of the regional plan and to evaluate the effects of national economic policy on their region. The Chairman, in theory, had direct access to the corridors of power in Whitehall but at least one Chairman resigned because he felt powerless. However the government's thinking soon returned to more conventional channels, although the Regional Planning Councils and Boards have never been officially killed. Indeed in the late 1970s they still exist in some peculiar limbo for they make no serious contribution to regional problems although occasionally one of them produces a plan which is soon lost in the monsoon of plans which currently flood the country (**22**).

(*d*) *1966 Industrial Development Act*. The Development Districts of 1960 were widened into Development Areas namely:

(*i*) The whole of Scotland except for an area around Edinburgh.

(*ii*) The whole of the northern region plus the Furness Peninsula.

(*iii*) An area in the north-west based on Merseyside.

(*iv*) Most of Wales.

(*v*) An area in the extreme south-west.

Capital aid was again increased but instead of giving money through tax allowances the aid came in direct grants.

17. 1967–1971.

(*a*) *1967 Special Areas*. These were small parts (based on Department of Employment offices) of Development Areas suffering from acute unemployment e.g. Workington and Ystalyfera and they qualified for more extensive aid. By 1971 when new areas were so classified, 8.5 per cent of Britain's insured population were living in Special Development Areas.

(*b*) *1967 Regional Employment Premium*. This was a system

springing from the now defunct Selective Employment Tax whereby employers in the Development Areas received a subsidy on the labour they employed. At first the measure was severely criticised for linking a subsidy not only to newly created jobs but also to existing ones and the Conservative administration of 1970 promised to abolish it in 1974. However, research showed R.E.P. was helpful to employment and it has been maintained.

(c) *1969 Hunt Report. Intermediate (Grey) Areas.* The Hunt Commission investigated those areas which claimed to suffer from economic depression but did not receive aid because their unemployment rates were insufficiently high. Examples of such places were North-East Lancashire, South Yorkshire, North-East Derbyshire and Plymouth. The common economic and social characteristics of Intermediate Areas were:

  (*i*) Falling or slow growing employment opportunities.
  (*ii*) Slow growth of personal incomes.
  (*iii*) A net emigration of population.
  (*iv*) Decaying environmental factors.
  (*v*) Poor communications.

Hunt's report acknowledged the problem and offered some solutions which were largely smaller amounts of aid than were going to the Development Areas. The Government accepted the report in principle, reduced the suggested levels of aid and narrowed the number of areas qualifying for intermediate status. The whole concept of Intermediate Areas was enshrined in the 1970 Employment Act.

(d) *1970 Conservative Government.* The new government of Mr. Heath was committed to the reapplication of market force ideas. Although they had no worked-out regional policy, in 1971 they replaced investment grants with allowances and indicated they wanted a switch of resources from direct industrial aid to infra-structure programmes. Suddenly in 1972 a new philosophy emerged in dealing with the regional policy.

18. 1972 onwards.

(a) 1972 *White Paper on Industrial and Regional Development* (*Cmnd.* 4942). The document made two points which had been obvious to some economists for a number of years:

(*i*) "The economic performance of the United Kingdom has been falling behind other major industrialised countries for a long time. We must devote a major effort to improving our industrial base."

(*ii*) "A faster rate of national economic growth is a necessary prerequisite for effective regional effort."

In other words, the illness of the regions cannot be treated independently of the national economic body and that body itself is becoming very unhealthy because of its industrial weaknesses.

(*b*) 1972 *Industry Act*. This Act gave large scale incentives for investment anywhere in the country. This policy would immediately reduce the attractiveness for industry of moving to the Development Areas so extra cash grants were given to establish buildings and machinery in the poorer areas. There was also assistance for projects which created or maintained employment. The Act also sanctioned more assistance for manpower schemes, e.g. retraining and mobility plus communication improvements. The number of Intermediate Areas was also increased. In practice the Act gave governments power to aid any firm or industry in any place for any reason so the Development Areas must have suffered relatively.

(*c*) 1972 *new bureaucracies*. All governments have the desire to create new efficient bureaucracies and the Conservatives were no exception. They established:

(*i*) A Minister for Industrial Development. He was responsible for all industrial development. The post was considered very important and was given to a political high flyer, Mr. Chataway, who eventually flew away from politics.

(*ii*) Industrial Development Board. Its membership was largely drawn from industry and financial services and its duties were to advise the Minister.

(*iii*) Industrial Development Executive. Manned by industrialists and staffed by the Department of Trade and Industry, the Executive had to implement the new policies and in particular to simplify the system for getting the money to industry. The Executive was housed in the regions, e.g. the fun spots of Bootle and Billington, again to underline the government's determination.

(*d*) 1974 *Labour Government*. Since 1974 the Labour Administrations have found that the fears of the 1972 White Paper have really materialised. Galloping inflation and rocketing unemployment have made specific regional problems seem meaningless. Particularly since the Eltis and Bacon campaign (*see* XIV, **12**) the government have concentrated on the basic national industrial structure and in the development of short-term palliatives, e.g. Temporary Employment Subsidy and Job Creation Schemes to attack unemployment. In 1975 the Labour Government produced their own Industry Act which centred on the setting up of the National Enterprise Board (*see* XIV, 11(*b*)). As with the 1972 Act, its prime intention is to assist all British industry but it might try to give some sort of preference to the regions. Politicians still pay lip service to the old regional concepts but the real fight is against national economic disaster.

19. Results.

(*a*) To accurately quantify the results of regional policy is very difficult and even if accuracy was possible the nature of the variables behind the statistics would be open to considerable controversy. Below are some figures which serve as a rough guide to assessing British regional policy.

(*b*) *Policies a success.* The main criteria of success is the employment situation. Table XXXIII clearly shows that compared to pre-1939 the regional discrepancies in unemployment rates have been significantly reduced and all researchers show that the policies have created or saved jobs. G. Manners ("Reinterpret-

TABLE XXXI. BASIC AID TO THE REGIONS (£m.)

	1963/4	*1966/7*	*1968/9*	*1973/4*	*1976/7**
Local Employment Acts	17	44	50	54.6	5
Regional Employment Premium	—	—	100	95.7	NA
Regional Account	—	25	85	260	335

(*Source: D. E. A. Progress Report, August 1969, Guardian, 17th January 1974, p. 15.*)

* Estimated figures

TABLE XXXII. ESTIMATED JOBS CREATED 1960–71

	Annual Av. p.a.	*Total 1960–71*
I.D.C. Policy	8,300	100,000
R.E.P. Policy	3,500–5,250	14,000–21,000
Investment Incentives	5,800	47,000
Special Development Areas	0–2,500	0–10,000

(*Source: B. Moore & J. Rhodes, Economica, February 1976.*)

TABLE XXXIII.   REGIONAL UNEMPLOYMENT RATES %

	1929	1932	1936	1959	1969	Dec. 1972	April 1977
London & South-East	4.5	13.0	6.2	1.3	1.6	1.8	4.4
South-West	6.8	15.8	7.7	2.1	2.7	3.2	6.8
Midlands	9.1	21.5	9.0	1.6	2.0	2.7	5.2
Northern	12.6	29.8	18.1	3.3	2.2	4.1	7.9
North-West	12.6	25.4	16.6	2.8	2.5	4.3	7.0
Scotland	11.0	26.8	17.1	4.4	3.7	5.8	7.8
Wales	18.2	37.4	30.4	3.8	4.1	4.7	7.7
Great Britain	9.6	22.4	12.8	2.2	2.4	3.3	5.8

(*Souce: Regional Policy for Ever, I.E.A. Readings II, p. 79, Department of Employment Gazette.*)

TABLE XXXIV.   CHANGES IN STRUCTURE OF WORKFORCE (000s)

	Wales		Scotland	
	1931	1970	1931	1970
Mining & Quarrying	210	54	146	41
Manufacturing	141	348	736	740
Construction	30	65	102	173
Distributive Trades	129	112	363	320
Professional & Scientific Services	27	124	78	285

(*Source: Regional Policy for Ever, I.E.A. Readings 11, p. 81.*)

ing the Regional Problem", *Three Banks Review*, September 1976), a critic of the policies, estimates that approximately 300,000 jobs were created in the period 1960–74. Also a reasonable case can be made to suggest that the regions now have a broader industrial base (*see* Table XXXIV) and their fortunes are no longer tied to the fates of one or two industries. Road and rail communications, particularly through Inter-City, and the motorway network have opened up many areas whilst educational facilities have also increased. So infrastructures have made forward progress.

    (*c*) *Policies a failure.* Three arguments tend to be used:

        (*i*) The geographical areas now receiving aid have increased frighteningly and about 45 per cent of the population now live in these areas. Outsiders have noticed this trend for in E.E.C. eyes (35) Britain, as a European regional problem, ranks with Italy and Ireland. Critics reasonably speculate why forty years of regional policies have apparently worsened the situation.

(*ii*) Nobody can deny the creation and saving of jobs (Table XXXII) but at what cost? Estimating the cost of each created job is a nightmare; so many schemes pump money into the regions whilst one has to substract from costs, savings on social security payments. Manners thinks in the 1970s about £600 million per annum has gone into the regions whilst an estimate in the late 1960s suggested each job created cost the Exchequer about £900–1,500. More recent evidence submitted by Moore and Rhodes to the House of Commons Committee on Expenditure (*Guardian*, 17th January 1974, p. 15) suggests the cost of each job is £6,000 (excluding extra tax revenue to the Government). Is this good or bad? Is the social benefit of reducing unemployment greater than any private economic cost?

(*iii*) Have regional policies contributed to the general economic malaise? Certainly they have created a considerable charge on government spending and at worst they might have damaged industrial efficiency by tempting companies to make irrational location decisions.

POSSIBLE CRITICISMS OF THE POLICY

20. Introduction. A divergence of opinion on the success of regional policy is shown in 19(*b*) and (*c*). Ultimately we are faced with the usual economic dilemma of not knowing what an alternative policy would have achieved. Nevertheless it is possible to discuss aspects of regional policy in which government thinking has been muddled.

21. Market forces and regionalism. Market forces are the main cause of structural employment and they determine the long run pattern of industrial location. Should governments be more cognisant of location decision taking if it wishes to influence these decisions? In fairness to governments it is argued that company thought in this field is by no means rational. It can be argued that many industries are footloose, i.e. the siting of their plants, within reason, is of no importance to their cost structures.

Locational theory teaches that companies must balance factors of distance (raw materials and markets) with factors of availability (labour and power) then economies and diseconomies of scale and concentration are introduced into the calculations. A location decision should resemble an investment appraisal project with the firm evaluating alternative site choices on a non-social cost basis.

However, Townroe has shown (P.M. Townroe, "How Managers Pick Plants", *Management Today*, October 1970) that companies have restricted alternatives because speed and secrecy of decision taking are important variables. The few sites are not seriously costed because companies have no simple location decision routines and managerial subjective views on their own quality of life intrude into the decisions.

Locational decisions end as satisfactory rather than best decisions with an inherent desire to build near existing plant. Companies giving evidence to the House of Commons Expenditure Committee on Regional Development in 1973–4 said regional incentives had a low priority in their location decisions. Dunlop summarised the general feeling by saying the primary consideration remained the validity of the commercial decision and Thorns argued that any financial gain was purely short term.

Governments must seek more direct co-operation with companies to understand their location motives. A quizzical mind might wonder why governments spend so much on regional aid when the main beneficiaries seemingly ignore the value of the incentives; would a tighter I.D.C. policy be cheaper yet more effective?

22. Role of the town planner. Within the last twenty-five years, governments have allowed the regional economic problems to become entangled with the town planner. Unfortunately, town planning is a pseudo-scientific discipline ravaged by the illness of Parkinson's Law and the onset of sociologists. Higher education institutions have churned out increasing numbers of planners all with the urge to plan our environment without any obvious understanding of man's social and economic needs. Local government re-organisation and new town expansion have been the powerful laxative enabling planners to run through our regions. (Warrington in Cheshire for example, has the benefit of five different groups of planners working on its behalf.)

Governments might have noted Marx's comments on the inherent power and importance of the economic structure of our lives. Hopefully light is dawning and even planners are talking of the role of industry and commerce in the fight to renew the nation's decaying town centres.

23. Policy changes. Industrialists have criticised governments for frequently changing the details of their policies. Two examples are given:

(*a*) *Capital grants or allowances.* Allowances are linked to company taxation and companies making high profits will receive more aid, however, the finance is paid after the time lags of the tax system and low profit companies may run into liquidity problems. (Rolls Royce in 1971.) Grants are direct payments to companies moving to development areas thus there is a specific link between moving and the aid but no link between the company's efficiency and the finance. Sudden switching, as often occurs, between grants and allowances undermines the industrialist's confidence, in the investment incentive programme.

(*b*) *Growth points and areas.* Conservatives have tended to concentrate aid into small geographical areas, i.e. growth points, in order to centralise the industrial growth and achieve external economies of scale, e.g. housing, education and communications. The created benefits then ripple out to larger areas. Labour governments have doubted the validity of the ripple theory and argued the growth point thesis would leave large areas of under-utilised resources.

24. Blanket solutions. Governments have tended to treat all development areas as homogeneous units with identical causes of under-development thus requiring identical solutions. This is an over-simplification, Scotland has suffered a vast emigration, Wales has pit closures and declining hill farming; none of these problems are inherent in the Merseyside situation. More varied aid schemes ought to be devised and areas could utilise the most relevant help available.

25. Over use of capital incentives. Most of the major incentive schemes are geared to reducing capital costs with the obvious consequence that they attract capital intensive firms to the regions (*N.I.E.R. Review*, November 1968) where the main identified problem is unemployment. Of course the thought of creating labour intensive industries in the 1970s may well be economic nonsense given the accelerating growth of technology and high labour costs.

26. The nature of unemployment. Generalised treatment of regional problems has already been criticised (**24**). Typical of this approach is the use, mainly, of a single criterion, unemployment, to judge the regional problem. Total figures of the unemployed are misleading; in terms of finding relevant industries for an area there is a need to identify the types of worker unemployed. Liverpool, for example, has an excessive supply of unskilled and semi-skilled workers, whereas many of the new companies which have come to Merseyside have had to import skilled workers to man their plant.

There is also a need to investigate the relationship between population changes and rates of unemployment. Moore and Rhodes ("Effects of British Regional Policy", *Economic Journal*, March 1973) have speculated whether regional policy has actually increased the supply of labour in the regions because the late 1960s saw a considerable reduction in the outward migration of population, yet we have no knowledge how this affected employment levels. Manpower planning is in its infancy but it could be useful in a regional analysis.

27. Basic changes in society. G. Manners ("Reinterpreting The Regional Problem", *Three Banks Review*, September 1976) argues that governments in viewing the regional problem have ignored some fundamental changes in the thinking and structure of society.

(*a*) *Economic environment.* Nobody now believes the old levels of full employment (in the 1950s 1.3 per cent) are attainable. The use of Keynesian demand management to control unemployment is under considerable attack (*see* IV), indeed the whole question of unemployment is a controversial one. Therefore views on the nature and treatment of unemployment must be established at national level before a meaningful regional policy is possible. A growing proportion of our industry is now owned by multinational organisations (*see* XVII) and their location decisions enter totally new areas. No longer is the choice, Essex or Wales, it is Nigeria or Belgium or Ireland or the United Kingdom. Location questions have become a global problem and regional policies may have to move in the same direction.

(*b*) *Employment patterns.* There has been a basic loss of manufacturing jobs in the U.K. over the last decade. V. H. Woodward (*Occupational Trends in Great Britain 1961–81*. Cambridge University Press, 1975) calculates that manufacturing will lose

530,000 jobs in the period 1971–81. The dominant areas of employment are becoming the service industries and public administration, i.e. a growth in white collar jobs. In terms of past cultural and educational traditions (2(*f*)) the regions are not equipped to deal with this phenomenon and it's only since the early 1970s that governments have tried to push new office jobs to the regions. Ideally governments should persuade companies to site head offices in the regions thus bringing higher income jobs and socially dynamic leadership to where it is most needed.

(*c*) *Socio/geographical changes.* The mid 1970s have witnessed a significant fall in rates of population growth, we may be entering a period of falling population. There are also shifts in population migration, e.g. out of the West Midlands. These two facts could undermine our long-established divisions of poor and rich areas and also invalidate many of the long-term plans about resource ultilisation, particularly land. For example, the inner boroughs of London are desperately poor and short of work whereas the north-east of Scotland is dripping with oil money, yet it is the latter area which receives regional aid. Politicians are recognising this switch of prosperity (market forces working again) and the cry is to regenerate life in the inner cities, a life extinguished by governments and planners who failed to note the simple economic fact that small firms provide work and work helps community life.

28. Lack of growth. The disappointing performance of the British economy has been the fundamental reason for the lack of work in the regions. If a company cannot sell its products it will not create new work anywhere. Since 1945 the constraints of inflation and the balance of payments have caused governments to reduce the level of aggregate demand, on average, two years out of five. The erratic nature of post-war policies and governments' desire to improve the quality of life by printing money have led to total industrial uncertainty and low levels of investment.

The stupidity of the political habit of raising industrial costs, attacking profits, lowering demand and then bribing companies to open new plant in far-away places has been exposed.

29. Lack of knowledge. Regional policy has been with us for thirty years, acres of words have been written, endless speeches made, yet do we really understand the underlying economic foundations of the regional problem (8)? Two quotes will suffice:

"There must be few areas of government expenditure in which so much is spent but so little known about the success of the policy." (*Public Money and Private Sector*, July 1972. House of Commons Paper 347.)

"Regional policy has been empiricism run mad, a game of hit and miss, played with more enthusiasm than success. There has been no proper evaluation of the costs and benefits of policies pursued." (*House of Commons Expenditure Committee Regional Development Incentives Report*. H.M.S.O. 1974.)

ALTERNATIVE IDEAS

30. Introduction. It has been argued that the problem of the regions is now becoming merged with national difficulties and the whole background thought of the regions is slowly changing. However, should the need for a distinctive policy re-emerge the following ideas may prove more useful than simply rehashing the ideas of the previous era.

31. Types of aid. There has been little change in the broad type of aid given; changes have come in the myriad of detail and administration, thus making the pursuit of assistance a time-wasting paperchase for industrialists. (Perhaps jobs have been created via the Civil Service.)

Would it be possible to devise a system where the company received a lump sum for each job created assuming the job lasted for a guaranteed period of time. (If it did not, money could be refunded.) The scheme links aid directly with jobs and cuts down the administration.

32. Mobility. There is a theoretical case for moving workers but policies have only dallied with the problem. The real root of the mobility problem is the housing situation, particularly if a person moves from a poorer to a more prosperous area. The system of allocating local authority housing subsidies to buildings and not people, plus the series of Rent Control Acts, has meant that any tenant of a private or public rented house is acting in an economically irrational way if he moves unless his new wage differential is enormous. Geographical job mobility depends on housing mobility. This fact is recognised by industry which often subsidises the job movement of its employees.

33. Adjusting labour costs. According to market force theory, wage levels in areas where there is an excess of labour ought to be relatively lower but because of national wage bargaining the regions do not develop a labour price differential. However, the government might do this in two administratively difficult ways:

(a) *Differential National Insurance contributions.* Companies in the development regions would pay lower N.I. contributions thus reducing their labour costs.

(b) *Pay roll tax.* A pay roll tax would be levied on all employees outside the development areas. Politically this would only be feasible if there were high levels of employment in the non-assisted areas.

34. Regionalism. The definition of British regions was done as an economic planning exercise (15(c)) but can it be argued that if the concept was transmitted into political terms, power and decision taking could be decentralised to the regions, thus improving their economic performance. The logical extension of the argument is devolution, when a whole country, e.g. Scotland or Wales, becomes self-governing. To the economist two big questions remain unanswered:

(a) Why should the decentralising of economic decisions make the decisions better ones. Is it valid to suggest that a local allocation of resources automatically creates greater welfare? Are the decisions of town halls noticably better than the decisions of Whitehall?

(b) Is the British economy big or strong enough to be split into small parts; regional economic policies and results so far suggest the answer is "no". Cynics might argue the growth of Scottish Nationalism is simply a function of the discovery of natural resources off the cost of Scotland and the prosperity of Scotland will develop from old-fashioned economics not from political musical chairs.

EUROPEAN ECONOMIC COMMUNITY AND REGIONAL PROBLEMS

35. Introduction. The problems of uneven levels of prosperity is by no means confined to Britain and from the beginning the E.E.C. has recognised the Community would face the problem of a maldistribution of affluence across a wide geographical area.

(In 1970 Hamburg's Gross Domestic Product *per capita* was five times higher than west Ireland and southern Italy, by 1975 the ratio was six.) The Preamble to the Treaty of Rome (1958) refers to "Reducing the differences existing between the various regions and mitigating the backwardness of the less favoured." Whilst Article 92 states, "Aids intended to promote the economic development of regions where the standard of living is abnormally low or where there exists serious under-employment are compatible with a Common Market."

This section looks at the broad pattern of E.E.C. thinking and policy on the regional problem.

36. Basic thinking. A prime fear of the E.E.C. is that industry, trade and prosperity will be concentrated in the central core of the Community (in British terms the Midlands and south-east England), whilst the peripheral areas, e.g. Scotland and northern England, north and south-west France and southern Italy will decline. To test this theory is difficult because these areas would be the recipients of national aid with or without the E.E.C.

The 1960s saw the original E.E.C. members enjoying growth and prosperity on an unprecedented scale and regional worries faded from the scene. However the 1970s have brought a distinct change of emphasis attributable to two new factors.

First, the slowing down of economic growth as the western world fought inflation. Secondly, the admittance to the E.E.C. of weaker countries, e.g. United Kingdom and Ireland and the application for membership of even weaker countries, e.g. Spain and Portugal. Suddenly regional problems were back on the E.E.C. agenda.

Several points developed as the centres of interest.

(*a*) To what extent would competing national regional policies produce distortions in the total E.E.C. economic objectives?

(*b*) Would the desire for a common fiscal and monetary policy worsen the regional imbalances?

(*c*) What policies and institutions could be developed to help the problem?

In fact two main strands can be discerned in the E.E.C.'s regional policy.

37. Policy. The commitment to regional policy can be seen in this statement. "The underlying gap between richer and poorer regions remains as intractable as ever. The market economy will not automatically resolve the problem even when growth revives. Without a strong regional and structural policy there can be no real progress towards greater economic integration or cohesion, the lack of which is a limitary factor in the Community's international role and influence." (1st Report European Regional Fund 1975, p. 5.)

The basis of the policy is a fund chanelling agency and some co-ordination of national policies.

(a) *European Regional Fund.* The Fund developed out of the 1972 Paris Summit meeting and a report prepared by Commissioner George Thompson (U.K.) in 1973. The fund was officially established in March 1975 and the first year's budget was 300 units of account. (Units of account are the E.E.C. standard measure and are turned into national currencies by an agreed rate of exchange. In June 1977, £1 = 2.4 U.A.) To be eligible for Fund assistance investments must fall in the framework of regional development programmes prepared by member states and must be receiving national aid. Not all applications for aid are granted. (In 1975, applications were 1,521, successes 1,183.) Britain has greatly benefited from the fund receiving, in 1976, 28 per cent of the allocated funds, which put her on a par with Italy and Ireland. In terms of projects the figures are even more staggering.

TABLE XXXV. PROJECTS APPROVED BY EUROPEAN REGIONAL FUND, 1975

Belgium	36
Denmark	34
Germany	64
France	232
Ireland	105
Italy	174
Luxembourg	1
Netherlands	3
United Kingdom	534
Total	1183

The main criteria for receiving aid is regional unemployment rates and the Fund tries to make not only quantitative but also qualitative decisions.

(b) *Co-ordination policies*. The Commissions are working in several areas.

(i) National aid should be transparent, i.e. capable of being expressed as a percentage of the cost of investment. They wish to avoid disguised subsidies which simply allow individual firms to enjoy competitive price advantages in the market. Some doubts have been expressed about Regional Employment Premiums (**16**(b)) on this score.

(ii) Where possible to have general policies, e.g. a common type of I.D.C. (**15**) policy to stop multinationals playing off one state against another (XVII).

(iii) To evaluate the impact of other E.E.C. policies in the regions. For example, the policy allowing in cheap Third World textile imports decimated parts of the Northern Ireland textile industry.

(iv) To develop methods of ensuring that Regional Fund investments are cost effective to avoid endless sums of money going down bottomless wells.

38. Other regional aid. Member states with regional problems may draw help from two other sources.

(a) *European Investment Bank*. The Bank was created by the Treaty of Rome, its basic function is to contribute to the balanced development of the Common Market. It grants long term loans and gives its guarantees to public and private institutions to finance projects which favour the less advanced regions or which serve the interests of the Community as a whole, e.g. a cross boundary motorway or generating scheme. Its capital comes from its members and it raises funds from international capital markets therefore its lending has to be commercially orientated although the bank itself is non-profit making. Generally the bank's loans go into infra structure programmes (**2**(h)). As with the Regional Fund, Britain is an important customer of the Bank. In 1975 the Bank made sixty-four loans totalling 917.5 million units of account. Italy took 39.1 per cent and Great Britain 36.5 per cent of the total, this represented a doubling of our share as compared to 1974. Some of the 1975 British projects were:

(i) Hartlepool nuclear power station.
(ii) New coal wagons for British Railways.
(iii) Petroleum harbour in Scotland.

    (*iv*) Modernising telecommunications in Wales.

    (*v*) Whisky bottling in Glasgow.

    (*b*) *European Social Fund.* From the start of the E.E.C. it was realised that a common market and economic growth would require change with consequent social problems. There have been a series of studies of groups who are losing out, e.g. young workers and migrant workers. The fund was set up to finance schemes to help people meet the change and most of the money goes to retraining schemes. Retraining is clearly a vital element in regional schemes and the Social Fund has been a useful addition to regional aid. It must be noted, however, that in the structure of the E.E.C., regional and social policies are distinct entities.

39. Conclusion. The E.E.C. is well aware of the regional problems in its midst but whether the Community can succeed where member governments have struggled is open to doubt.

PROGRESS TEST 19

    1. Describe the characteristics of the poorer regions of the advanced nations. **(2)**

    2. Explain congestion costs. **(6)**

    3. What are the difficulties of moving workers out of a region? **(10)**

    4. Outline the underlying principles of British regional legislation. **(13)**

    5. What is an intermediate area? **(17(*c*))**

    6. In what ways have regional policies been a success? **(19(*b*))**

    7. Discuss the impact of market forces on regionalism. **(21)**

    8. Why do capital incentives for the regions have drawbacks? **(25)**

    9. How could worker mobility be increased? **(32)**

    10. What is the European Regional Fund? **(37(*a*))**

APPENDIX I

Bibliography

PART ONE: THE MACROECONOMIC APPROACH

Beveridge, W. H. *Full Employment in a Free Society.* Allen & Unwin.

Brittain, Sir Herbert. *The British Budgetary System.* Allen & Unwin, 1959.

Brittan, S. *Steering the Economy.* Penguin Books, 1971.

Brooman, F. S. *Macroeconomics.* Allen & Unwin, 1967.

Caves, Richard E. *Britain's Economic Prospects.* Allen & Unwin, 1968.

Chubb, Basil. *The Control of Public Expenditure.* Oxford University Press, 1952.

Dicks-Mireaux, L. A. *The Inter-relationship between Cost and Price Changes 1946–1949.* Oxford Economic Papers, October, 1961.

Dow, J. C. R. *The Management of the British Economy 1945–1960.* Cambridge University Press, 1964.

Galbraith, J. K. *Economic Development.* Oxford University Press.

Gill, R. T. *Economics.* Prentice Hall, 1974.

Hansen, A. H. *A Guide to Keynes.* McGraw–Hill.

Lewis, W. Arthur. *Theory of Economic Growth.* Allen & Unwin.

Lipsey, R. G. "The Relation between Unemployment and the Rate of Change of Money Wage Rates in the United Kingdom 1862–1957." *Economica,* February 1960.

Morris D. J. *The Economic System in the U.K.* Oxford University Press 1977.

Nevin, E. *The Problem of the National Debt.* University of Wales Press.

Phillips, A. W. "The Relation between Unemployment and the Rate of Change of Money Wage Rates in the United Kingdom 1861–1957." *Economica,* November 1958.

Prest, A. R. *Public Finance in Theory and Practice.* Weidenfeld & Nicolson, 1967.

Seddon, E. *Economics of Public Finance.* Macdonald & Evans, 1969.

OFFICIAL PUBLICATIONS

Appropriation Accounts. Annual. H.M.S.O.
The British System of Taxation. Central Office of Information, Reference Pamphlet No. 10. H.M.S.O., 1965.
Estimates. Annual. H.M.S.O.
Economic Trends. H.M.S.O.
Finance Accounts of the U.K. Annual. H.M.S.O.
Finance Act. Annual. H.M.S.O.
Finance Statement. Annual. H.M.S.O.
Loans from the National Loans Fund. Annual White Paper. H.M.S.O.
National Income and Expenditure. Annual Blue Book. H.M.S.O.
National Income Statistics: Sources and Methods. H.M.S.O.
Preliminary Estimates of National Income and Expenditure. Annual White Paper. H.M.S.O.
Prices and Incomes Act, 1966. H.M.S.O.
Public Expenditure 1968–9 to 1973–4. Cmnd. 4234. H.M.S.O., 1970.
Value-added Tax. 1971 Green Paper. Cmnd. 4621. H.M.S.O.

PART TWO: THE MONETARY SYSTEM

Crockett, A. *Money: Theory, Policy and Institutions*. Nelson, 1973.

Dacey, W. Manning. *The British Banking Mechanism*. Hutchinson, 1962.

Day, A. C. L. *An Outline of Monetary Economics*. Clarendon Press, 1957.

Friedman, M. *The Counter-Revolution in Monetary Theory*. Occasional Paper 33, Institute of Economic Affairs, 1970.

Gibson, N. J. *Financial Intermediaries and Monetary Policy*. Hobart Paper 39, Institute of Economic Affairs, 1967.

Hanson, J. L. *Monetary Theory and Practice*. Macdonald & Evans, 1965.

Hobson, Sir Oscar. *How the City Works*. Dickens Press, 1962.

Macrae, N. *London Capital Market*. Staples Press, 1957.

Morgan, E. Victor. *Monetary Policy for Stable Growth*. Hobart Paper 27, Institute of Economic Affairs, 1966.

Paish, F. W. *Business Finance*. Pitman, 1965.

Revell, J. *The British Financial System*. Macmillan, 1973.

Sayers, R. A. *Modern Banking*. Oxford University Press, 1967.

BANKING PUBLICATIONS

Bank of England Annual Report.
Bank of England Quarterly Bulletin.
The Banker.
The Bankers' Magazine.
Journal of the Institute of Bankers.
The reviews of the London clearing banks.

OFFICIAL PUBLICATIONS

The British Banking System. Central Office of Information Pamphlet No. 65. H.M.S.O.
British Financial Institutions. Central Office of Information Pamphlet No. 24. H.M.S.O.
Report of the Committee on the Working of the Monetary System (Radcliffe Report). Cmnd. 827. H.M.S.O., 1959.

PART THREE: INTERNATIONAL TRADE AND PAYMENTS

Friedman, M. "The Case for Flexible Exchange Rates." *Essays in Positive Economics*, pp. 157–187. University of Chicago Press, 1953.
Haberler, G. von. *The Theory of International Trade.* Macmillan, 1937.
Hodgman, D. *National Monetary Policies and International Monetary Co-operation.* Little, Brown & Co., 1974.
Kindleberger, C. P. *International Economics.* Irwin, 1963.
Machlup, F. *Plans for Reform of the International Monetary System.* Special Papers in International Economics No. 3. Princeton University Press, 1962.
Scammell, W. M. *International Monetary Policy, Bretton Woods and After.* Macmillan, 1975.
Triffin, R. *Gold and the Dollar Crisis.* Yale University Press, 1961.
Worswick, G. D. N., and Ady, P. H. *The British Economy in the 1950s.* Oxford University Press, 1962.

OFFICIAL PUBLICATIONS

The Activities of GATT. Annual. Geneva.
Britain and the European Communities: An Economic Assessment. 1970 White Paper. Cmnd. 4289. H.M.S.O.
Britain's Financial Services for Overseas. Reference Paper R.4881/65. C.O.I.
Britain's Overseas Investment. Reference Paper R.5732/66. C.O.I.

European Free Trade Association. Annual Report. Geneva.
I.M.F. Annual Report. Washington.
Preliminary Estimates of National Income and Balance of Payments. Annual White Paper. H.M.S.O.
U.K. Balance of Payments. Annual Orange Book. H.M.S.O.

PART FOUR: GOVERNMENT AND INDUSTRY

Allen, G. C. *Monopoly and Restrictive Practices*. Allen & Unwin.

Cameron, G. C., and Clark B. D. *Industrial Movement and the Regional Problem*. Oliver & Boyd.

Caves, Richard E. *Britain's Economic Prospects*. Allen & Unwin.

Evely, R., and Little, I. M. D. *Concentration in British Industry*. Cambridge University Press.

Hague, D. C. *Managerial Economics*. Longmans.

Hartley, I. C. *Problems of Economic Policy*. Allen & Unwin, 1977.

Henderson, P. *Economic Growth in Britain*. Weidenfeld & Nicolson.

McCrone, G. *Regional Policy in Britain*. Allen & Unwin.

Newbould, G. *Management and Mergers Activity*. Guthstead (Liverpool).

Pickering, J. F. *Industrial Structure and Market Conduct*. Martin Robinson, 1975.

Pryke, R. *Public Enterprise in Practice*. MacGibbon & Kee, 1971.

Schonfield, A. *Modern Capitalism*. Oxford University Press.

Shepherd, W. G. *Economic Performance under Public Ownership*. Yale University Press.

Sutherland, A. *Monopolies Commission in Action*. Cambridge University Press.

Thornhill, W. *Nationalised Industries*. Nelson.

Tindall, R. E. *Multinational Enterprise*. Oceania Publications, New York, 1975.

Tugendhat, C. *The Multinationals*. Penguin, 1973.

Webb, M. *Economics of Nationalized Industries*. Nelson, 1973.

OFFICIAL PUBLICATIONS

Financial and Economic Obligations of Nationalised Industries. Cmnd. 1337, 1961. H.M.S.O.

Mergers: A Guide to Board of Trade Practices. H.M.S.O., 1969.

Monopolies and Restrictive Practices Commission Reports. H.M.S.O.

Nationalised Industries: A review of Economic and Financial Objectives. Cmnd. 3437, 1967. H.M.S.O.
Registrar of Restrictive Trading Agreements Reports. H.M.S.O.
Survey of Mergers Report 1958–1968. H.M.S.O., 1970.

Examination Technique

Success in examination depends not only upon a knowledge of facts but also upon the ability to marshal evidence systematically in a succinct answer to a specific question. In developing an examination technique the candidate will benefit from the following advice:

1. Read the whole paper carefully and unhurriedly and make a selection of those questions you intend to answer. You should be confident that you understand quite clearly the meaning of the questions selected. Avoid those questions where it seems that you will simply duplicate what you will write elsewhere.

2. Having understood a question let it remain uppermost in your mind so that your answer is wholly relevant. Too many failures result from candidates answering questions which do not appear in the paper.

3. Apportion your time so that you are certain of answering the required number of questions. Failure to complete the paper automatically lowers your maximum possible marks.

4. Many problems in Applied Economics have a highly controversial content with no clear-cut solutions. You should therefore avoid dogmatic answers. It is preferable to present the arguments of opposing schools of thought and to arrive at a balanced conclusion. You must certainly avoid the superficial and politically emotive approach of popular journalism.

5. Plan your answers systematically so that there is a logical progression of ideas leading to a natural conclusion. Avoid arguments based upon a series of disconnected points which do nothing to support your conclusion.

6. Finally, it is important to give attention to the composition of your script. A slipshod presentation immediately creates an unfavourable impression.

Examination Questions

PART ONE: THE MACROECONOMIC APPROACH

This selection of examination questions is related to the four parts of the text. However, it should be understood that in some cases it will be necessary to refer to material covered elsewhere in the book.

1. Explain how the level of income and employment are determined in a private enterprise economy. (*G.C.E.(A)*, *J.M.B.*)

2. Consider the relative merits of direct and indirect taxation. What are the advantages and disadvantages of increasing the proportion of revenue derived from indirect taxation in the United Kingdom? (*G.C.E.(A)*, *J.M.B.*)

3. Is it possible to reconcile the views that (*a*) savings are necessary for growth and (*b*) savings create unemployment? (*G.C.E.(A)*, *J.M.B.*)

4. To what extent, if any, is the National Debt a burden? (*G.C.E.(A)*, *J.M.B.*)

5. How may redistribution of income offset the level of total demand? (*B.Sc. (Econ.)*, *Part I*, *London Internal*)

6. Explain the multiplier concept and discuss its implications for economic policy. (*B.Sc. (Econ.)*, *Part I*, *London External*)

7. Control over the money supply is increasingly advocated as a means of preventing inflation. Examine briefly the theoretical rationale of this argument. (*B.Sc.(Econ.)*, *Part I*, *London External*)

8. "Higher taxes will never solve our problems." (Mr. Edward Heath, 22nd March, 1969.) Explain how the pressure of demand on the country's productive capacity is reduced:

(*a*) by higher taxes;

(*b*) by higher saving. (*B.Sc.(Econ.)*, *Part I*, *London Internal*)

9. Discuss the policy implications of the Phillips Curve which relates changes in money wages and prices to the percentage of unemployment. (*B.Sc.(Econ.)*, *Part I*, *London Internal*)

10. How do you distinguish between macroeconomic and microeconomic theories? (*B.Sc.(Econ.)*, *Part I, London Internal*)

11. Why has the British economy experienced a relatively low level of unemployment since the war? (*B.Sc.(Econ.)*, *Part I, London Internal*)

12. Discuss critically recent developments in the forecasting and control of public expenditure in the U.K. (*B.Sc.(Econ.)*, *Part II, Public Finance, London Internal and External*)

13. "Post-war stabilisation policy has replaced ten-yearly major depressions with much more frequent minor recessions." Discuss. (*B.Sc.(Econ.)*, *Part II, Public Finance, London Internal and External*)

14. Discuss the influence of short-term stabilisation policies on long-term growth. (*B.Sc.(Econ.)*, *Part II, Public Finance, London Internal and External*)

15. Discuss the influence of the progressivity of the income tax on the aggregate supply of labour. (*B.Sc.(Econ.)*, *Part II, Public Finance, London Internal and External*)

16. What measures would you recommend to improve the built-in stability of the U.K. economy? (*B.Sc.(Econ.)*, *Part II, Public Finance, London Internal and External*)

17. How would you explain the comparatively slow rate of growth in the British economy in recent years? In what ways do you consider that public finance may best be directed to achieving an improvement? (*H.N.D. Business Studies, Liverpool Polytechnic*)

18. Explain why measures to sustain the level of effective demand are not appropriate in dealing with all forms of unemployment. What alternative measures have been developed and with what results? (*H.N.D. Business Studies, Liverpool Polytechnic*)

19. Explain the belief that it is not necessarily sound public finance to insist upon balancing the national budget. (*H.N.D. Business Studies, Liverpool Polytechnic*)

20. Detail the structure of the National Debt. Examine the significance of its burden and the possibilities of reducing this burden. (*H.N.D. Business Studies, Liverpool Polytechnic*)

21. What difficulties hinder a prices and incomes policy in conditions of full employment and free collective bargaining? (*H.N.C. Business Studies, Liverpool Polytechnic*)

22. "The acceptance by governments of responsibility for the level of employment cannot be understood without reference to the changes in economic theory associated with Keynes." What

in economic thought do you associate with Keynes? (*H.N.C. Business Studies, Liverpool Polytechnic*)

23. Present government economic policy faces a conflict of interest between short term "stop-go" and long term planning for growth. Explain, with examples, why this is so. (*H.N.C. Business Studies, Liverpool Polytechnic*)

24. Outline the main characteristics of the "national debt." How far is such a debt a burden on a country's economy? (*I.O.B.*)

25. Outline the general principles a government should adopt when levying taxation. (*I.O.B.*)

26. Contrast the place of the budget in the modern economy with its position before 1939, illustrating your answer by reference to any particular country. (*I.O.B.*)

27. Discuss the relationship between rising wages and rising costs. (*I.M.T.A.*)

28. "Since the Second World War the centre of interest in economics has shifted from the study of equilibrium to the study of growth." How do you explain the change? (*Economics, Final Part I, I.M.T.A.*)

29. To what extent can the Government use the level of public expenditure as an instrument of economic stabilisation? (*Public Finance, Final Part I, I.M.T.A.*)

30. Is the short-run control over the supply of money a necessary condition for ensuring price stability? (*Public Finance, Final Part I, I.M.T.A.*)

31. "Savings and investment are always equal."

"In equilibrium savings equal investment."

Reconcile these two statements. (*Public Finance, Final Part I, I.M.T.A.*)

32. What are the causes of unemployment? Illustrate your answer with examples. (*I.C.W.A.*)

33. Why has the United Kingdom experienced inflation since 1945? (*I.C.W.A.*)

34. "Savings and investment are done by different people at different times for different reasons." Explain this statement. (*I.C.W.A.*)

35. In what ways may the budget be used as an instrument of economic policy? (*I.C.W.A.*)

36. What do you understand by the "multiplier"? Explain its usefulness to a government seeking to control an economy. (*I.O.T.*)

37. Is it true to say that the trade cycle belongs nowadays to Economic History? (*I.O.T.*)

38. What do you understand by a full employment policy? How likely is it to cause inflation? (*I.O.T.*)

39. What do you understand by inflation? Why do governments seek to control it? (*I.O.T.*)

PART TWO: THE MONETARY SYSTEM

40. What factors determine the supply of money in the United Kingdom? (*G.C.E.(A), J.M.B.*)

41. What part do the discount houses play in the system of monetary control operated by the Bank of England? (*G.C.E. (A), J.M.B.*)

42. What are the main instruments of monetary policy? Assess their efficacy as economic stabilisers. (*G.C.E.(A), J.M.B.*)

43. Outline the chief problems involved in the value of money in time. (*G.C.E.(A), J.M.B.*)

44. Explain how the London discount market acts as a buffer between the monetary authorities on the one hand and the clearing banks on the other. (*B.Sc.(Econ.), Part I, London External*)

45. "Bankers cannot create anything; they merely exchange one kind of asset for another." Discuss. (*B.Sc.(Econ.), Part I, London External*)

46. Discuss fully the meaning attached to the concept of liquidity in the Radcliffe Report. (*B.Sc.(Econ.), Part I, London External*)

47. Outline the ways in which an efficient capital market can assist the finance of industry. (*B.Sc.(Econ.), Part I, London External*)

48. "Recent theoretical attempts to arrive at a definition of money suggest that the problem can be usefully pursued only as en empirical question." Discuss. (*B.Sc.(Econ.), Part II, Principles of Monetary Economics, London Internal*)

49. The experience of the 1960s seems to suggest that rising interest rates are associated with an expansion rather than a contraction of the money supply. How can this experience be explained? (*B.Sc.(Econ.), Part II, Principles of Monetary Economics, London Internal*)

50. Non-bank financial intermediaries have grown in size and number in the past two decades. What effects may this have had on the supply of money, rates of interest and the effectiveness of

monetary policy? (*B.Sc.(Econ.)*, *Part II*, *Principles of Monetary Economics*, *London Internal*)

51. "The quantity of money in the United Kingdom since 1945 has been entirely demand determined." Consider whether this statement is true and, if so, why. (*B.Sc.(Econ.)*, *Part II*, *Principles of Monetary Economics*, *London External*)

52. "The authorities can choose interest rates or the supply of money but cannot choose both independently of each other" (Sayers). On what basis should the authorities make their choice? (*B.Sc.(Econ.)*, *Part II*, *Principles of Monetary Economics*, *London External*)

53. "A firm control of the money supply is both necessary and sufficient to control inflation." Discuss. (*B.Sc(Econ.)*, *Part II*, *Principles of Monetary Economics*, *London External*)

54. To what extent is it true to say that money is the creation of the banking system? (*H.N.D. Business Studies*, *Liverpool Polytechnic*)

55. Describe the structure and operation of the London discount market. Do you believe that it performs a useful function? (*H.N.D. Business Studies*, *Liverpool Polytechnic*)

56. The methods by which the Bank of England traditionally exercised the ultimate control over the supply of money are no longer effective. Explain and evaluate this statement. (*H.N.D. Business Studies*, *Liverpool Polytechnic*)

57. "The commercial banker's basic problem is to achieve a proper balance between liquidity and profitability." Explain. (*H.N.C. Business Studies*, *Liverpool Polytechnic*)

58. How can the authorities control the amount of money and why should they wish to do so? (*H.N.C. Business Studies*, *Liverpool Polytechnic*)

59. Why is it that whilst opinion seems to be that Bank-rate changes are an outmoded instrument of economic policy, the authorities continue to attribute to them an important role? (*H.N.C. Business Studies*, *Liverpool Polytechnic*)

60. Describe the structure and operations of the London money market. (*I.O.B.*)

61. Discuss the special characteristics that distinguish money from other economic goods. (*I.O.B.*)

62. Examine the various factors which in present-day Britain set a limit to an increase in the money supply. (*I.O.B.*)

63. Describe the demand for, and the supply of, funds in the London money market. (*I.O.B.*)

64. Examine the present-day effectiveness of Bank rate as a deflationary control. (*I.O.B.*)

65. To what extent is the ability of money to fulfil its functions affected by changes in its value? (*I.O.B.*)

66. "It is impossible in practice to achieve together all the objectives of monetary policy." Discuss this statement. (*I.O.B.*)

67. Describe the components of the supply of money in Britain and examine carefully the consequences of a reduction in the supply. (*S.B.I.*)

68. "The effectiveness of Bank Rate as an instrument of economic policy depends more on the fact that it changes than on its particular level." Discuss. (*S.B.I.*)

69. Set out the sources of borrowing by the central government in Britain and show the importance of the Savings Banks in this borrowing. (*S.B.I.*)

70. Explain the function of the Bank of England as "lender of last resort." What role does the discount market play in the fulfilment of this function? (*S.B.I.*)

71. Consider the consequences on the supply of money of my withdrawing a deposit from a savings bank and depositing it instead with a commercial bank. (*S.B.I.*)

72. Discuss briefly the asset structure of joint-stock banks. How is it influenced by changes in interest rates? (*Public Finance, Final, Part I, I.M.T.A.*)

73. "The Discount Market makes a living by borrowing short and lending long." Discuss. (*Public Finance, Final Part I, I.M.T.A.*)

74. Assess the view that the management of the national debt is an integral part of monetary policy. (*Public Finance, Final Part I, I.M.T.A.*)

75. Outline the economic services provided by a Joint Stock Bank. (*I.C.W.A.*)

76. Define Bank rate and describe the possible economic effects of a rise in Bank rate. (*I.C.W.A.*)

77. Distinguish between the characteristics of the Bank of England and those of the Joint-Stock Banks. (*I.C.W.A.*)

78. What do you understand by the supply of, and the demand for, money? (*I.C.W.A.*)

79. Distinguish between (*a*) finance houses and (*b*) building societies, making clear the economic role of each. (*I.C.W.A.*)

80. If Banks are merely financial intermediaries, how can they create credit? (*I.O.T.*)

81. Why is Bank rate raised or lowered? (*I.O.T.*)

82. Bankers claim that they can only lend what is lent to them. How then is it possible for them to "create credit"? (*I.O.T.*)

83. Contrast the functions of a central bank and a commercial bank. (*I.O.T.*)

PART THREE: INTERNATIONAL TRADE AND PAYMENTS

84. Explain what is meant by the *terms of trade* and the *balance of trade*. What relationship exists between these two concepts? (*G.C.E.(A), J.M.B.*)

85. Explain what is meant by "devaluation". How is a devaluation likely to affect the balance of payments of an economy? (*G.C.E.(A), J.M.B.*)

86. State precisely what you understand by the "fundamental disequilibrium" in the British balance of payments. (*G.C.E.(A), J.M.B.*)

87. Assess the relative merits of devaluation and tariff imposition as instruments for correcting an adverse current balance. (*G.C.E.(A), J.M.B.*)

88. Consider the relative merits of devaluation and deflation as correctives of a Balance of Payments deficit. (*B.Sc.(Econ.), Part I, London External*)

89. Why is it mutually profitable for two or more countries to engage in international trade? Can the existence of unemployment modify your conclusions? (*B.Sc.(Econ.), Part I, London External*)

90. Argue the case for and against flexible exchange rates. (*B.Sc.(Econ.), Part I, London External*)

91. Consider the view that restrictions on British investment can secure short-run improvement in the balance of payments only at the expense of a long-run worsening. (*B.Sc.(Econ.), Part I, London External*)

92. Under what conditions would you expect a fixed exchange rate system to permit major trading countries to maximise their own welfare? (*B.Sc.(Econ.), Part II, Principles of Monetary Economics, London Internal*)

93. "The problems surrounding the supply of international means of payment arise because the countries which are the world's bankers are also its chief traders; these problems will be solved only when these roles are separated." Discuss. (*B.Sc.*

(*Econ.*), *Part II*, *Principles of Monetary Economics, London Internal*)

94. Discuss the merits of the "crawling peg" scheme for exchange-rate adjustments. (*B.Sc.(Econ.)*, *Part II*, *Principles of Monetary Economics, London External*)

95. "Under a regime of fixed exchange rates a government cannot maintain both internal and external balance." Comment. (*B.Sc.(Econ.)*, *Part II*, *Principles of Monetary Economics, London External*)

96. "The general adoption of flexible exchange rates would increase, not lessen, both the need for the authorities to intervene in the foreign exchange market and the need for international co-operation." Discuss. (*B.Sc.(Econ.)*, *Part II*, *Principles of Monetary Economics, London External*)

97. Explain the concepts of over-valuation and under-valuation when applied to a currency. What are the possible remedies in each case? (*H.N.D. Business Studies, Liverpool Polytechnic*)

98. Explain the composition of the balance of payments and assess the relative importance of each of its components. Consider some of the measures which might be applied to the improvement of this balance. (*H.N.D. Business Studies, Liverpool Polytechnic*)

99. Examine the advantages and disadvantages to the British balance of payments of sterling's function as a world reserve and trading currency. Could this function be abandoned? (*H.N.D. Business Studies, Liverpool Polytechnic*)

100. Despite the advantages of international trade based upon the principle of comparative costs, countries do in fact impose restrictions on trade. Why is this? (*H.N.C. Business Studies, Liverpool Polytechnic*)

101. Argue the merits of devaluation rather than deflation as an answer to balance of payments problems. (*H.N.C. Business Studies, Liverpool Polytechnic*)

102. For what reasons do some economists advocate a rise in the price of gold? What objections are raised to such a proposal? (*H.N.C. Business Studies, Liverpool Polytechnic*)

103. Show how the total of the debits and credits on a country's balance of payments account must always equal one another. (*I.O.B.*)

104. "Deflation and devaluation are not alternatives. Some deflation is necessary if devaluation is to succeed." Comment on this statement. (*I.O.B.*)

105. "For international monetary equilibrium a properly functioning adjustment process is as important as sufficient liquidity." Discuss this statement. (*I.O.B.*)

106. Define the term "international liquidity" and comment on the main elements of such liquidity today. (*I.O.B.*)

107. How can a country have a surplus in its balance of trade but a deficit in its balance of payments? Why must a country take steps to reduce a persistent payments deficit? (*S.B.I.*)

108. Why has the present international monetary system been described as the New Gold Standard? Indicate the chief defects of the present system and how they might be resolved. (*S.B.I.*)

109. Give an account of the objectives and principles of operation of the International Monetary Fund. (*S.B.I.*)

110. What are the "sterling balances"? In what way do they create a problem for Britain? Suggest possible solutions. (*S.B.I.*)

111. Outline the functions of the International Monetary Fund. Will the issue of Special Drawing Rights enable the Fund to play a more effective role in the international monetary system? (*S.B.I.*)

112. "Whatever policy is used, a Balance of Payments deficit can only be corrected through a reduction in the standard of living of the economy as a whole." Discuss. (*Public Finance, Final Part I, I.M.T.A.*)

113. Will export subsidies increase the competitiveness of British exports in the long run? (*Public Finance, Final Part I, I.M.T.A.*)

114. Why may it pay a country to import goods which it can produce itself? (*I.C.W.A.*)

115. How may the Government finance a deficit on the balance of payments in the short run? (*I.C.W.A.*)

116. Discuss the advantages and disadvantages of imposing restrictions on international trading relations. (*I.O.T.*)

117. Why does the economist suggest that international trade is gainful? (*I.O.T.*)

118. "Overseas investment merely creates overseas competitors and should be discouraged." Discuss. (*I.O.T.*)

PART FOUR: GOVERNMENT AND INDUSTRY

119. Why are monopolistic practices in general thought to be against the public interest? How has the Government attempted to deal with them? (*G.C.E.(A), J.M.B.*)

120. "In the industrial structure of the U.K., all competition is monopolistic, all monopoly is to some extent competitive." Discuss this statement. (*G.C.E.(A), J.M.B.*)

121. What factors encourage (*a*) horizontal integration and (*b*) vertical integration in an industry? (*G.C.E.(A), J.M.B.*)

122. Is increasing concentration in industrial markets inevitable? (*G.C.E.(A), J.M.B.*)

123. How and why has the Government intervened in the location of industry since 1945? (*G.C.E.(A), J.M.B.*)

124. Examine the view that public sector industry should be run like ordinary commercial enterprises. (*G.C.E.(A), J.M.B.*)

125. What criteria of efficiency can and should be applied to nationalised industries? (*G.C.E.(A), J.M.B.*)

126. What are the advantages and disadvantages of setting price equal to marginal cost in public enterprises? (*G.C.E.(A), J.M.B.*)

127. In what ways does the functioning of a "planned" economy differ from that of a "free" economy? (*G.C.E.(A), J.M.B.*)

128. "To check and reverse the drift of population to the South-East and Midlands would be to impose an unwarrantable cost upon the national economy." Discuss. (*B.Sc.(Econ.), Part II, London*)

129. Should the financial targets for nationalised industries be based on the rate of return on capital earned by private industry? (*B.Sc.(Econ.), Part II, London*)

130. Would a policy to outlaw monopolies necessarily be in the public interest? (*H.N.D. Business Studies, Liverpool Polytechnic*)

131. Governments have tried to cure regional economic imbalance for over thirty years, yet the problem remains. Discuss possible reasons for this lack of success. (*H.N.D. Business Studies, Liverpool Polytechnic*)

132. What difficulties arise in applying commercial criteria as a measure of efficiency to nationalised industries? (*H.N.D. Business Studies, Liverpool Polytechnic*)

133. Discuss the assertion that a ruthless breaking up of

monopolies might create more inefficiency than it would eliminate. (*H.N.C. Business Studies, Liverpool Polytechnic*)

134. "No policy for dealing with the regional problem ought
to interfere with the fundamentals of economic efficiency" (Professor Wilson). In what ways might Government policy have
offended this precept? (*H.N.C. Business Studies, Liverpool
Polytechnic*)

135. What main factors influence an entrepreneur in his choice
of locality for a new factory? (*I.O.B.*)

136. Monopoly is usually regarded as undesirable. Outline the
case that can be made against this view. (*I.O.B.*)

137. To what extent do you agree that nationalised industries
should finance their capital investment out of profits? (*I.O.B.*)

138. How may companies with "Monopoly Powers" attempt
to strengthen their market position? (*I.C.W.A.*)

139. Some authorities take the view that the security of monopoly provides conditions in which the most rapid technical progress will take place in industry. Others hold that the pressure of
competitive conditions is more favourable to this process.
Discuss. (*C.I.S.*)

140. "The taking over of one company by another is always in
the interest of the shareholders but rarely in the interest of the
country as a whole." Discuss this statement. (*C.I.S.*)

141. "The main disadvantage of monopoly is not that it
causes high prices but that it is inefficient." Discuss. (*C.I.S.*)

142. Does economic theory indicate any rules which should
govern the policies pursued by nationalised industries? (*C.I.S.*)

143. "Planning without specific targets is a useless operation
for raising economic growth." Do you agree? (*C.I.S.*)

144. "The economic activities of the state have increased and
are increasing." How far economically is such increase (*a*) desirable, (*b*) undesirable? (*C.I.S.*)

Index